P9-DWJ-634

LOW-INTENSITY WARFARE

MICHAEL T. KLARE
PETER KORNBLUH
EDITORS

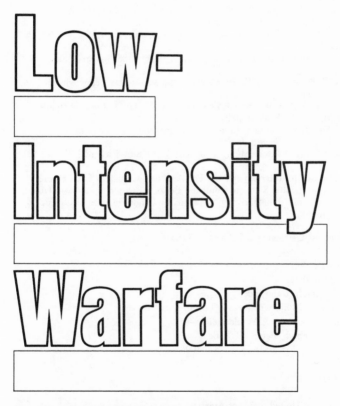

Low-Intensity Warfare

**COUNTERINSURGENCY, PROINSURGENCY,
AND ANTITERRORISM IN THE EIGHTIES**

PANTHEON BOOKS   NEW YORK

TO ANDREA, ELIANA, GABRIEL
AND THE LITTLE ONE TO COME.

Compilation and "The New Interventionism: Low-Intensity Warfare in the 1980s and Beyond," copyright © 1988 by Michael T. Klare and Peter Kornbluh.
"Counterinsurgency: The First Ordeal by Fire," copyright © 1988 by Charles Maechling, Jr.
"The Interventionist Impulse: U.S. Military Doctrine for Low-Intensity Warfare," copyright © 1988 by Michael T. Klare.
"Low-Intensity Warfare: The Warriors and Their Weapons," copyright © 1988 by Stephen D. Goose.
"El Salvador: Counterinsurgency Revisited," copyright © 1988 by Daniel Siegel and Joy Hackel.
"Nicaragua: U.S. Proinsurgency Warfare Against the Sandinistas," copyright © 1988 by Peter Kornbluh.
"Counterinsurgency's Proving Ground: Low-Intensity Warfare in the Philippines," copyright © 1988 by Walden Bello.
"Afghanistan: Soviet Intervention, Afghan Resistance, and the American Role," copyright © 1988 by Selig S. Harrison.
"The Costs and Perils of Intervention," copyright © 1988 by Richard J. Barnet.

All rights reserved under International and Pan-American Copyright Conventions. Published in the United States by Pantheon Books, a division of Random House, Inc., New York, and simultaneously in Canada by Random House of Canada Limited, Toronto.

Library of Congress Cataloging-in-Publication Data

Klare, Michael T., 1942–
  Low intensity warfare.
  Includes bibliographies and index.
  1. United States—Military policy.   2. Low-intensity
conflicts (Military science)   3. World politics—
1985–1995.   I. Kornbluh, Peter   II. Title.
UA23.K62   1987   355'.0335'73   87-43008
ISBN 0-394-55579-1
ISBN0-394-74653-8 (pbk.)

Manufactured in the United States of America

98765432

CONTENTS

1 The New Interventionism:
Low-Intensity Warfare in the 1980s and Beyond   3
MICHAEL T. KLARE AND PETER KORNBLUH

2 Counterinsurgency: The First Ordeal by Fire   21
CHARLES MAECHLING, JR.

3 The Interventionist Impulse:
U.S. Military Doctrine for Low-Intensity Warfare   49
MICHAEL T. KLARE

4 Low-Intensity Warfare:
The Warriors and Their Weapons   80
STEPHEN D. GOOSE

5 El Salvador: Counterinsurgency Revisited   112
DANIEL SIEGEL AND JOY HACKEL

6 Nicaragua: U.S. Proinsurgency Warfare
Against the Sandinistas   136
PETER KORNBLUH

7 Counterinsurgency's Proving Ground:
Low-Intensity Warfare in the Philippines   158
WALDEN BELLO

8 Afghanistan: Soviet Intervention,
Afghan Resistance, and the American Role   183
SELIG S. HARRISON

9 The Costs and Perils of Intervention   207
RICHARD J. BARNET

Notes   223

Bibliography   246

Contributors   249

LOW-INTENSITY WARFARE

1

THE NEW INTERVENTIONISM: LOW-INTENSITY WARFARE IN THE 1980s AND BEYOND

MICHAEL T. KLARE AND PETER KORNBLUH

TWENTY-FIVE years after the doctrine of "counterinsurgency" transformed American military thinking and swept the nation into the Vietnam War, a new strategy of intervention is ascending in Washington: the Reagan administration's aggressive doctrine of "low-intensity conflict," or "LIC" as it is known in Pentagon circles. LIC begins with counterinsurgency, and extends to a wide variety of other politicomilitary operations, both overt and covert. For U.S. policy-makers and war planners, however, low-intensity conflict has come to mean far more than a specialized category of armed struggle; it represents a strategic reorientation of the U.S. military establishment, and a renewed commitment to employ force in a global crusade against Third World revolutionary movements and governments.

In the mind-set of many senior officials, the decisive battle of this century is now unfolding in this "long twilight struggle" between America's LIC warriors and the revolutionary combatants of the Third World.[1] Theirs is an outlook that identifies Third World insurgencies—and not Soviet troop concentrations in Europe—as the predominant threat to U.S. security; it is, moreover, an outlook that calls on the United States to "take the offensive"—in contrast to the passive stance of "deterrence"—to overcome the revolutionary peril. Indeed, LIC has become the battle cry of the late Reagan era—a clarion call for resurgent U.S. intervention abroad.

In justifying the new interventionism, LIC advocates invariably begin with a grim assessment of the global political and military environment. "The plain fact is that the United States is at war," military expert Neil C. Livingstone told senior officers at the National Defense University in 1983, and "nothing less than the survival of our country and way of life" is at stake in that struggle. This is not, however, warfare in the classic sense of armies fighting armies on a common battlefield. "The most plausible scenario for the future," he affirmed, is that of "a continuous succession of hostage crises, peacekeeping operations, rescue missions, and counterinsurgency efforts, or what some have called 'low frontier warfare.' " This being the case, it is essential "that the American people and our policy-makers be educated as to the realities of contemporary conflict and the need to fight little wars successfully."[2]

Today, this outlook reflects the prevailing mind-set within the national security bureaucracy. "It is very important for the American people to know that this is a dangerous world; that we live at risk and that this nation is at risk in a dangerous world," Lieutenant Colonel Oliver North, director of the National Security Council's Counterterrorism and Low-Intensity Warfare Group, told the Joint House-Senate Select Committee on Iran and the Contras in July 1987.[3] Similar views were expressed by Secretary of Defense Caspar Weinberger in his 1987 annual report to Congress: "Today there seems to be no shortage of adversaries who seek to undermine our security by persistently nibbling away at our interests through these shadow wars carried on by guerrillas, assassins, terrorists, and subversives in the hope that they have found a weak point in our defenses." Unless the United States adopted a comprehensive "national strategy" to combat low-level wars, he asserted, "these forms of aggression will remain the most likely and the most enduring threats to our security."[4]

To meet this perceived threat, the United States has now begun to transform its national security apparatus—to rethink, reorganize, and rearm for current and future engagements in the Third World. In January 1986, Secretary Weinberger hosted the Pentagon's first "Low-Intensity Warfare Conference" at Fort Lesley J. McNair in Washington, D.C.[5] That same month, the Army/Air Force Center for Low-Intensity Conflict (CLIC) was established "to improve the Army/ Air Force posture for engaging in low-intensity conflict [and to] elevate awareness throughout the Army/Air Force of the role of military power in low-intensity conflict."[6] In addition, a Joint Low-Intensity Conflict Project (JLIC) was established in 1985 and one year later released a two-volume, thousand-page *Final Report* on the concepts, strategy, guidelines, and application of low-level war-fighting doctrine in the Third World.[7]

These initiatives have been accompanied by a major overhaul of America's war-making capability. To provide Washington with an enhanced capacity for counterguerrilla and "unconventional" operations, as Stephen Goose shows in Chapter 4, the Reagan administration has ordered a 100 percent increase in the Pentagon's "Special Operations Forces" (SOF)—the Army's "Green Berets," the Navy's "SEALs" and other elite commando formations. For covert operations of the sort managed by Lieutenant Colonel North of the NSC, there is the supersecret "Delta Force," the 160th Army Aviation Task Force ("the Night Stalkers"), and other paramilitary "assets" controlled by the Central Intelligence Agency. And, for more demanding military engagements, there are the four new light infantry divisions (LIDs) established by the Department of the Army since 1984.

More important, in the Pentagon's view, is the development of an appropriate doctrine for low-intensity operations. By focusing on the Soviet military threat in Europe, it is argued, present doctrine has left U.S. troops wholly unprepared for the unconventional challenges they are likely to face on Third World battlefields. "Given the proposition that low-intensity conflict is our most likely form of involvement in the Third World," LIC proponent Colonel John D. Waghelstein wrote in 1985, "it appears that the army is still preparing for the wrong war by emphasizing the Soviet threat on the plains of Europe."[8] To ready U.S. forces for the "right" war, Waghelstein and other senior officers have crusaded for the rapid introduction of specialized strategy and tactics. For American troops to prevail in low-intensity warfare, Colonel James B. Motley wrote in *Military Review*, "the United States should reorient its forces and traditional policies away from an almost exclusive concentration on NATO to better influence politico-military outcomes in the resource-rich and strategically located Third World areas."[9]

Because the challenge posed by Third World revolution is political as much as it is military in nature, the U.S. response must, according to the Pentagon, be equally comprehensive. "Low-intensity conflicts cannot be won or even contained by military power alone," General

Donald R. Morelli and Major Michael M. Ferguson of the U.S. Army Training and Doctrine Command affirmed in 1984. "It requires the sychronized application of all elements of national power across the entire range of conditions which are the sources of the conflict."[10]

The foundation of LIC doctrine, as Charles Maechling, Jr., writes in Chapter 2, lies in the "counterinsurgency" programs—the coordinated integration of economic assistance with psychological operations and security measures—developed for Latin America after the 1959 Cuban revolution, and for South Vietnam in the early 1960s. "Counterinsurgency is the old name for low-intensity conflict," according to Colonel Waghelstein, former head of the U.S. military group in El Salvador.[11] However, as Michael Klare writes in Chapter 3, the Reagan administration has gone beyond counterinsurgency as it was seen twenty-five years ago by publicly committing the United States to a policy of undermining not just revolutionary movements coming into being, but also revolutionary regimes which already exist and are perceived as allies of the Soviet Union. A modernized version of John Foster Dulles's concept of "rollback" in a counterinsurgency guise, the "Reagan Doctrine" proclaims a "global offensive against communism at the fringes of the Soviet Empire." According to the president, "the tide of Soviet communism can be reversed. All it takes is the will and the resources to get the job done."[12]

Under Reagan, LIC doctrine has been institutionalized in the national security bureaucracy. In early 1987, the president signed legislation that created a unified command for special operations and established a "Board for Low Intensity Conflict" within the National Security Council. It also mandated a new bureaucratic position—deputy assistant to the president for low-intensity conflict. And, in June 1987, Mr. Reagan signed a highly classified National Security Decision Directive (NSDD) that authorizes the bureaucracy to develop and implement a unified national strategy for low-intensity warfare.

"How does one begin to bring understanding to this complex issue?" asks the *Joint Low-Intensity Conflict Project Final Report.*[13] The term itself derives from the Pentagon's image of the "spectrum of conflict"— a theoretical division of armed conflict into "low," "medium," and "high" levels, depending on the degree of force and violence. Guerrilla wars and other limited conflicts fought with irregular units are labeled "low-intensity conflicts" (even though the impact of such wars on underdeveloped Third World countries, like El Salvador, can be quite devastating); regional wars fought with modern weapons (such as the Iran-Iraq conflict) are considered "mid-intensity conflicts"; and a global nonnuclear conflagration (like World Wars I and II) or a nuclear engagement fall into the "high-intensity" category.[13]

For the Pentagon, however, the definition of LIC encompasses more than a category of violence: "It is, first, an environment in which conflict occurs and, second, a series of diverse civil-military activities and operations which are conducted in that environment."[14] So deliberately broad and ambiguous is the official description of low-intensity warfare that it embraces drug interdiction in Bolivia, the occupation of Beirut, the invasion of Grenada, and the 1986 air strikes on Libya. Also included are a wide range of covert political and psychological operations variously described as "special operations," "special activities," and "unconventional warfare."[15]

But while military strategists depict LIC as a war for all seasons, in essence it is a doctrine for countering revolution. The "LIC pie," as Pentagon insiders call it, is largely divided between counterinsurgency and proinsurgency operations—what the *JLIC Final Report* describes as "diplomatic, economic and military support for either a government under attack by insurgents or an insurgent force seeking freedom from an adversary government."[16] In other words, LIC doctrine is meant to be applied in countries such as El Salvador, Nicaragua, the Philippines, Angola, Cambodia, and Afghanistan, where the United States is either trying to bolster a client government against a revolutionary upheaval or fostering a counterrevolutionary insurgency against an unfriendly Third World regime.

BEHIND THE LIC PHENOMENON

Washington's growing adherence to LIC doctrine stems from two interrelated factors. The first is a consensus among policy-makers and military planners that the United States has been preparing for an unlikely war in Europe while the "real war" for the Third World has gone unattended. In the mind-set of U.S. national security managers, the surge of revolutions, the escalation of terrorist incidents, and other forms of "ambiguous aggression" in the 1970s and early 1980s reflected not a nationalist effort to redress socioeconomic inequality in the Third World but an attempt by the Soviet Union to "nibble" away at U.S. interests on the periphery while avoiding a nuclear confrontation in Europe. Through the Kremlin's use of proxies, and the calculated exploitation of the political and economic instability endemic to many Third World societies, it was felt that the Soviets had successfully challenged U.S. credibility, authority, and, perhaps most significantly, access to raw materials and markets of considerable economic importance to the West. "We depend heavily on some of these nations for strategic minerals and energy resources," Weinberger informed Congress in 1984. "Our economies and the economies of our allies are, therefore, especially susceptible to disruption from conflicts far from our own borders."[17]

For many U.S. strategists, the Third World has become the primary locus of low-intensity warfare. Given the strategic importance of many underdeveloped countries, Livingstone averred, "it is mastery of this type of conflict upon which the fate of the world is likely to turn."[18] Adherents of this view are highly critical of the military policies of the Ford and Carter periods, which placed overwhelming emphasis on the threat posed by conventional Soviet forces in Central Europe. As the former head of the Defense Intelligence Agency, Lieutenant General Samuel Wilson summarizes this critique: "There is little likelihood of a strategic nuclear confrontation with the Soviets. It is almost as unlikely that Soviet Warsaw Pact forces will come tearing through the Fulda Gap [of West Germany] in a conventional thrust. We live today with conflict of a different sort."[19]

This "different sort" of conflict, according to LIC planners, requires a "different sort" of U.S. response. "The roots of insurgencies are not military in origin," Secretary of the Army John Marsh explained, "nor will they be military in resolution."[20] This analysis has led to an emphasis on nontraditional forms of coercion—economic, diplomatic, psychological, and paramilitary—what Colonel Waghelstein bluntly describes as "total war at the grass-roots level."[21]

The deemphasis of conventional military tactics dovetails with the second major impetus for the ascendency of LIC doctrine—the search for a politically acceptable mechanism to wage war in the underdeveloped areas. Bringing the power of the United States to bear in regional Third World conflicts has been an obsession of the Reagan administration. Indeed, the administration's desire to restore intervention as a primary tool of U.S. foreign policy has dominated Washington's foreign-policy agenda over the last seven years—despite the fact that it has been constrained by the reality of an international and domestic environment inhospitable to the bald assertion of power.[22]

To a great extent, the militant posture of the administration was a reaction to the changing international environment Reagan encountered when he assumed office in 1981. Between 1974 and 1980, a spate of revolutions had swept the Third World. Beginning with Vietnam, the wave of change brought the ouster of corrupt or colonial regimes the United States had once supported in at least a dozen countries, including Angola, Mozambique, Ethiopia, Iran, Grenada, and Nicaragua.[23]

For the Reagan team, this accumulation of U.S. "defeats" in the Third World was a bitter pill. "The escalating setbacks to our interests abroad," Secretary of State Alexander Haig proclaimed when the administration took office in 1981, "and the so-called wars of national liberation, are putting in jeopardy our ability to influence world events."[24] Given the long history of America's quest for world paramountcy, it was inevitable that Washington would seek to redress its losses, reassert its power, and attempt to restore its global dominion to the halcyon days of the Cold War.

Yet any such assertion of imperial will was conditioned by the domestic repercussions of America's debacle in Vietnam. The U.S. public had lost much of its innocence during the long and futile conflict in Indochina. Despite intensive White House efforts to erase it, the "Vietnam syndrome"—a clear and pervasive reluctance of American citizens to support overt U.S. intervention in local Third World conflicts— placed severe political constraints on the use of U.S. military power abroad.

Low-intensity conflict doctrine offered the Reaganauts an irresistible solution to this dilemma. It presented the prospect of waging a war not defined as such. No draft would be necessary; few soldiers would be deployed, and even fewer would be sent home in body bags. Therein lay the great appeal of LIC doctrine: the ability to overcome the limits on American power while pursuing the counterrevolutionary goals of a president determined to restore U.S. dominion where once it had been lost.

THE HISTORICAL ORIGINS OF LIC

But while the terminology and some of the tactics of current LIC doctrine may be original, much of the intent is consistent with previous episodes in American history. Under one banner or another, the United States has been waging low-level wars in the Third World for many decades—from the Philippines at the turn of the century to Nicaragua in the early 1930s. The end of World War II, moreover, ushered in a new era of low-level engagement. With the Truman Doctrine in 1946, the United States began to develop a rudimentary counterinsurgency strategy for combating Communist guerrillas in Greece. In 1947, the clandestine apparatus that had conducted "special activities" behind enemy lines during the war was reorganized under the National Security Act as the Central Intelligence Agency. Under successive administrations, the CIA became deeply embroiled in paramilitary activities in Europe, the Middle East, Southeast Asia, and Latin America.[25]

To be sure, U.S. strategists focused most of their attention during the early Cold War period on the threat posed by Soviet conventional forces in Europe and the threat of Communist military encroachment elsewhere. Korea was the first manifestation of Washington's commitment to wage conventional conflict in the nuclear age; it was also the first manifestation of the American reluctance to embrace a protracted military campaign of unclear purpose and meaning. By the time Washington negotiated a cease-fire in 1953, most Americans were weary of the war and eager to avoid similar entanglements in the future.

To reduce military expenditures while providing a credible counterweight to Soviet conventional strength, President Eisenhower adopted the strategy of "Massive Retaliation"—a doctrine relying on the threat of a U.S. nuclear strike to prevent nonnuclear incursions by the Soviet Union in Europe and elsewhere. In accordance with this approach, Eisenhower presided over a major buildup of U.S. nuclear forces and a corresponding reduction in America's nonnuclear ground and naval strength.[26]

Although Eisenhower quietly unleashed the CIA to overthrow nationalist governments in Iran and Guatemala, the doctrine of Massive Retaliation dominated formal U.S. strategic policy between 1952 and 1960. But Massive Retaliation did not, and could not, deter the emergence of revolutionary guerrilla upheavals in Vietnam, Algeria, Cuba, and other far-flung corners of the Third World. Political and economic instability in the underdeveloped regions was, in large part, attributable to the dissolution of colonial empires in the aftermath of World War II. Yet, U.S. policy-makers chose to portray the so-called "wars of national liberation" as Soviet-instigated proxy wars against the West meant to circumvent U.S. nuclear superiority. "Massive Retaliation as a guiding strategic concept has reached a dead end," General Maxwell Taylor wrote in his 1960 best-seller, *The Uncertain Trumpet.* "While our massive retaliatory strategy may have prevented the Great War—a World War III—it has not maintained the Little Peace: that is, peace from disturbances which are little only in comparison with the disaster of general war."[27]

To provide a credible, realistic response to future such "disturbances" in the Third World, General Taylor advocated a strategy of Flexible Response—the development of a large and multifunctional conventional force of unprecedented flexibility. The term Flexible Response, he noted, "suggests the need for a capability to react across the entire spectrum of possible challenge, for coping with anything from general atomic war to infiltrations and aggressions such as threaten Laos and Berlin." The new strategy, moreover, "would recognize that it is just as necessary to deter or win quickly a limited war as to deter general war."[28]

This strategic doctrine, which theoretically incorporated a capability to engage simultaneously or serially in irregular, conventional, or nuclear warfare, was enthusiastically embraced by John F. Kennedy upon his election as president in 1960. One of Kennedy's first acts in office was to order his secretary of defense, Robert McNamara, to plan and manage an across-the-board buildup of America's conventional military forces. Seeking a vigorous response to the Cuban revolution and to mounting turmoil in Southeast Asia, he also mandated that the U.S. military, in coordination with other national security agencies, be mobilized to wage wars of suppression against revolutionary guerrilla upheavals in the Third World. In National Security Action Memorandum No. 124, signed January 18, 1962, Kennedy called for "proper recognition throughout the U.S. government that subversive insurgency ('wars of liberation') is a major form of politico-military conflict equal in importance to conventional warfare."[29]

As a result, the U.S. Army was ordered to expand its Special Forces detachments and to step up training in counterguerrilla operations. Interagency committees were established to coordinate State Department, Defense Department, CIA, and USIA political, economic, and psychological operations. "Subversive insurgency is another type of war, new in its intensity, ancient in its origins," the president told West Point graduates in 1962. "It requires in those situations where we must counter it . . . a whole new kind of strategy, a wholly different kind of force, and therefore a new and wholly different kind of training."[30]

Kennedy's near-obsession with guerrilla warfare gave rise to the doctrine of counterinsurgency, which inexorably led the United States into the jungles of Indochina. Vietnam was to be the first "test case" of America's counterinsurgency capability under realistic battlefield conditions. In his last year in office, President Kennedy authorized a buildup of Special Forces advisers, the deployment of U.S. combat aircraft, and the initiation of a broad "civic action" program in South Vietnam in order to counter stepped-up guerrilla activity by the National Liberation Front (NLF). "Here we have a going laboratory," General Taylor informed Congress in 1963, "where we see subversive insurgency, the Ho Chi Minh doctrine, being applied in all its forms."[31]

Once Vietnam was designated as a proving ground for U.S. counterinsurgency, it became essential for Washington to avoid defeat—lest America's failure encourage leftist insurgents in other countries to employ the "Ho Chi Minh doctrine." With U.S. credibility on the line in Vietnam, the option of retreat became increasingly difficult to contemplate. As Taylor suggested in a secret 1964 memorandum to McNamara, "The failure of our programs in South Vietnam would have heavy influence on the judgements of Burma, India, Indonesia, Malaysia, Japan, Taiwan, the Republic of Korea, and the Republic of the Philippines with respect to U.S. durability, resolution and trustworthiness."[32] Unable to resist such arguments, Kennedy, and then Lyndon Johnson, ordered more U.S. advisers and counterinsurgency teams into Southeast Asia. And when it became apparent that South Vietnamese government forces were no match for the North Vietnamese-backed NLF, five hundred thousand U.S. troops were deployed in a futile effort to rescue American "credibility."

As casualties mounted without any corresponding sign of military success, American public opinion turned against the war. By the end of the 1960s, this opposition was variously manifested in massive student uprisings, militant resistance to the draft, a split among American elite between the prowar "hawks" and the antiwar "doves," and other symptoms of public discontent. Ultimately, the schisms at home became so volatile that most U.S. leaders—McNamara among them—concluded that the war was lost and withdrawal was essential. On April 15, 1975, the last American helicopter lifted off the U.S. Embassy rooftop in Saigon as North Vietnamese troops took over the city.

RESURRECTING INTERVENTIONISM

Vietnam inspired a deep-seated public resistance to protracted U.S. military involvement abroad. In a political climate hostile to war, the antiwar forces secured the passage of significant restrictions on direct U.S. involvement in future regional conflicts in the Third World. The draft was abolished. Congressional oversight of the CIA was mandated. The "War Powers Act" was passed; no longer could a president order the extended deployment of U.S. troops abroad without congressional approval.

Predictably, this domestic political backlash also contributed to the discrediting of the doctrines and a dismantling of the forces that had spearheaded the United States involvement in Indochina. The budget for the Pentagon's Special Operations Forces was cut; the CIA's paramilitary capabilities were curtailed; and counterinsurgency quickly disappeared from the Pentagon lexicon as the Department of Defense turned its attention once again to the less controversial task of enhancing U.S. capabilities in the European theater. "The lesson of Vietnam is that we must throw off the cumbersome mantle of world policeman," is the way Senator Edward Kennedy summarized the prevailing liberal postwar attitude regarding future intervention in the Third World.[33]

Nevertheless, a small contingent of officers, analysts, and political operators inside the national security establishment, supported by a growing neoconservative movement, committed themselves to restoring the United States as the "guardian at the gate" of a global hegemonic order. Jimmy Carter's halfhearted attempt to move America beyond what he called "an inordinate fear of communism" provided the grist for a right-wing offensive mounted by such groups as the Committee on the Present Danger, the Heritage Foundation, the Hoover Institution, and Georgetown University's Center for Strategic and International Studies. Carter's foreign and military policies were characterized by weakness and vacillation, these groups argued, permitting the Soviet Union to undermine U.S. security by sponsoring revolution in the Third World.[34] "Containment of the Soviet Union is not enough," averred a policy paper drafted by a group of would-be Reagan advisers, and published by the Council for Inter-American Security in mid-1980. "Détente is dead. Survival demands a new US foreign policy. America must seize the initiative or perish. For World War III is almost over."[35]

To successfully wage "World War III," the proponents of low-intensity warfare advocated a complete overhaul of U.S. strategies and capabilities for waging counterrevolution in the Third World. With the dynamic of revolution in Central America as a catalyst, in the early 1980s their policy recommendations began to garner widespread attention within the national security bureaucracy. In forum after forum, LIC theorists advanced their case. One 1983 conference on "Special Operations in U.S. Strategy," hosted by the National Defense University (NDU) at Fort McNair, called for the United States "to develop diverse and even novel ways to defend its economic and geopolitical interests when these are affected by unconventional conflicts."[36] In the audience was a then unknown staff officer of the NSC, Lieutenant Colonel (then Major) Oliver North.[37]

As the Reagan period proceeded, advocates of LIC doctrine were given ever-expanded authority to convert their theories into practice. In the essays that follow, we see some of the results of these endeavors. Hence, in Chapter 5, Daniel Siegel and Joy Hackel show how the State and Defense Departments have directed an increasingly bitter and violent counterinsurgency campaign against El Salvadoran guerrillas. In Chapter 6, Peter Kornbluh discloses how the Pentagon and the CIA have collaborated in the management of a bloody proxy war against the Sandinista government of Nicaragua. And in Chapter 7, Walden Bello explores America's growing politicomilitary involvement in the Philippines. Not since the heyday of CIA Director Allen Dulles has Washington undertaken as extensive and ambitious an array of "special activities."

"HEARTS AND MINDS" AT HOME

To sustain these campaigns abroad, and to consolidate LIC as a standard tool of U.S. intervention, U.S. policy-makers perceive an urgent need to wage a war at home—to fight for the "hearts and minds" of the American people. Given the public's continuing adherence to the "Vietnam syndrome," a political campaign to garner grass-roots support for renewed interventionism is considered an essential component of LIC doctrine. "In order to promote a broad understanding of the issues involved, a carefully created, sophisticated and ongoing public diplomacy effort is necessary," the *JLIC Final Report* avows.[38] The need for public politicization has also been underlined by the deputy assistant secretary of the Air Force, J. Michael Kelly. "I think the most critical special operations mission we have today is to persuade the American public that the Communists are out to get us," he declared at the 1983 NDU conference attended by Colonel North. "If we win the war of ideas, we will win everywhere else."[39] Clearly, the Reagan administration's heavy-handed rhetoric about Central American "freedom fighters," Nicaragua's "totalitarian dungeons," and the constant peril of terrorism is all part of this "war of ideas"—a synchronized effort to legitimize intervention as a paramount feature of America's political and military landscape.

Such efforts are considered particularly crucial because low-intensity conflict—almost by definition—entails an alliance with right-wing forces and regimes that are not known for their democratic sensibilities or respect for the rules of war. "The American view of war is generally incompatible with the characteristics and demands of counterrevolution," LIC theorist Sam C. Sarkesian observed in *Air University Review*. To defeat a revolutionary movement, insurgent leaders must be identified, abducted, or somehow eliminated—a process that normally involves the widespread use of torture and assassination. "If American involvement [in counterrevolution] is justified and necessary," Sarkesian notes,

> national leaders and the public must understand that low-intensity conflicts do not conform to democratic notions of strategy or tactics. Revolution and counterrevolution develop their own morality and ethics that justify *any means* to achieve success. Survival is the ultimate morality.[40] [Emphasis added.]

This belief that "any means" are justified in conducting counterrevolutionary warfare is a common subtheme in current discussions of low-intensity warfare. "The 'dirty little wars' of our time are not pretty," Neil Livingstone told senior U.S. officers in 1983, but if we shrink back from harsh and brutal measures, "we abrogate our ability to engage successfully in low-level conflict." Among his suggestions for success in low-intensity warfare: restrictions on media access to foreign war zones; diminished congressional "micromanagement" of LIC operations; and the employment of bounty hunters to track down and assassinate suspected terrorists. "While such recommendations would surely provoke an outcry from civil libertarians," he noted, the United States is "at war" in the Third World, "and in wartime the only thing that counts is winning."[41]

By any standard, the most dramatic explication of this point of view was contained in Colonel North's July 1987 testimony to the select congressional committee on the Iran-contra affair. Arguing that the United States was vitally threatened by Soviet-backed forces in the Third World, North repeatedly affirmed that U.S. national security justifies the employment of covert paramilitary operations, and, to help conceal such operations from our adversaries, the calculated dissemination of false and misleading information by (and to) U.S. officials. "There is great deceit [and] deception practiced in the conduct of covert operations," he declared. "They are at essence a lie."[42]

To a large degree, the pervasive secrecy favored by North and his associates at the NSC was intended to avert public disclosure of controversial—and probably illegal—administration dealings with Iran and the contras. But closer analysis suggests that the emphasis on covert warfare stems from a deeper cause: the Reagan administration's growing frustration with the military contraints associated with continuing public adherence to the Vietnam syndrome.

Given continuing public resistance to overt intervention abroad, it is likely that secrecy, deception, and intrigue will remain essential features of the domestic political landscape. Indeed, whatever the immediate consequences of the Iran-contra disclosures, there is no evidence that American leaders—be they Democrats or Republicans—have any intention of repudiating current LIC doctrine or of dismantling the Pentagon's "special" military forces. If anything, one can detect growing support among U.S. policy-makers for an expansion of America's LIC capabilities: witness, for instance, the bipartisan congressional support accorded the administration's plans for a multibillion-dollar buildup of U.S. special operations capabilities (see Chapter 3). Low-intensity conflict has been anointed as the paramount strategic concern of the late Reagan era, and we will feel its repercussions for many years to come.

This being the case, the authors believe it essential that the American people become more familiar with official thinking on low-intensity warfare, and press for an open national debate on the costs and perils of LIC doctrine. Such a debate must consider two broad issues: the probable military consequences of U.S. intervention abroad, and the political and moral consequences at home.

The military debate has, of course, already been initiated by the proponents of LIC doctrine. Without a vigorous U.S. response to

Soviet-sponsored expansionism, they argue, the United States will be deprived of access to critical raw materials and will ultimately experience an irreversible loss of power to the Soviet bloc. These are serious concerns, and they merit careful consideration. All too often, however, their purveyors fail to acknowledge that Soviet influence in the Third World has been declining in recent years as once-radical regimes turn to the West for capital and technology; similarly, they often overlook the fact that the United States has not experienced any significant difficulties in obtaining the strategic raw materials it requires for its high-tech industries.[43] More than this, however, the pro-LIC argument fails to consider the perils we face by *engaging* in intervention, rather than by avoiding it.

In assessing these perils, it is useful to recall the paramount lesson of Vietnam: that even a "limited" deployment of U.S. military and political power has a way of expanding into a much larger commitment of American strength. As suggested by Charles Maechling in Chapter 2, "the slippery slope from advice and assistance to commitment of combat forces has always been steeper for the United States than for other countries." Current LIC doctrine seeks to minimize that risk by enhancing the military capabilities of host-nation forces. But such forces can fail, as they did in Vietnam, and then the pressures to salvage an American ally by deploying American forces can become overpowering. Secretary Weinberger alluded to this risk in his 1987 report to Congress: "Although we seek to counter subversion through the methods [prescribed by LIC doctrine], the United States has, in the past, responded effectively with force to blunt this kind of aggression . . . and retains the capability *and the will* to do so again should it be deemed necessary." Surely, he added, "no one can contend that it is to our advantage to allow a communist-supported subversion to convert a friendly government into a communist enemy, and particularly not in our own hemisphere."[44] (Emphasis added.)

Such an intervention, however "low-intensity" in theory, would not be without significant costs or perils. Direct U.S. involvement in a politically charged Third World conflict would surely provoke considerable dissent at home, and possibly within the American military itself. A protracted struggle, moreover, could result in considerable American casualties and would certainly generate pressures for reinstatement of the draft. In the Third World itself, the consequences would be even more severe: American firepower would inevitably produce some civilian casualties (no matter how "surgical" the delivery of munitions), and the ravages of war would leave many people homeless, hungry, and stripped of their means of livelihood. Indeed, we can already witness the devastating consequences of "low-intensity warfare" in both El Salvador (see Chapter 5) and Afghanistan (see Chapter 8). As these wars grind on, the social and economic infrastructure is shattered, thus destroying any chance of escaping from poverty and underdevelopment.

We must also recognize that the growing worldwide availability of high-tech conventional weapons is systematically eroding the gap between "low-" and "mid-intensity conflict," and likewise between "mid-" and "high-intensity conflict." As the 1987 Iraqi missile attack on the USS *Stark* demonstrated, our major military systems are highly vulnerable to sophisticated weapons of the sort now possessed by many Third World nations. Previously, as noted by two Army theorists in *Military Review,* distinctly different forces and weapons were developed for each type of warfare; today, "with the greater dispersion, increased kill probabilities and improved mobility [of modern weapons], those types of war along the spectrum of conflict may be more similar than they are dissimilar."[45] What this means, of course, is that a war that starts out as "low-intensity conflict" can escalate overnight to the "mid" or "high" category—a risk that is particularly acute in the highly militarized Persian Gulf area. As Selig Harrison suggests in Chapter 8, moreover, low-intensity conflict can lead to a U.S.-Soviet confrontation, if intervention by one superpower invites countermoves by the other (as has occurred in Afghanistan) and triggers an uncontrolled spiral of escalation.

Turning to the domestic political consequences of the new interventionism, we can see a variety of threats to American rights and liberties. First and foremost is the threat to public information. LIC theorists have made no secret of their belief that an active press and Congress represent a significant obstacle to military effectiveness. "The United States will never win a war fought daily in the U.S. media or on the floor of Congress," Livingstone told senior officers at the National Defense University.[46] Similarly, Colonel North went out of his way to justify the concealment of information—even from the appropriate committees of Congress—on covert LIC operations abroad.

But the public's access to information is only one casualty of the war at home. As Richard Barnet suggests in the concluding chapter of this book, any sustained effort to mislead and circumvent Congress poses a serious threat to the integrity of the constitutional process. If the Executive considers itself above the law, and NSC operatives are authorized to conduct an independent foreign policy, then we can no longer rely on the checks and balances that are our ultimate safeguard against tyranny. Just how vulnerable these protections have become was dramatically revealed in Colonel North's July 10, 1987, testimony, when he disclosed that former CIA Director William J. Casey had proposed the establishment of an "off-the-shelf, self-sustaining, stand-alone entity" that could perform covert political and military operations without accountability to Congress. "If you carry this to its logical extreme," Senator Warren B. Rudman observed two days later, "you don't have a democracy anymore."[47]

And not only democracy is at risk, but also our basic moral values. While U.S. leaders *always* claim that they seek to promote American values when authorizing military intervention abroad, the outcome is often quite another matter. As Sam Sarkesian has suggested in the passage cited above, U.S. support for counterrevolution inevitably risks American entanglement in the repressive behavior of Third World autocrats and their heavy-handed security forces. Once committed to the survival of these regimes, we often compound our sins by failing to curb blatant abuses or worse, by telling ourselves that occasional atrocities can be overlooked in the name of "democracy." From there, it is but a short distance to the view that *any means* are justified in the pursuit of victory, even the wholesale liquidation of civilian communities. Thus, however assiduously Washington seeks to minimize the risks, deepened U.S. involvement in low-intensity conflict abroad could impose intolerable strains on the moral fabric of the nation.

In their preface to the *JLIC Final Report*, the members of the Joint Low-Intensity Conflict Project affirm that their intention was to initiate an "enlightened debate" on the type of conflict most likely to engage American forces in the years ahead. "In this sense," they affirmed, the *Final Report* "is not a prescription but an invitation."[48] In editing this book, the authors have taken up this invitation. We believe that the essays contained herein represent an important contribution to an "enlightened debate" on low-intensity conflict. But we do not believe that the debate is now concluded; there are too many aspects of low-intensity conflict—some still only dimly understood—and too many risks to leave it at that. Only through a broad and open discussion of LIC theory and practice can the American citizens make intelligent decisions on policies that are likely to affect our lives and liberties for many years to come.

COUNTERINSURGENCY:
THE FIRST ORDEAL BY FIRE

CHARLES MAECHLING, JR.

"WHAT are we doing about guerrilla warfare?" said President John F. Kennedy in January 1961, almost on the day he took office.[1] The answer: not very much. Revolution, insurgency, and guerrilla warfare were well down the agenda of policy-makers in the Pentagon and the State Department; terrorism was viewed as the province of the FBI and the Justice Department. From the end of World War II until the closing days of the Eisenhower administration, the primary concerns of U.S. strategic thinking had been the Soviet conventional threat to Europe and the Chinese Communist threat to East Asia. Deeply implanted in the mentality of the Joint Chiefs of Staff was the lesson of Korea—never to get bogged down in unwinnable wars on the mainland of Asia. With the possible exception of Cuba, Taiwan, and South Korea, the less-developed countries were largely viewed as peripheral to U.S. national security interests.

Nevertheless, by 1961 it was widely felt that some shift in strategic focus from conventional and nuclear warfare to unconventional forms of conflict was long overdue. Containment of the Soviet Union through nuclear deterrence had not proved to be an adequate response to insurgency and indirect aggression against vulnerable Third World governments friendly to the United States. Even a conventional-warfare response seemed inappropriate to cope with the tide of revolution sweeping through the Third World. To President Kennedy, the triumph of insurgency movements in Algeria and Indochina, the defeat of

Chiang Kai-shek and the Chinese Nationalists at the hands of Mao Tse-tung, the overthrow of the Batista dictatorship in Cuba by Fidel Castro, and incipient insurgencies in South Vietnam and Latin America were ominous portents of trouble to come from unexpected quarters.

In reaction to these emerging threats, Kennedy ordered his new team of senior advisers—some of whom professed specialized knowledge of military and strategic affairs—to develop a vigorous, multilevel response to the revolutionary threat. What slowly emerged was the first comprehensive effort of the U.S. government to devise a politicomilitary strategic program to deal with guerrilla and counterguerrilla warfare—the domain described today as "low-intensity conflict." Even before this effort could get underway, however, Kennedy's advisers were scanning the Third World for possible sites to "draw the line" against Communist insurgency.

These efforts were brought into sharp focus by Soviet Chairman Nikita Khrushchev's speech of January 6, 1961, endorsing "wars of national liberation" in the Third World. Taken in the context of Communist writings on guerrilla warfare, which the new breed of civilian "defense intellectuals" in Kennedy's entourage had been studying in think tanks and universities, the speech seemed to portend a Communist strategy of protracted conflict aimed at eroding the U.S. alliance system from the periphery rather than by attacking it directly.[2] The same intellectuals, led by Professor Walt W. Rostow of MIT, the new deputy national security adviser, discovered a perfect symmetry between Communist guerrilla doctrine and Rostow's theory of the "stages of economic growth," set forth in his book of the same name. It was easy for them to forge a plausible link between a supposed Communist master plan for world revolution and their own blueprint of the development process, based on the premise that developing nations are most vulnerable to subversion and revolt during the "takeoff" stage when societal stresses are at their maximum. By amalgamating guerrilla warfare doctrine with development theory, these instant experts were able to construct alarming scenarios that depicted Moscow and Peking as plotting to "confiscate the revolution of rising expectations" by exploiting the growing pains of Third World nations.[3]

To those familiar with the regions in question, this apocalyptic vision was, to say the least, simplistic. The Foreign Service professionals of the Department of State generally took the view that postwar insurgencies in Asia and Africa had their roots in the social and economic upheaval of World War II and were fomented by the anticolonial movements that followed in its wake. Everyone with firsthand acquaintance of South and Central America knew that their revolutionary troubles were a response to the social and economic injustice built into the hierarchical structure of the Latin nations, and to the political violence—often accompanied by sadistic brutality—traditionally employed by local tyrants and oligarchies to maintain power and suppress peaceful reform.[4]

The upheavals of the 1950s and 1960s did, however, differ from their predecessors in that their political direction was often shaped by Marxist ideology, which united traditional anticolonialism and nationalism with the struggle of the impoverished masses against economic exploitation. Another difference was that the new doctrines of guerrilla warfare sought to extend the arena of conflict to the entire population, including its economic and political infrastructure. The military tactics employed by guerrilla movements were not, however, novel per se—ambush and hit-and-run attacks had always been the tactics of the weak against the strong, and had most recently been employed by World War II resistance movements against the occupying forces of the Axis.

In modern history, guerrilla warfare begins with its use by Spanish insurgents (who coined the name) against the French in the Napoleonic Wars. It was the strategy of the Indian against the white man in North America; of the Cuban insurgents against Spain in the 1890s; of the Philippine insurgents under Aguinaldo against the U.S. Army in 1899; of Augusto Sandino against U.S. Marines in Nicaragua in the 1920s; and of countless other independence movements. The distinguishing feature of all these insurgencies was the effort of the contestants to capture the loyalty of the uncommitted majority through some combination of intimidation, promises of reform, and appeal to grievances.

In Asia, the classic case of a recent Communist insurgency—in this case an unsuccessful one—was in Malaya. Between 1948 and 1956, a Communist guerrilla movement composed of ethnic Chinese plantation workers fought the British colonial government and the emerging Malayan state. Operating from jungle hideouts, the guerrillas waged a campaign of hit-and-run attacks not only against British security forces but also against the rubber plantations and their Malayan work force. At first ineffectual, the British response to the "Emergency" (as it was called) became more effective after the appointment of General Sir Gerald Templer as supreme commander. Templer built up an efficient intelligence network and adopted a strategy of aggressive small-unit patrolling aimed at relentless pursuit of guerrilla forces and encirclement of their jungle hideouts.

Despite a reputation for ruthlessness, Templer operated on the presumption that civilians were friendly or uncommitted in the absence of overwhelming evidence to the contrary. He also insisted that London first take immediate steps to broaden local autonomy and then negotiate complete independence without waiting for the termination of hostilities. British military tactics kept the guerrillas on the run while British political strategy cut the ground out from under the nationalistic appeal of the guerrillas.

In the early days of the Kennedy administration, the Malayan experience was held up as a model of how to deal with an Asian Communist insurgency. Unfortunately, the Americans never profited from, or even understood, its lessons, which were later set out in two noteworthy books by Sir Robert Thompson, one of General Templer's staff officers.[5] Incomprehensible to a nation committed to massive effects and military deployments was a policy predicated on the principle of limited investment. At no time during the Emergency did the British use more than twenty-five infantry and police battalions; nor did they employ artillery, airborne units, tanks, or air bombardment. As a consequence, there was no mass destruction; civilian deaths were minimal, and the civilian economy emerged sufficiently unscathed to put the new state of Malaysia on the road to its present prosperity.[6]

Closer to home was the Hukbalahap rebellion of the mid-1950s in the Philippines. This was a wartime liberation movement that was later transformed into a Communist-led insurgency as a result of continued exploitation of the rural peasantry by large landowners. The "Huk" rebellion subsided only after a gifted Philippine defense minister (and subsequent president), Ramón Magsaysay, developed a carrot-and-stick counterinsurgency program entailing the same sort of aggressive small-unit patrolling as in Malaya and a program of amnesty and rehabilitation for defecting rebels (supplemented by housing grants). Magsaysay's strategy depended on lavish U.S. economic aid to provide housing for amnestied families, and to assist in the implementation of land reform.

Neither in Malaya nor in the Philippines did military "doctrine" per se play much of a role. In Malaya, General Templer, who had a virtual blank check from the British government, followed the British tradition of treating insurgencies as unique local problems, with exclusive reliance on military and police professionals. Only the most far-reaching political decisions were referred to the Cabinet in London. In the Philippines, Colonel Edward Lansdale of the CIA had a relatively free hand to recommend innovative counterinsurgency techniques of his own (see Chapter 7).

In contrast, the Kennedy administration took the view that local insurgencies were either part of the Communist grand design or so open to Communist exploitation as to call for the same response. Whatever their qualifications in other areas, the "best and the brightest" who formed Kennedy's foreign-policy brain trust had little knowledge of the developing areas. The result was an abstract approach to Third World political violence that treated countries as counters in an East-West game and failed to set revolutionary movements in a regional context. Moreover, despite a new international panorama made up of a multiplicity of emergent national states, the national security bureaucracies at State and Defense continued to cling to an outdated vision of American "responsibilities" that extended U.S. strategic interests to virtually the entire globe. Without quite realizing it, the new president's global rhetoric and sweeping policy formulations were committing his administration and the nation to an ambitious program of countering left-wing revolution around the world.

FORGING THE
DOCTRINE OF COUNTERINSURGENCY

Driven by his own magniloquent rhetoric to seek dramatic results, President Kennedy moved quickly to establish the institutional framework for a global crusade against Third World revolution. Barely recovered from the fiasco of the Bay of Pigs, the new president included a section on "subliminal warfare" (as low-intensity conflict was termed at the time) and the need for counterinsurgency measures in his Special Message to Congress on Urgent National Needs of May 16, 1961.[7] Moreover, as one of his first assignments, the president's new special military representative, General Maxwell D. Taylor, was instructed to prod the Pentagon into building up the Army's counterguerrilla capabilities. As a result, the Special Forces training center at Fort Bragg, North Carolina, was given added responsibilities, and the secretary of defense appointed a special assistant for unconventional warfare. The secretary of state followed suit by appointing a "director for internal defense" to his politicomilitary staff—a position occupied by the author from 1961 to 1963.[8]

The president's fascination with guerrilla warfare and counterinsurgency—the two were wholly confused in his mind, and the term "low-intensity conflict" had not yet been invented—nevertheless presented problems for the Pentagon. Despite a long and on the whole successful record of irregular warfare in the Indian Wars and the Philippine Insurrection, the U.S. Army before World War II regarded counterguerrilla operations as a subsidiary branch of warfare to be handled by "aggressive small-unit activity."[9] The only U.S. Army counterguerrilla doctrine to appear before 1961, Field Manual 31-20, *Operations Against Guerrilla Forces* (1951), was based on Soviet and Yugoslav partisan activities in World War II. The manual was designed for U.S. troop operations alone, and assumed the existence of a U.S. military government or U.S. control of the local political structure—i.e., a typical occupation situation. Wholly lacking was any reference to a protracted revolutionary war scenario or to the mission of training and supporting local forces.

The Pentagon, in short, had a rudimentary counterguerrilla doctrine (i.e., a doctrine for armed combat against guerrilla forces) but not a comprehensive *counterinsurgency* doctrine (i.e., a politicomilitary strategy for overcoming an ideologically driven revolutionary struggle). Without the latter, the Army lacked a uniform and multilevel approach to the new strategy of protracted warfare. Moreover, there was resistance at high levels in the Pentagon to overemphasis on guerrilla warfare: such a focus, it was feared, would generate images of "elite" units which could disturb morale and raise unwarranted expectations of rapid promotion. It would also open the door to noncombat missions that could divert resources from regular military missions.

The State Department was equally wary of the new White House interest in counterguerrilla warfare. It smacked of a fad that could identify the United States with repression and political reaction abroad, and could lead to overinvolvement in the internal affairs of other countries. Moreover, it threatened further militarization of the foreign aid program, and distortion of the latter's objectives. The Agency for International Development (AID) in particular resisted any contamination of its economic development programs, especially the Alliance for Progress, by the inclusion of internal security ingredients.

During the final six months of 1961, President Kennedy tried without success to get the State Department to assume leadership for a government-wide counterinsurgency effort. State, however, had neither the staff, the experience, nor the authority to coordinate programs of this scale involving coequal government agencies like the Department of Defense and the CIA. Finally, in frustration at State's incapacity to exert "leadership," and at the urging of General Taylor and other key advisers, Kennedy authorized the formation of a new Cabinet-level body, the Special Group (Counter-Insurgency). On January 18, 1962, he promulgated National Security Action Memorandum No. 124 (NSAM-124), which initiated a government-wide counterinsurgency effort and directed the Special Group (CI) to manage it.[10]

According to NSAM-124, the functions of the Special Group were:

a. To insure proper recognition throughout the U.S. Government that subversive insurgency ("wars of national liberation") is a major form of politico-military conflict equal in importance to conventional warfare.

b. To insure that such recognition is reflected in the organization, training, equipment and doctrine of the U.S. Armed Forces and other U.S. agencies abroad and in the political, economic, intelligence, military and informational programs conducted abroad by State, Defense, AID, USIA and CIA. . . .

d. To insure the development of adequate interdepartmental programs aimed at preventing or defeating subversive insurgency and indirect aggression in countries and regions specifically assigned to the Special Group.

As originally constituted, the Special Group consisted of General Maxwell D. Taylor, the chairman of the Joint Chiefs of Staff; the director of the CIA; the deputy secretary of defense; the heads of AID and the U.S. Information Agency (USIA); and the attorney general, Robert F. Kennedy; State was represented first by Deputy Undersecretary U. Alexis Johnson, and then by Averell Harriman, who assumed the chairmanship. With Harriman and Bobby Kennedy on the committee, the White House was assured of policy control and rapid action. The "Counterinsurgency Era" could now begin in earnest.[11]

For the next five years, the Special Group (CI) acted as the presidential vehicle for launching, executing, and monitoring a worldwide counterinsurgency effort. In its first session, the Group designated three Southeast Asian countries—Laos, Thailand, and South Vietnam—as falling within its cognizance.[12] Subsequently, three Latin American countries with incipient guerrilla movements—Colombia, Venezuela, and Bolivia—were added to the list. After the U.S.-Soviet Geneva conference of 1961–1962 resulted in the neutralization of

Laos, that country was deleted; in due course, Iran, Indonesia, and Ecuador were added.

At first, country-specific programs did not dominate the Group's agenda. Instead, priority went to reorientation of the civilian and military bureaucracy to reflect the new emphasis on counterinsurgency. Particular attention was given to drafting a government-wide counterinsurgency doctrine and then submitting it to an interdepartmental clearance process. Entitled the *U.S. Overseas Internal Defense Policy* (OIDP), this document finally surfaced in August 1962. After being approved by the Special Group, the OIDP was made official policy by President Kennedy in a secret directive, National Security Action Memorandum No. 182 (NSAM-182).[13]

The OIDP immediately became the basic policy guide of the government's counterinsurgency effort. More than any other document, it spelled out the purpose, principles, and applicability of the new doctrine. Suggesting that "a most pressing U.S. national security problem now, and for the foreseeable future, is the continuing threat presented by communist-inspired, supported, or directed insurgency," it asserted that "our task is to fashion on an urgent basis an effective plan of action to combat this critical communist threat." The main thrust of U.S. action was to be support of friendly Third World governments that were threatened by revolutionary guerrilla movements. After describing the nature of the insurgency threat and the techniques of protracted revolutionary war, it specified initial steps for making local governments aware of the threat, and then enumerated the U.S. assistance programs that could be brought to bear to overcome it.

Drawing on the Philippines and Malaya as examples of successful counterinsurgency operations, the OIDP called for a strategy of "internal defense" against revolutionary movements. "Success in preventing or defeating these movements depends on identifying and understanding the nature of the threat and combatting it with properly balanced action." These actions included fostering indigenous military and police capabilities through training and aid; promoting development through economic assistance; urging social and political reforms; and bolstering non-Communist labor unions, youth groups, and political parties. All of these activities were to be woven together in a "coordinated and integrated approach" to undermine the appeal of radical movements and to "minimize the likelihood of direct U.S. military involvement in internal war."[14]

To effectively apply counterinsurgency methods, the OIDP called for the expansion of U.S. intelligence capabilities and American military and economic programs in target countries. The document also spelled out departmental roles and missions. The Department of State was charged with encouraging "diplomatic, political, economic, psychological and military support for countries under indirect attack by communists."[15] The Agency for International Development was to "plan and implement programs having as their long-term aim the creation of economic and social conditions of sufficient vitality to eliminate the causes of discontent on which the communist appeal breeds." AID was also enjoined to enhance the counterinsurgency capabilities of police and security organizations in Third World countries. The Defense Department and its military assistance advisory groups (MAAGs) were mandated to provide counterinsurgency training and equipment to Third World military and paramilitary forces, and to reorient them toward nation-building and military civic action. The USIA was to expand its own psychological operations programs and to improve mass communication techniques in target countries. The CIA, meanwhile, was to conduct unspecified covert missions. Each particular counterinsurgency program was to be tailored to a "country internal defense plan," drafted by U.S. embassy officials in consultation with local governments and approved by the Special Group (CI).

Reflecting the divergent priorities of the agencies represented on the drafting group, the OIDP contained some rather contradictory language as to the relative balance between military and nonmilitary efforts in counterinsurgency. At State's insistence, the document stressed the social and economic causes of insurgency, flatly declaring that these stem from "the failures or inadequacies of the local government to requite or remove popular or group dissatisfaction." Accordingly, the OIDP cautioned against an overly visible U.S. participation and stated that "the major counter-insurgency effort must be indigenous." In apparent contradiction, however, were other paragraphs of an explicitly interventionist nature, included at the insistence of the Pentagon. Thus, the document stated that at "higher levels of insurgency, or where there is a threat of Communist takeover, the commitment of U.S. operational forces may be required." More sweepingly, the document was made applicable to the prevention and defeat of both "Communist-inspired" insurgencies and any others that might be "inimical to U.S. national security interests."

Notably absent in the OIDP was any reference to human rights, international law, the Geneva Conventions on prisoner treatment, U.S. legislative authority, or the conditions of its application other than presidential fiat. Repeated efforts to include even cursory mention of these factors were rejected by the Pentagon and General Taylor's office as "superfluous."

IMPLEMENTING THE DOCTRINE

The formal adoption of NSAM-182 provided the impetus for a broad expansion of U.S. counterinsurgency operations. In April 1962, the Joint Chiefs of Staff (JCS) published a Joint Counter-Insurgency Concept and Doctrinal Guidance of its own.[16] Shortly thereafter, it established the office of special assistant to the director of the Joint Staff for Counter-Insurgency, who also became the Pentagon's deputy representative on the Special Group and the writer's opposite number.[17] The Joint Chiefs also ordered revision of war college courses and field manuals. Scores of new courses were introduced on such subjects as guerrilla and counterguerrilla tactics, psychological warfare, and helicopter operations in a counterinsurgency environment.[18] All this sounded impressive, but according to one military authority there was nothing in the revised curricula to reflect a U.S. *advisory* (as distinct from a direct combat) role, and little change from Ranger tactics of long standing.[19] Although the basic Army operational manual expanded its coverage of unconventional warfare from 2 percent to 20 percent, U.S. doctrine still assumed that American forces would do all the fighting.[20]

The Pentagon next took steps to reorient the Military Assistance Program (MAP). Under the prodding of General Maxwell Taylor, much emphasis was placed on military civic action—the employment of local armed forces in projects that would bring them closer to the population, such as literacy instruction, disease inoculation, construction of roads and sanitary facilities, disaster relief, and so forth. Taylor, a more imaginative counterinsurgent than most, was convinced that Third World armies needed to play a constructive role in rural societies in order to build a sympathetic image of the military and thereby win the support of the civilian population. Another of Taylor's goals was to "professionalize" the officer corps of Third World countries by including civil government courses in the training programs for foreign officers at U.S. staff colleges, and encouraging them to participate in the political process. In

Latin America, U.S. MAAGs and military missions sought to reorient indigenous military establishments away from their traditional focus on external defense toward internal security and counterinsurgency.

At first glance, these innovations may have appeared as a logical and indeed enlightened response to the new challenge. In practice, however, they inevitably led to unprecedented military involvement in the political process, especially in South and Central America. In virtually every Latin American country, the elite officer corps constituted the single most disciplined and motivated political force. General Taylor's philosophy of "getting the Army out of the barracks and into the life of the people" broke down the flimsy partition separating civilian and military authority. Instead of periodic military coups by overweight generals who traditionally left the humdrum aspects of government to civilian bureaucrats, middle- and senior-grade military officers—acting on the premises of the new gospel—began taking over functions of civil administration. In the ensuing decade, many of the majors and colonels who had attended the U.S. Army School of the Americas in the Panama Canal Zone or the Inter-American Defense College in Washington during the 1960s helped overthrow constitutional governments all over Latin America. The regimes they installed were invariably maintained by intimidation, and sometimes, as in the case of Argentina, by mass murder.[21]

When a few voices in the State Department suggested that reforms that made good sense for democratic governments with strong civilian control over the military might be fatal to the fragile democracies of the Third World, their warnings were dismissed. One State Department policy paper that endorsed the new role of the Latin American military while incorporating civilian control and human rights safeguards as a condition of U.S. military assistance was peremptorily rejected by General Taylor as "unresponsive."[22]

The Kennedy administration's desire to make AID programs an integral part of the counterinsurgency effort also ran into resistance. The foreign-aid agency had always been hypersensitive to pressure from U.S. ambassadors to fund high-visibility projects aimed at enhancing the public image of client governments. With a more "liberal" administration in office, the new team at AID was determined to shape country programs exclusively in accordance with long-term economic development plans. The AID leadership conceded that there might be a broad correlation between economic misery and political violence, but it saw no justification for diverting badly needed development funding to "quick fix" projects tied to counterinsurgency campaigns.

Even greater obstacles were encountered when the Special Group, under the goading of Robert Kennedy, put heavy pressure on AID to accept responsibility for a greatly expanded U.S. police assistance program. The attorney general was a committed advocate of the notion that local police forces could be transformed into an "early warning system" for the detection—and subsequent suppression—of left-wing political movements before they erupted into armed rebellion. This was not, of course, an entirely new idea. The U.S. foreign aid agency, in its various incarnations, had for years included small police advisory teams in some of its overseas missions, on the rationale that domestic stability was necessary to protect the development process. But this early program had attracted the attention of the CIA, which, in the Dulles years, had secured permission to infiltrate intelligence officers under the guise of police advisers. By the time Kennedy took office, the resistance of the AID bureaucracy to what they saw as perversion of police assistance for intelligence purposes had reached such a pitch that the whole police program had been drastically cut back to avoid tainting the U.S. foreign-aid image.

Nonetheless, the attorney general was determined to convert friendly foreign police forces into a vital element of the U.S.-sponsored counterinsurgency effort. He did, however, recognize the suspicion attaching to a police assistance program when its personnel were automatically assumed to be intelligence operatives. Accordingly, a special interagency task force convened to reorganize the programs devised a solution: the program would be centralized, purged of its covert aspects, and bona fide police specialists would be recruited to serve as advisers.

These proposals were formalized in National Security Action Memorandum No. 177 (NSAM-177), signed by President Kennedy on August 7, 1962. In essence, NSAM-177 gave presidential authority to the attorney general's plan for an expanded police role in counterinsurgency operations abroad. "The U.S. should give considerably greater emphasis to police assistance programs in appropriate less developed countries where there is an actual or potential threat of internal subversion or insurgency," the document avowed. Such programs were to involve training by specialized U.S. personnel at overseas missions, advanced schooling at an "international police academy" to be established in

Washington, and the delivery of specialized arms and equipment. Management of this program was to be the responsibility of a new office in AID, but special permission was given to the Department of Defense (DOD) to participate directly in police missions in certain countries.[23]

With the signing of NSAM-177, an Office of Public Safety (OPS) was established within AID, and the former administrator of the CIA undercover program, Byron Engle, emerged from his CIA cover and was installed as OPS program director. Senior technical specialists and chiefs of small-city police departments were recruited from all over the United States to serve as overseas advisers. The emphasis of the new program was on improved police administration, the modernization of communications and intelligence operations, the teaching of modern methods of riot control, and the establishment of centralized command-and-control centers. The International Police Academy was established in an old streetcar barn in Georgetown, at which senior police officers from client states received advanced instruction in counterinsurgency and police administration. At its peak in 1969, the program had an annual budget of over $37 million and maintained advisory and training missions in some forty countries, of which the largest was in South Vietnam.[24]

(In 1974, Congress phased out the Public Safety program and closed down the International Police Academy amid a furor of allegations that the program had become inseparably associated with state terrorism and repression of political dissent. Particular damage to the program's image resulted from charges that OPS advisers had participated in or condoned the use of torture to silence dissidents or to obtain information on left-wing political formations. While these charges were never substantiated, there is no doubt that in modernizing foreign police forces while failing to insist on rigorous standards of criminal justice and civil liberties, the United States was often guilty of creating efficient instruments of repression where none had existed before.)

To the State Department fell the uncomfortable task of "exercising leadership" over the entire counterinsurgency effort by coordinating the new government-wide effort. As the department responsible for the conduct of U.S. foreign relations, State chaired most of the new interagency task forces and committees, including the OIDP drafting group. Beginning in April 1963, moreover, State presided over the Special Group (CI), with the redoubtable Averell Harriman in the chair. In the field, the U.S. ambassador—as head of the U.S. "Country Team"—was responsible for drafting the host country's "internal defense plan" and for coordinating the counterinsurgency assistance programs of other U.S. agencies.

The most unlikely mission foisted on the State Department, however, was "consciousness raising"—spreading the counterinsurgency gospel throughout the government by means of foreign-policy pronouncements, indoctrination lectures, and articles for publication.[25] The core of this effort was the development of an inderdepartmental seminar for senior officers destined for posts in Third World countries called "Problems of Development and Internal Defense." In its heyday, the six-week course featured lectures on such subjects as developmental economics, the sociology of military elites, Marxist-Leninist ideology, Communist infiltration tactics, and causes of political unrest—many given by professors from well-known universities.[26]

By 1966, when the Special Group was dissolved—or rather merged, into a larger interdepartmental coordination mechanism[27]—it had approved country internal defense plans for twenty countries and programs for over thirty more. In South Vietnam, the plan ran to over a hundred pages, incorporating the strategic hamlet program and the entire AID effort. In Thailand, the plan covered training and reequipment of the Thai Border Patrol Police, and strategic road construction. In Latin America, individual country plans typically entailed the modernization of police forces; in Iran, the plan included provision of counterguerrilla training for the shah's paramilitary Gendarmerie.

Prepared in the field by foreign-service and military professionals, country internal defense plans proved to be useful informational and analytical tools. When shown in whole or part to friendly local leaders— which U.S. ambassadors were authorized to do at their discretion—they served to pinpoint weaknesses and to suggest remedies. But as operational plans they were virtually useless. They depended for successful implementation on local authorities who had neither the funds, the experience, nor, in many cases, the inclination to put them into execution. In some cases, literal implementation would have torn up the existing social and economic fabric, including age-old systems of rewards and punishments; this might have resulted in genuine progress, but it might also have weakened the authority of the prevailing regime (upon which the entire counterinsurgency effort depended).

In the end, only a small part of all this high-level ferment in Washington had much impact on the regimes they were intended to instruct.

Except for Vietnam, the insurgency tide that was supposed to inundate the "free world" either never materialized or churned along at a reduced pace. Generally speaking, U.S. counterinsurgency programs had only a minor effect in countering domestic subversion and revolution. For the most part, U.S.-devised internal defense plans were accepted without cavil by governments eager to increase the flow of U.S. security assistance; adoption of their recommendations for economic and social reform was, however, another matter—in general, American ambassadors rarely pressed their clients too insistently.

On the military side, improvements in the counterinsurgency capabilities of U.S.-aided Asian and Latin American security forces went slowly. U.S. funds and military equipment were welcomed; advice was often ignored. In Latin America, U.S. military missions were loath to imperil relationships painstakingly built up after World War II by cutting out "prestige" military items—tanks, personnel carriers, self-propelled artillery—from military-aid programs, even though counterinsurgency doctrine prescribed such changes. This made it even harder to induce changes in the conventional-force structures into which this hardware fitted.

In Washington, however, these obstacles were minimized: by now counterinsurgency had developed a life of its own. Within the Departments of State and Defense, counterinsurgency committees and task forces proliferated. Insatiable White House demands for "fresh ideas" led to the recruitment of outside consultants. A wave of "defense intellectuals" from think tanks and universities descended on Washington in search of research contracts. To these spirited amateurs, counterinsurgency represented an exciting new discipline which allowed them to play armchair warrior while promoting social and economic reform.

VIETNAM:
THE ULTIMATE TEST OF DOCTRINE

Meanwhile, in the minds of Mr. Kennedy and his entourage, the global insurgency threat was beginning to crystallize around the deteriorating situation in South Vietnam. An interdepartmental task force replaced the handful of military and foreign-service personnel concerned with the Indochina problem in Washington. After the creation of the Special Group (CI) in 1962, a status report on Vietnam became the first action item on the agenda of the Group's weekly meetings. Throughout the

Special Group's first year, endless hours were devoted to discussions on the capabilities of South Vietnamese Army and civil defense forces, the design of strategic hamlets, and ways of strengthening the South Vietnamese economy, to name only a few of the recurring items. Senior military officers and civilian program heads from Saigon were summoned before the Group whenever they were in Washington for consultations. Their testimony often had disturbing effects on the mind-set of some of the Group's high-level membership, since they were under no compulsion to paint a rosy picture of the situation in the field.

In fact, since the spring of 1961, South Vietnam had been in "Phase II" of a classic Asian insurgency conducted along Maoist lines. It will be recalled that in Mao Tse-tung's concept of "People's War," Phase I was a grass-roots organizational effort, Phase II was armed action building up to a guerrilla war of attrition, and Phase III was a rising tempo of guerrilla attacks culminating in a final offensive of a conventional military character. The essence of Mao's doctrine was that the guerrilla avoids pitched battle except under conditions of his own choosing: he retreats when the enemy advances; harasses when the enemy stands still; and advances when the enemy retreats. Mao's most famous dictum is that "guerrillas are fish, and the people are the water in which they swim. If the temperature is right the fish will thrive and multiply."[28]

General Vo Nguyen Giap, the North Vietnamese military leader who masterminded the war of liberation against the French, had already made innovations of his own in adapting Mao's precepts to conditions in Vietnam. Before initiating hostilities in the South in the late 1950s, Ho Chi Minh and Giap had carefully built a formidable underground guerrilla organization on the foundation of the Viet Minh independence movement that had won the war against the French. Called the National Liberation Front (NLF) by its adherents and the Viet Cong (VC) by opponents, this organization created a grass-roots shadow government at the local level, complete with tax collection, informal land distribution, and a system of "people's justice" to mete out punishment (usually lethal) to "traitors" and agents of the Saigon regime.[29] By the end of 1961, Viet Cong strength in the South had reached twelve thousand, and its political network had expanded to the point where government control in many areas, especially the Mekong Delta, was largely fictional, with the Saigon government ruling by day, the NLF by night.[30] The Diem government made repeated attempts to penetrate and liquidate the NLF cells, but such was the regime's unpopularity and ineffectiveness that each act of repression tended to swell the ranks of the VC underground.

That South Vietnam was under threat of an attempt at forcible unification by the North had been recognized ever since President Ngo Dinh Diem canceled the elections mandated by the Geneva Accords of 1954. From the beginning, however, this threat had been viewed in terms of a Korean-style cross-border invasion, and the lavish U.S. military aid program had been fashioned accordingly. The South Vietnamese Army—the ARVN (for Army of the Republic of Vietnam)—had therefore been trained and equipped along conventional lines, with the country divided up into four large "corps areas." The standard response of the ARVN to guerrilla activity, when it reacted at all, was to detach a motorized company or battalion from its divisional base and send it in pursuit of the guerrillas along highways and roads; if guerrillas were spotted, the ARVN units would fan out in formation along front and flanks, and attack in formation under a heavy screen of mortar and rifle fire. Success was usually defined in terms of overrunning the hamlet or paddy fields temporarily held or infiltrated by the Viet Cong, not in destroying the guerrillas or their organization. And woe betide the villagers who had the misfortune to tolerate a Viet Cong presence, whether under duress or not: the ARVN's treatment of VC sympathizers was savage.

Large-scale U.S. involvement in Vietnam first began in late 1961. Worried by intelligence reports on the corruption and ineffectiveness of the Saigon regime, and on the corresponding growth of the National Liberation Front, President Kennedy dispatched a high-level investigative mission to Saigon in October of 1961. Headed by Maxwell Taylor and Walt Rostow, the mission discovered a far more serious situation than had been portrayed in the rosy reports of the U.S. military assistance advisory group. Taylor and Rostow found a reclusive chief of state surrounded by a corrupt and domineering family clique; an army of 150,000 trained to fight the wrong kind of war; an impoverished and disaffected rural population, alienated from the government in Saigon by persistent corruption and arbitrary misrule; and a society vulnerable to propaganda from Hanoi and ready to swing left or right depending on the degree of intimidation and pressure.

In its report, the Taylor-Rostow mission made no judgment as to whether South Vietnam was intrinsically important to the security of the United States—only that the spreading insurgency was part of a global Communist offensive of "wars of national liberation." As seen by Taylor and Rostow, the VC insurgency posed a threat to a friendly ally in a region where U.S. prestige was on the line and any sign of flagging commitment would trigger a massive loss of confidence on the part of America's allies. The report recommended a major counterinsurgency effort to prevent the collapse of the Diem regime, entailing the delivery of military vehicles, communications equipment, automatic weapons, and U.S. helicopters to give the ARVN greater firepower and offensive mobility. The report also recommended the immediate deployment of ten thousand U.S. ground troops, to be followed ultimately by the commitment of six Army divisions. These forces were to serve as a defensive screen to protect South Vietnam against invasion from the North while the ARVN took on the internal task of destroying the Viet Cong. On the political side, the Taylor-Rostow mission recommended a wide range of political and economic reforms, including redistribution of land from large properties and plantations to small holdings, together with an increased economic aid program to support the rural economy and stabilize South Vietnamese finances.

President Kennedy accepted all the Taylor-Rostow recommendations except for deployment of U.S. ground forces. As a result, for the next four years—until President Johnson dispatched U.S. combat troops in 1965—the United States was committed to the prosecution of a counterinsurgency war by proxy, to pouring in equipment and advisers, and using every device of persuasion and coercion to mobilize the government and armed forces of South Vietnam according to a master plan largely framed in Washington.

The administration's first task in shaping this effort was to establish the dimensions of the problem and to devise a scheme for U.S. support. When in January 1962 President Kennedy met in Honolulu with General Paul D. Harkins, the new commander of what had become the U.S. Military Assistance Command, Vietnam (MACV), U.S. intelligence estimated Viet Cong guerrilla strength in the South at 16,000. The ARVN at this time consisted of 175,000 regulars, organized and trained along conventional lines, plus a paramilitary Civil Guard of 67,000 and a newly recruited "self-defense force"—villagers armed with rifles—

numbering 54,000. This provided a theoretical fifteen-to-one ratio of government forces to guerrillas (excluding the self-defense force). Actually, in terms of combat troops, it was closer to eight-to-one—too low, in the opinion of the military experts, to produce anything better than a stalemate.

In consultation with Sir Robert Thompson, of Malayan Emergency fame, MACV then devised a plan to improve the ratio by the multiplier effects of technology and mobility. The plan envisioned the use of helicopters for airlift and gunfire, and of overage fighters and bombers for air support, so as to enable the ARVN to encircle and destroy the principal Viet Cong pockets. It also proposed the use of chemical defoliants (the notorious Agent Orange) to deprive the Viet Cong of ground cover. In order to separate the guerrillas from the population (in Maoist metaphor, to dry up the waters used by the fish), the core of the plan was a "strategic hamlet" program—forced resettlement of rural villagers into fortified compounds, linked together in an interdependent network—that would eventually squeeze the Viet Cong into isolated jungle areas.[31]

For the next four years, the strategic hamlet program became the centerpiece of U.S. strategy. The idea was not a novel one: it had been tried with varying success by the Spaniards in the Cuban revolution of 1895–97, by the British in the closing phases of the Boer War, by the French in Indochina, and, in modified form, by the British in Malaya. But for all the expense and effort—AID poured in vast amounts of supplies and equipment—the U.S. program turned out to be a failure.

As devised by Sir Robert Thompson, the hamlet network should have been expanded outward from one or more secure centers. The hamlets themselves were supposed to displace a minimum number of villagers, with only the most outlying families physically moved inside the perimeter so as not to separate them from their farming plots. Instead, the Saigon government first constructed a few elaborate model hamlets and then began designating hamlets as strategic on a random basis, some being hardly fortified at all and others displacing whole villages that were relocated in hastily built quarters with no means of livelihood.[32] The hamlets were supposed to be self-sustaining economic units, designed to help loyal peasants pursue their way of life under secure conditions; in fact, the people of many hamlets were disaffected or pro-NLF to begin with, and dislocation made their discontent more acute. Only a miraculous combination of peace, prosperity, genuine land reform, and an end to government mismanagement would have satisfied the villagers—and this the Saigon government was unable to provide.

To supplement the hamlet program and drive out the Viet Cong, Thompson and other insurgency experts advocated the same counter-guerrilla tactics that had been successful in Malaya: aggressive patrolling and surprise attacks by small commando units rigorously indoctrinated to distinguish between active guerrillas and hapless villagers caught in between.[33] Instead, the South Vietnamese Army, when it went on the offensive at all, followed the U.S. philosophy of wide-reaching sweeps and massive expenditure of firepower. These tactics killed civilians and devastated the countryside without rooting out the guerrillas; needless to say, they also solidified the antigovernment orientation of the villagers.

Meanwhile, the constructive features of the U.S. counterinsurgency plan ground to a halt, or rather proved impossible to carry out. The Diem regime first dragged its feet on land distribution, and then declared reform impossible to implement because of wartime conditions and the exigencies of the strategic hamlet program. Some AID-sponsored agricultural, road-building, and sanitation projects were started, but in general the disruption of rural economic life required diversion of much of the AID effort to humanitarian relief.

On top of the spreading insurgency came mounting political turmoil in Saigon and the other major cities. Internal opposition to Diem finally exploded into violence in the unexpected form of antigovernment demonstrations by the Buddhist minority, followed by attacks on the Buddhist temples by government security forces. Within the State Department's Far Eastern bureau there was universal agreement that in any fair election in the South, Ho Chi Minh and his slate of leftist candidates would win over the Saigon regime hands down. Diem was well aware of this, but his harsh police repression only isolated him further from the rest of the population. In the spring of 1963, the U.S. embassy established secret contact with disaffected Vietnamese generals, and in August the Kennedy administration sent a cable approving a military plot to get rid of Diem and his hated entourage.[34] The plot succeeded, and with it the United States became committed to the fortunes of the generals that took over from Diem.

Nineteen sixty-four was a watershed year. President Kennedy, for all his willingness to send in equipment and advisers, never tired of reiterating, "It's their war; we can't win it for them." By contrast, his successor, Lyndon Johnson, made it his war even before he committed U.S. combat troops. Action-oriented, impatient for quick results, with overweening confidence in American know-how and breathtaking ignorance of Southeast Asia, President Johnson blindly accepted the judgment of the academic coterie he had inherited from Kennedy that American prestige was at stake and that it was time to draw the line against Communist encroachment in Asia. On the advice of Dean Rusk, McGeorge Bundy, Walt Rostow, and Robert McNamara, Johnson decided to end the charade of acting through South Vietnamese proxies. It was time to "Americanize" the war against Ho Chi Minh and the Viet Cong and bring it to a rapid and successful conclusion.

Urged on by his advisers, and fortified by the blank check given to him by Congress after the Tonkin Gulf incident,[35] Johnson raised the number of U.S. military "advisers" from sixteen thousand at the beginning of 1964 to over twenty-three thousand at the end. He vastly increased the commitment of U.S.-manned helicopters and transport planes. He authorized an enlarged Public Safety program to equip and train the Vietnamese paramilitary Civil Guard and National Police. He ordered an increase in CIA covert programs, especially the creation of people's action teams (PATs) to act as village security forces, and counterterror teams (CTTs) to liquidate the Viet Cong political network. Finally, he authorized retaliatory bombing strikes by U.S. planes against the North. Without saying so, Johnson had opened the way to full-scale U.S. involvement.

None of this, however, slowed the deterioration in the Saigon government's control over South Vietnam. The turmoil in civilian administration after the downfall of Diem brought the strategic hamlet program to a halt; a 1965 report showed the actual number of "secure" hamlets to be only three thousand instead of the eighty-five hundred claimed in 1963.[36] By midyear the Viet Cong, whose main-strength forces were now estimated at thirty-four thousand, had increased their hold over the provinces to the point where they controlled most of the Delta and in northern South Vietnam threatened to cut the country in two. By the end of 1964, Giap and his colleagues in Hanoi felt confident enough to respond to the growing U.S. involvement by infiltrating units of their regular forces into the South along the Ho Chi Minh Trail.[37]

In 1965, the character of the war changed dramatically. After Diem's overthrow, Viet Cong guerrilla activity in the provinces reached a level of intensity that reduced the ARVN to holding actions around the towns and arterial highways. In contrast, after the Tonkin Gulf Resolution, the American reaction continued to be defensive and limited to the provision of airlift, tactical air support, and protection of airfields and supply depots. In February 1965, after the usual publicity about presidential agonizing, Lyndon Johnson adopted the punitive strategy advocated by General Taylor and authorized Operation "Rolling Thunder," the sustained air bombardment of North Vietnam. The president's hope was that steady pulverization of the North's base areas, power plants, and key industrial facilities would force them to abandon the war in the South. Instead, the only visible reaction was increased defiance and an augmented flow of North Vietnamese men and munitions into the South.

In the spring of 1965, a panicky reappraisal by Secretary of Defense Robert S. McNamara, coupled with the obvious failure of Rolling Thunder to produce results, led President Johnson to the fatal decision to commit U.S. combat troops. But to what sort of war? The concept of the commander designated to lead the U.S. intervention force, General William C. Westmoreland, was to commit enough divisions to arrest the losing trend in the South, and then to take the offensive in "high-priority areas" by methodically destroying the guerrilla pockets and proceeding with "pacification."[38] In concrete terms, this meant taking over the counterinsurgency war from the South Vietnamese—but doing it the American way, by deploying the full arsenal of U.S. conventional weaponry and technology.

The full implications of this approach were not understood at the time, and only became apparent after the effects were brought home by television to the American public in the family living room. Instead of using the first hundred thousand U.S. combat troops as a concentrated mass of maneuver to cut infiltration routes and go after North Vietnamese main-force units in the northern part of South Vietnam (while leaving the ARVN to deal with the insurgency in the southern provinces), General Westmoreland spread his divisions around the country and tried to root out the Viet Cong by means of "search-and-destroy" tactics—i.e., large-scale ground sweeps preceded by air strikes and artillery bombardment, and accompanied by helicopter landings on the enemy flanks and rear.[39] Despite attempts to limit the destruction of property and civilian loss of life, the results were devastating. Villages and hamlets controlled or infiltrated by the Viet Cong were labeled enemy territory—and then all the destructive power of high explosives intended for heavily fortified enemy positions was brought to bear on primitive bunkers in straw-thatched villages. There is no need to quote opponents of the Vietnam War as to the impact of this strategy; the words of the top U.S. Army field commander (and General Westmoreland's successor) will suffice: "War is death and destruction. The American way of war is particularly violent, deadly and dreadful. We believe in using 'things'—artillery, bombs, massive firepower—in order to conserve our soldier's lives."[40]

In a word, the U.S. Army fell into the trap of using conventional tactics and weaponry to fight a counterinsurgency war. Since the object was not to seize and hold territory, but to destroy an unseen enemy, Viet Cong casualties and to a lesser extent captured weapons became the only measure of success. Hence, the grisly and barbaric "body count," enthusiastically adopted by the statistically minded secretary of defense, Robert S. McNamara, and systematically publicized by MACV to a horrified world to demonstrate U.S. "progress." This is not to say that in purely military terms, search-and-destroy tactics were a failure. The U.S. Army and Marine Corps inflicted heavy losses on the Viet Cong whenever they could flush them out or bring them to battle. Areas sympathetic to the Viet Cong were so devastated that the guerrillas' political infrastructure was wrecked. But the price for this was civilian loss of life, the generation of refugees, disruption of the local economy and way of life, and alienation of public opinion back home.[41]

The second prong of U.S. strategy, termed "pacification," was a plan to gradually bring the entire rural population under Saigon administrative control (in contrast to the hamlet-by-hamlet approach), thereby insulating it from the Viet Cong while preserving its economic viability. An immense "nonmilitary" advisory organization called Civil Operations and Revolutionary Development Support (CORDS) was set up under MACV to train and advise village defense militias and reestablish central government administration. The CORDS program was one of method, not substance. Its purpose was to extend—under American supervision—the traditional South Vietnamese system of local government, law enforcement, and tax collection to villages and rural areas ruled at night by the NLF. At its peak in 1969, CORDS had a staff of sixty-five hundred U.S. military and eleven hundred civilian personnel and a budget of over $500 million in U.S. funds plus matching Vietnamese funds.[42]

CORDS was supplemented by the notorious Operation Phoenix assassination program, a CIA-inspired South Vietnamese campaign aimed at identifying and liquidating the Viet Cong political apparatus in the villages.[43] Although supposedly targeted exclusively against NLF stalwarts, the Phoenix program was largely used by the Saigon regime to liquidate the non-Communist political opposition and NLF "sympathizers"—an effort that further alienated the mass of civilians. Pacification was rounded out by an amnesty-and-rehabilitation program (Chieu Hoi) that was much publicized by MACV but whose statistics were grossly inflated by the inclusion of large numbers of villagers arbitrarily classified as sympathizers.

Despite a massive expenditure of money and effort, the nonmilitary side of the U.S. pacification program had one intrinsic weakness—it depended for execution on the South Vietnamese leadership. Not only was the Vietnamese civil administration inefficient and corrupt, but the central bureaucracy in Saigon—under both Diem and the generals—was utterly inexperienced in, and unsympathetic to, the implementation of nationwide programs that depended for success on the active cooperation of the populace. Moreover, many of the Saigon officials charged with carrying out these plans were drawn from the privileged Catholic minority linked to Diem, or from the landlord class whose attitude toward land reform was, to say the least, unenthusiastic. The U.S. bureaucracy in Saigon displayed a high level of energy in conferring, planning, and traveling madly around the countryside and back to Washington, but this frenetic activity translated into little progress in the field.[44] In comparison to the French, the Americans displayed almost no interest in the culture of Southeast Asia and no empathy with the natives—and thus the most essential element of "winning hearts and minds" was missing.

Nineteen sixty-eight was another watershed year. At the end of January, during the Tet religious holiday, the Viet Cong staged surprise attacks in thirty-four towns and cities of South Vietnam, including Saigon. The attacks were eventually repulsed, and towns temporarily held by the insurgents were ultimately recaptured, but the political consequences for the United States were traumatic. From a purely military standpoint, the Tet offensive was a disaster for the Viet Cong, which suffered personnel losses estimated as high as one hundred thousand—a setback from which they were never able to recover. But from a psychological standpoint the offensive was a stunning success. Not only were presidential claims of imminent success—the "light at the end of the tunnel"—proved hopelessly fallacious, but the fact that a few suicide commandos had been able for a brief period to penetrate the U.S. embassy compound before being wiped out was seen by the media as a major U.S. defeat.

What everyone overlooked at the time was that Tet changed the nature of the war. Before Tet, the Viet Cong, reinforced by North Vietnamese regulars acting in a guerrilla role, had borne the brunt of the war. After Tet, the North Vietnamese command increasingly relied on main-force regulars, leaving the Viet Cong as a guerrilla screen to keep the ARVN dispersed and pinned down. In the final stages of the war, from 1970 to 1975, "Vietnamization" and the withdrawal of U.S. ground forces reinforced the defensive character of the ARVN deployment. When General Giap launched his final "victory offensive" in 1975, he did so with seventeen conventionally deployed divisions equipped with tanks and artillery that he maneuvered in a Schlieffen-like swinging-door movement through the Central Highlands. The dispersal of the ARVN to protect its strong points from the Viet Cong enabled the North Vietnamese to strike in overwhelming force at every point of impact. Hanoi's final strategy owed more to Clausewitz than to Mao.[45]

COUNTERINSURGENCY AFTER VIETNAM

The writer has neither the space nor the qualifications to write an authoritative postmortem of the Vietnam War. But a few key lessons stand out. Whether viewed as a local insurgency, or as Communist aggression from the North, or as a combination of both, the war was at all times an inherently Asian struggle with deeply indigenous roots. Unlike Malaya, the scale of the conflict was too vast to be contained by a limited investment of U.S. combat troops, at least as long as the insurgent forces could draw on immense reserves of manpower in the North. Crucial to the success of any guerrilla movement is the existence of sanctuaries in which to regroup and resupply, and the Viet Cong had two kinds to fall back on—an external one in the North and across the border in Cambodia, and an internal one among its sympathizers in the South. Conversely, on the American side, there never was (nor, in all probability, could there be) a governmental structure in Saigon that

could call upon strong indigenous support. Given these conditions, the
war could go on as long as the Viet Cong were able to replenish their
losses and preserve the will to fight.

The original counterinsurgency strategy of the United States—before it was vitiated by the massive deployment of American ground
troops—may have been sound in theory but was hopelessly unworkable
in practice. It had to be implemented by an unpopular, unrepresentative
local regime without a strong governmental structure in either the
capital or the provinces, and without an adequate communications and
transportation network. The hamlet program in particular could not be
imposed on a fragile, wartime subsistence economy without disrupting
rural society. When the United States tried to take over "pacification"
through the CORDS program, it faced the almost insuperable task of
attempting to train and organize cadres wholly different in language,
culture, and outlook from their advisers.

When one considers the difficulties of successive U.S. administrations in understanding the ethos of the countries of Western Europe,
the presumption of the Kennedy and Johnson administrations in suppos-
ing that middle-grade U.S. Army officers and civil servants from the
American heartland could create a viable rural society in a primitive and
densely populated Asian country in the middle of a civil war is stagger-
ing. There was no way for the Americans to get beneath the surface of
Vietnamese life despite all the resources and goodwill that they brought
to bear on the task.

After 1965, American military strategy further complicated the picture. As stated earlier, conventional tactics, including search-and-destroy
missions employing air strikes and massive artillery fire, proved too
destructive to permit anything but transitory success in a purely military
sense. As long as the enemy's internal and external sanctuaries remained
intact, he could follow a strategy of protracted war, shifting from the
offensive to the defensive according to a schedule of his own choosing.
The escalating U.S. bombing offensive was never a substitute for severing enemy supply and infiltration routes or bringing North Vietnamese
main-force units to battle, especially since public opinion declined to
tolerate extensive bombing of civilian targets.

Limits on the U.S. conventional response were inevitable in any case.
The Joint Chiefs repeatedly served notice that there was no way of
increasing the 250,000-man ceiling on ground forces without resorting
to some sort of national mobilization or drawing on U.S. forces commit-

ted to NATO. With these options ruled out, and with the external sanctuary likewise inviolate, there was no way for the United States to win the war by decisive military action. Nor was there any prospect of internal pacification and reconstruction given the devastation and disruption wrought by the American style of warfare and the omnipresence of an enormous occupation force.

Despite the record of Vietnam, it would be presumptuous to predict that because counterinsurgency failed in Southeast Asia it would necessarily fail in, say, Central America. The latter arena is smaller and totally accessible to U.S. sea and air power; it is also one where cultural and language barriers are readily surmountable. What *can* be said, however, is that any U.S. involvement in Third World internal conflicts in general and Central America in particular will have disruptive social and political consequences both in the target country and in the surrounding area. It will also generate commitments that will make extrication difficult if not impossible later on. The slippery slope from advice and assistance to commitment of combat forces has always been steeper for the United States than for other countries. We have no tradition of treating colonial wars and other overseas ventures as limited investments in which reverses and military defeats are part of the game, where you cut your losses and get out if the investment goes sour. American administrations have to "sell" their commitments to Congress and the public, and habitually do so by wildly exaggerating the threat, whitewashing their clients, distorting the facts, and consecrating their own actions as part of a crusade. With political and psychological vulnerabilities like these, the risk of more Vietnams is infinite.

The dilemma that confronts the United States in its policy of preventing the revolution of rising expectations from being "confiscated" by the other side goes deeper. In Central America and elsewhere, current discontents are the product of three centuries of social inequity and economic exploitation. Violence, brutality, and cold-blooded slaughter are endemic to civil conflict and for centuries have been employed by the armed retainers of the prevailing order to repress popular upheavals. Even in nominal democracies, internal security forces are often autonomous and brutal. Because U.S. counterinsurgency strategy rests to such a significant degree on the utilization of indigenous military and security forces, intensified repression and polarization are almost inevitable, and the potential for reform is diminished accordingly.

Consciously or unconsciously, the goal of U.S. policy continues to be preservation of the status quo. We pay lip service to reform but only to the extent that it can be comfortably accommodated to the containment of radicalism. Because, after Vietnam, the American craving for stability in the Third World has had to be reconciled with the political need to keep direct U.S. military involvement to a minimum, the inevitable result has been reliance on local power structures whose sole objective is self-preservation.

This is hardly a prescription for identifying the United States with the forces of progress and reform, let alone with the aspirations of the impoverished masses. As long as this approach undergirds U.S. policy, association with the forces of repression is inevitable. Until Washington has the courage and foresight to ride the wave of revolutionary change in the Third World, it will continue to play King Canute to waves lapping higher and higher about its ankles.

THE INTERVENTIONIST IMPULSE: U.S. MILITARY DOCTRINE FOR LOW-INTENSITY WARFARE

MICHAEL T. KLARE

"THE Army's dilemma," Robert H. Kupperman wrote in a seminal 1983 study on low-intensity warfare, "is that the conflict least likely to occur—extended conventional superpower hostilities in Europe—nevertheless dominates Army thinking, training, and resource allocation." Chiding the Army for its excessive preoccupation with improbable European contingencies, Kupperman argued that the American military was least prepared for the wars most likely to entail its involvement—"those small but critical low-intensity conflicts proliferating at the periphery of the great powers." To adequately meet future challenges at this "low end of the violence spectrum," he asserted, "the Army will require new doctrine, organization, tactics, and equipment."[1]

The belief that the United States lacks both the forces and, more importantly, the strategic outlook to successfully conduct low-level operations in the Third World is a common theme in the professional literature on low-intensity conflict (LIC). In many respects, this perspective mirrors that assumed by President John F. Kennedy in 1961, when he concluded that the United States lacked an effective response to the threat of revolutionary guerrilla warfare (see Chapter 2). Just as Mr. Kennedy called for a shift in priorities from conventional conflicts to counterinsurgency warfare, many of today's military leaders are urging a comparable change in strategic orientation.[2] "Current U.S. defense policy . . . [is] becoming increasingly inappropriate to the global power shifts under way and the new identifiable threat environments in non-NATO areas," Colonel James B. Motley wrote in 1985. To cope successfully with "the low-intensity battlefields of the future," he argued, "the United States will require forces with greater strategic and tactical utility to counter the more likely low-intensity contingencies that will confront the United States in ever-increasing numbers for the rest of this decade and beyond."[3]

Such views, considered heretical by most military professionals until very recently, are now regarded as the common wisdom by top Pentagon officials. "Low-level conflict will likely remain the most immediate threat to free-world security for the rest of this century," Defense Secretary Caspar Weinberger told Congress in 1985, and thus "specially trained forces" would be assembled to combat this potent threat.[4] This turnaround in priorities has led to the formation of new U.S. combat organizations (see Chapter 4), and to a new emphasis on the development of LIC doctrine. "Like St. Paul on the road to Damascus," Colonel John D. Waghelstein wrote in 1985, many U.S. strategists "have become converts [to LIC doctrine] and begun to reassess our capability" for combat in this arena.[5]

In the wake of this "conversion," Pentagon officials have made the development of LIC doctrine a major military objective. As in the heyday of counterinsurgency, military journals are full of articles by aspiring young officers—captains, majors, and lieutenant colonels—on the strategy and tactics of low-intensity combat. Many of these officers were selected to participate in the Joint Low-Intensity Conflict Project, a year-long doctrinal assessment commissioned by the Army chief of staff in 1985. To acquaint senior commanders with these efforts, Defense Secretary Weinberger sponsored a Low-Intensity Warfare Conference at the National Defense University (NDU) in January 1986.[6] In the same month, the Army and the Air Force established the Joint Center for Low-Intensity Conflict at Langley Air Force Base, Virginia.[7]

This commitment to the development of LIC doctrine has been accompanied by a renewed interest in "special operations"—i.e., the use of specialized military forces in clandestine paramilitary operations with high political payoff (examples include the early U.S. efforts to prop up the regime of Ngo Dinh Diem in South Vietnam and the U.S.-sponsored campaign to hunt down and kill the Argentinian-born guerrilla leader Ernesto "Che" Guevara in Bolivia). Such operations were largely spurned after Vietnam, but in 1981 Secretary Weinberger ordered a major "revitalization" of America's Special Operations Forces (SOF). This effort has entailed the expansion of America's SOF capabilities (see Chapter 4), and the refinement of military doctrine for special operations in an LIC environment. In support of this endeavor, the NDU in 1983 cosponsored a conference on "Special Operations in U.S. Strategy," a meeting attended by some 125 military and intelligence officials, including then Major Oliver L. North of the National Security Council (NSC).[8]

These endeavors have resulted in a significant outpouring of doctrinal materials on low-intensity conflict. Of particular significance is a collection of articles from the mid-1980s that appeared in *Military Review* and *Parameters,* the theoretical journals of the Army's Command and General Staff College (USACGSC) and the Army War College, respectively. Much of this thinking was subsequently synthesized in a series of new Army manuals, including Field Circular 100-20, *Low-Intensity Conflict,* published by the USACGSC in 1986.[9]

The new LIC manuals and the many articles they have generated constitute the core of an emerging body of doctrine on low-intensity warfare. Although American strategists are still debating and refining various aspects of LIC doctrine, a broad consensus has developed on the basic points of policy. This strategic outlook has already begun to govern U.S. planning for the LIC battlefield and, as the United States becomes more deeply involved in the actual conduct of such operations, will increasingly shape the training, tactics, and outlook of U.S. military personnel.

THE ROLE OF DOCTRINE

The Department of Defense defines "doctrine" as the "fundamental principles by which the military forces or elements thereof guide their actions in support of national objectives."[10] Put another way, doctrine represents the basic precepts that determine how U.S. forces are armed, trained, and organized for the conduct of military operations. Doctrine thus constitutes something of a middle ground between "grand strategy," the enduring geopolitical objectives of a nation (for example, "containment" of the Soviet system), and "tactics," the basic principles of war that govern day-to-day combat operations by discrete military formations.

Since doctrine often determines the orientation and structure of military forces, it can have a significant impact on the allocation of institutional and budgetary resources. Because, in peacetime, the various branches of the military are in perpetual competition over the disposition of basic resources, a major shift in doctrine can result in a significant realignment of power and authority within the military services—and so may be fiercely resisted by those who have a vested interest in the prevailing bureaucratic structure. To effect a change in doctrine, therefore, advocates of a new policy are often forced to wage a major political effort among senior policy-makers to win support for their innovations. Low-intensity conflict doctrine is a notable case in point, having risen to its present level of prominence only after vigorous efforts by zealous officers persuaded senior officials of the need to gird for a new round of military encounters with Third World revolutionaries.[11]

Low-intensity conflict doctrine is also notable for its strong ideological content. Because the Pentagon's focus on NATO from 1972 to 1982 reflected the American public's aversion to U.S. military involvement in regional Third World conflicts—the stance we know as the "Vietnam syndrome"—proponents of an enhanced LIC capability have felt it necessary to challenge and transform public as well as official attitudes. "Neither our political nor our military establishment is properly attuned to the new realities of conflict in our time," Neil C. Livingstone affirmed at a 1983 conference at the National Defense University. "Only when [U.S. citizens and policy-makers] comprehend what is at stake will we as a nation be able to develop the clarity of vision necessary to build and sustain a national consensus needed to underwrite a new policy . . . governing the application of force in low-level conflict situations."[12] Consonant with this outlook, President Reagan and his top lieutenants have made frequent statements on our need to overcome the Vietnam syndrome and to countenance the use of military force in protecting vital U.S. interests in the Third World.[13]

In the case of low-intensity conflict, then, "doctrine" has a far broader meaning than is generally the case for professional military matters. Indeed, the very definition of low-intensity conflict has become a matter of dispute. The dilemma posed by low-intensity conflict "begins with our inability to find the words to describe what it is that we have under consideration," General Paul F. Gorman observed in 1986. In fact, "the phenomenon presents a series of dilemmas for the United States, kind of a quandary within a puzzle, within a dilemma."[14]

DEFINING THE THREAT

This quandary was in no significant way overcome by the Pentagon's adoption of a formal definition for low-intensity conflict. In 1985, after much internal debate, the Joint Chiefs of Staff agreed on the following language:

> Low-intensity conflict is a limited politico-military struggle to achieve political, social, economic, or psychological objectives. It is often protracted and ranges from diplomatic, economic, and psycho-social pressures through terrorism and insurgency. Low-intensity conflict is generally confined to a geographic area and is often characterized by constraints on the weaponry, tactics, and the level of violence.[15]

Although generally considered useful as a starting point, this language has not satisfied those who seek a more exact characterization of low-intensity conflict. "This definition," Major Mitchell M. Zais wrote in 1986, "is so broad and encompassing that it is almost meaningless."[16] Similar comments have been made by other LIC theorists, many of whom continue to search for a more precise definition.

At stake in this dispute over language is the determination of just how deeply involved the United States should become in the prosecution of low-intensity conflicts in the Third World. Defined narrowly, as a peripheral strategic issue, low-intensity warfare presumably entails rather limited opportunities for U.S. military involvement; defined broadly, as a major strategic threat, LIC entails a correspondingly expanded role for U.S. forces. The position finally occupied by low-intensity warfare on this scale of potential danger will, in effect, set the nation's military agenda for years to come.

On one side of this debate are those analysts who equate low-intensity conflict with guerrilla war and counterinsurgency, as was generally the practice during the Kennedy period. For Colonel Waghelstein, who commanded U.S. advisers in El Salvador, the term "low-intensity conflict" is little more than a euphemism for counterinsurgency, which, he suggests, dropped out of formal military usage in the 1970s because of its close association with the U.S. failure in Southeast Asia.[17] Those U.S. strategists who share this view generally argue that the United States was wrong to employ regular ground forces in Vietnam, and suggest that any future U.S. involvement in low-intensity conflict be limited to the de-

ployment of advisers and relatively inconspicuous "special" forces.
Hence, according to Major Robert J. Ward of the Army, LIC doctrine
should focus "primarily on U.S. assistance and advice to allied or friendly
nations threatened by insurgencies, rather than the commitment of U.S.
combat forces."[18]

For other strategists, however, low-intensity conflict encompasses a
much wider range of threats, and thus requires, in response, a significantly
greater military effort on the part of the United States. "LIC is not simply
Vietnam revisited," Lieutenant Colonel Peter A. Bond wrote in 1986,
nor does it "equate to counterinsurgency." Rather, "LIC is a very broad
concept that spans the spectrum of conflict from relative peace to
conventional war."[19] Included in this spectrum, according to Lieutenant
Colonel John M. Oseth, are "insurgency and counterinsurgency operations, terrorism and counterterrorism, surgical direct action military
operations, psychological warfare, and even operations by conventional or
general purpose forces."[20] Adherents to this view generally argue that the
United States must maintain a large and varied assortment of forces so as
to be able to undertake a wide variety of LIC operations.

While debate on the scope of LIC operations will undoubtedly continue, most U.S. strategists appear to have reached consensus on an
assessment that sees LIC as lying at the upper rather than the lower end
of the scale of threats. According to this view, low-intensity conflict
encompasses a wide variety of potential threats to U.S. security—none
of which by themselves may represent a major peril, but which, as
elements of a larger pattern of Third World violence, take on a very
threatening character indeed. "While it can be argued that, in isolation,
a single episode [of LIC] poses no significant threat to the United
States," Major General Donald R. Morelli and Major Michael M.
Ferguson of the Army's Training and Doctrine Command (TRADOC)
wrote in 1984, "the cumulative effect of these subtle but growing challenges to U.S. interests places us at considerable risk—*now.*"[21]

Flowing naturally from this perception is the belief that the United
States must actively respond to the LIC threat, with military force if
necessary. In perhaps the most eloquent expression of this view, Secretary of State George Shultz told participants at the Pentagon's 1986 LIC
Conference:

> We have seen and we will continue to see a wide range of ambiguous threats
> in the shadow area between major war and millenial peace. Americans must

understand . . . that a number of small challenges, year after year, can add up to a more serious challenge to our interests. The time to act, to help our friends by adding our strength to the equation, is not when the threat is at our doorstep, when the stakes are highest and the needed resources enormous. We must be prepared to commit our political, economic, and, if necessary, military power when the threat is still manageable and when its prudent use can prevent the threat from growing.[22]

With these words, we glimpse the interventionist impulse that underlies the emerging consensus on low-intensity conflict; while rarely expressed in such forceful terms, this outlook provides the framework for the more technical discourses on LIC doctrine.

THE LIC SPECTRUM

In line with the prevailing consensus on low-intensity conflict, current U.S. doctrine envisions a wide spectrum of potential missions for American forces. Accordingly, the professional literature in this field tends to consist of extensive discussion of the strategies and tactics to employ in each of these "mission areas." To fully appreciate the thrust of LIC doctrine, therefore, it is necessary to examine U.S. military thinking in each of the major categories of LIC combat.

Current doctrine for low-intensity conflict is spelled out in several key documents, most notably: Field Circular 100-20, *Low-Intensity Conflict* (FC 100-20); TRADOC Pamphlet 525-44, *U.S. Army Operational Concept for Low Intensity Conflict*; and the two-volume *Final Report* of the Joint Low-Intensity Conflict Project (JLICP).[23]

Six specific "mission categories" are identified in the now-voluminous literature on low-intensity warfare:

☐ *Foreign internal defense:* counterinsurgency, encompassing those actions taken by the United States to assist friendly governments resisting insurgent threats.

☐ *"Proinsurgency":* the sponsorship and support of anti-Communist insurgencies in the Third World.

☐ *Peacetime contingency operations:* short-term military activities— rescue missions, show-of-force operations, punitive strikes—taken in support of U.S. foreign policy.

☐ *Terrorism counteraction:* the defensive and offensive measures taken by the armed forces to prevent or counter international terrorism.

☐ *Antidrug operations:* the use of military resources to attack and destroy overseas sources of illegal narcotics, and to curb the flow of drugs into the United States.

☐ *Peacekeeping operations:* the use of American forces (usually under international auspices) to police cease-fire agreements or to establish a buffer between hostile armies.

FOREIGN INTERNAL DEFENSE

Foreign internal defense, or FID, is defined as "those actions taken by civilian and military agencies of [the United States] in any program taken by another government to preclude or defeat insurgency."[24] Such programs are assumed to incorporate both military measures for isolating and defeating the guerrillas and nonmilitary measures aimed at undercutting popular support for the insurgent cause. Together, these measures are classified by the Army as "internal defense and development" (IDAD), and their generation by U.S. strategists is described as "the art and science of developing and using the political, economic, psychological, and military powers of a government, including all police and internal security forces, to prevent or defeat insurgency."[25]

For those familiar with the evolution of U.S. military policy, this will sound a great deal like the "counterinsurgency" strategy of the Kennedy era (see Chapter 2). Indeed, Major Zais wrote in *Military Review* that IDAD "is merely a new name for an old concept: counterinsurgency."[26] As in the original policy, IDAD doctrine assumes that "winning the hearts and minds" of the populace is as essential as defeating the insurgents on the battlefield. And while much effort is being made to distance current policy from U.S. military behavior in Vietnam, this does not represent a repudiation of 1960s-style counterinsurgency but rather signals a return to its original, "classical" form.

As originally conceived, counterinsurgency entailed a political-economic effort by host-nation agencies to secure the loyalty of the rural population, thus depriving the guerrillas of a popular base (or, borrowing from the Maoist image, "drying up the sea in which the guerrillas swim"). Such efforts, to be successful, were thought to require a genuine government commitment to improve the conditions of the peasantry, even if this meant curbing the privileges of the military and the landed gentry. The U.S. role, in such a setting, was theoretically limited to the provision of development aid and military advisory support—with the former taking precedence over the latter.[27]

"Classical" counterinsurgency of this type was attempted during the early years of U.S. involvement in Vietnam, but was ultimately abandoned when it became apparent that President Ngo Dinh Diem and his successors were too preoccupied with the accumulation of wealth and the preservation of their own vested interests to undertake any sort of popular transformation in the countryside. In place of counterinsurgency, U.S. officials came to rely on "pacification"—a largely military effort intended to cow the peasantry into submission through the threat of or the employment of violence, rather than to win them over through the promise of reform. American firepower thus became the principal agency of social control, robbing the Saigon regime of all remaining legitimacy and enhancing the nationalist credentials of the National Liberation Front.[28] (See Chapter 2.)

Today U.S. strategists appear to be making a concerted effort to restore the teachings, not to speak of the badly tarnished reputation, of classical counterinsurgency. "The goal of the host government in foreign internal defense is to win the support of its people," Major Ward wrote in 1985. In terms highly reminiscent of classical doctrine, Ward wrote that the military should confine itself to providing "a secure atmosphere so that the government can attempt to eliminate the causes of the insurgency through establishment of medical and educational facilities, agricultural and other forms of assistance . . . . [and by introducing] normal functions of government. . . ."[29]

In consonance with this approach, the Army's FID doctrine calls for the initiation of social, political, and economic measures intended to alleviate popular discontent and to win support for the prevailing regime. If popular grievances "are not addressed by a counterinsurgency program," the *JLICP Final Report* notes, "they make dealing with an insurgency immeasurably more difficult."[30] Normally, remedial efforts of this sort are the responsibility of host-nation agencies acting under the supervision of the central government. The U.S. role, in such a setting, is to guide and facilitate—but not to supplant—the host government's efforts to win popular support in the countryside.[31]

A critical feature of this approach is the functional integration of all indigenous police, paramilitary, and military forces into a unified counterinsurgency effort. Police forces are considered a particularly vital component of counterinsurgency, as they are usually better informed than the military about the political loyalties of ordinary citizens, and so are better able to penetrate and neutralize the insurgent support network. The police are "the first line of defense" against insurgent activity, FC 100-20 affirms, and in many countries are "better trained, organized, and equipped than the military for gathering intelligence on the local situation and handling low levels of violence, conspiracy, and subversion."[32]

While such bureaucratic and security considerations tend to dominate the articulation of IDAD doctrine, considerable emphasis is also placed on social and political reform—or at least the appearance of reform. American strategists recognize that initiatives of this sort are not likely to be undertaken with great enthusiasm by threatened governments, especially those based on narrow, oligarchical regimes. Nonetheless, they insist that the nature of revolutionary warfare makes such efforts essential.[33] "The [host] government . . . must realize that the true nature of the insurgent threat lies in its political claims and not in the military movement," the JLICP report notes. "Although the armed elements must be dealt with, a concentration on the military aspect of the threat resembles the bull charging the matador's cape; it is a diversion masking the real danger." To overcome the "real" danger, a determined leader "must overcome the inertia and incompetence of his own political system" in order to push through "unpalatable reforms that must be undertaken at a time of crisis."[34] As expressed in FC 100-20, this precept is reduced to the comment that "the [host] government must clearly demonstrate that it is a better choice than the insurgent organization."[35]

This, of course, is the central paradox of the whole IDAD strategy: If the prevailing government represented "a better choice" in the first place, it probably would not be threatened by a significant insurgent challenge; for the most part, it is only those governments that represent *inferior* choices—because of their resistance to social and political reform—that tend to inspire revolt. Consequently, the United States tends to become involved in counterinsurgency in those countries where the regime in power faces a significant insurgent threat precisely because it has proved itself *incapable* of meaningful reform. It is precisely this tendency that constitutes the "Achilles heel" of low-intensity conflict, Professor William M. LeoGrande of American University observed in 1987. "LIC is designed to stabilize, politically as well as militarily, societies in crisis—societies that are, most often, dominated by a wealthy minority ruling at the expense of the rest of the population. The inequality of such societies is the cause of their crisis, and so long as the basic structure remains unchanged, they are inherently unstable."[36]

Confronted with this paradox in Vietnam, the United States tried repeatedly to install a credible, reform-minded regime in Saigon; when those efforts failed, it attempted to manage civil reform on its own (through the Civil Operations and Revolutionary Development Support program, or CORDS), with equally disappointing results. As a result of this experience, U.S. strategy now appears to rest on the early installation of a reformist government: hence the decisive U.S. role in orchestrating Napoleón Duarte's ascendancy in El Salvador, and Washington's evident readiness to exchange Ferdinand Marcos for Corazon Aquino in the Philippines. These moves have not, however, eliminated the major sources of discontent in the countryside, nor have they persuaded the revolutionary opposition to abandon its struggle against the central government.

As a result, Washington is again facing a situation in which it feels compelled to increase U.S. military involvement in the counterinsurgency struggle (see Chapters 5 and 7). Yet, in accordance with the "classic" approach to counterinsurgency, American personnel are expected to perform a relatively inconspicuous support role in order to sustain the impression that the host government is in command. This support role, according to Army documents, is intended to help host nation forces acquire proficiency in the principal facts of counterinsurgency warfare: military civic action, PSYOP, intelligence, and counterguerrilla warfare.

Military civic action (CA) involves the use of military forces in rural development projects designed to win popular support for the established government. As defined by the Army, CA entails "the use of predominantly indigenous military forces on projects beneficial to the local population at all levels. This includes areas such as education, training, public works, agriculture, transportation, communications, health, sanitation, and other contributions to economic and social development, which would also serve to improve the standing of the military forces with the population."[37] The idea, of course, is to try to erase the peasantry's perception of the military as an oppressive occupation force, and to promote a more benign image of the central government. Only when the military is viewed in a favorable light, it is reasoned, will rural citizens welcome government protection and help the Army to find and disable any insurgent forces operating in the area.[38]

Psychological operations(PSYOP), like civic action, is intended to enhance the popular image of the government and to isolate and discredit the insurgent movement. According to the Army, PSYOP entails the utilization of multiple communications channels "in order to create attitudes and behavior favorable to the achievement of political and military objectives."[39] Such activities are considered to play an especially vital role in counterinsurgency, where the struggle over public attitudes is so critical. Typically, such efforts include the dissemination of audio, visual, and printed materials designed to portray the government in the best possible light while characterizing the insurgents as Moscow-backed terrorists. PSYOP can also entail the dissemination of faked enemy documents designed to discredit the insurgents or to stir up divisions within their ranks.[40]

Military intelligence is an essential component of counterinsurgency. Because insurgent forces tend to operate in remote and unfamiliar areas, and because they rely on support from the indigenous population, antiguerrilla forces cannot operate effectively unless they acquire sufficient intelligence on insurgent supply routes and base areas. Of particular importance are the "assessment and exploitation [of intelligence on] the insurgent infrastructure to include its command, control, and communications system, recruiting system, logistic support, and mass civil organizations."[41] Once possessed of such information—normally acquired through the interrogation (often forced) of captured guerrillas and their sympathizers—government forces can isolate and attack the clandestine infrastructure on which the insurgent movement depends.[42]

Combat operations in a counterinsurgency setting are intended "to destroy or neutralize insurgent tactical forces and bases and to establish a secure environment in which balanced development programs can be carried out."[43] In planning such operations, U.S. counterinsurgency strategists often speak favorably of the *tache d'huile* or "spreading oil stain" method, whereby host nation forces secure an ever-expanding zone of government control. "The most effective foreign internal defense strategy," Major Ward wrote in *Military Intelligence,* "consists of establishing a secure base of government support, often around the capital and other major cities, then slowly expanding the area of control until the insurgents are forced farther and farther away from their support base—the people."[44] As the insurgents are driven further afield, government forces are encouraged to conduct mobile "strike" operations designed to break up and destroy remaining guerrilla units and to deny them a "rear" in which to regroup for further action.[45]

When conducting armed combat operations, government forces are advised to employ the *surgical* use of force, and to scrupulously avoid unintended civilian casualties. "Anti-insurgency security measures must avoid alienating the general population with excessive violence or repression," Captain Steven E. Daskal wrote in *Military Review*. Successful counterinsurgency relies on small-unit operations, "not artillery or air power which can destroy everything within a given area."[46] Similar comments have been made by other strategists, often with the observation that the military's preference for massive air and artillery strikes contributed to the U.S. failure in Vietnam.[47]

Here too, however, U.S. strategists face a critical paradox: many embattled governments would rather bomb or shell a rebel-infested area than risk sending in ground troops that might scatter or disintegrate in the face of more capable insurgent forces. Hence, many counterinsurgency campaigns harbor an inherent tendency toward military escalation—a tendency clearly shown in El Salvador, where government forces have continually stepped up their air attacks against villages considered friendly to insurgent forces despite much criticism in the professional counterinsurgency literature. While considered effective in disrupting the rebels' logistical support system, these air strikes have killed and wounded many civilians, thus undercutting the legitimacy of the Duarte government and complicating the U.S.-sponsored effort to "win hearts and minds."[48]

This failure of some U.S.-backed regimes to fully carry out the strictures of current LIC doctrine brings us to the most difficult policy dilemma of them all: at what point, and to what degree, should the United States commit its own combat forces to a counterinsurgency struggle?

In line with the classical approach, current U.S. doctrine holds that American personnel committed to internal conflicts abroad should take a backseat position to the host government forces engaged in counterinsurgency. But what if government forces prove unequal to this task and begin to crumble under the pressure of constant guerrilla harassment and progressive internal decay? At this point, U.S. leaders must choose between withdrawal and defeat, or the direct use of American combat forces.

In pondering this choice, some U.S. strategists—believing that American military involvement in such conflicts would provoke significant opposition at home and would accelerate the erosion of host government legitimacy—argue that withdrawal is preferable to outright intervention. Others, however, believe that the United States cannot allow friendly regimes to be overwhelmed by insurgent armies, even if it means contemplating the direct use of U.S. combat forces. "It is possible that a threat to US interests will not be identified until it has reached serious proportions or has grown beyond the capability of local forces to contain," Morelli and Ferguson wrote in 1984. "In such cases, the commitment of US forces in direct support of indigenous forces engaged in combat and, at the extreme, directly to combat on behalf of US interests is possible."[49]

Ultimately, the decision of whether or not to commit U.S. military forces in such a situation is a political, not a military, one. At this point, no one can predict with certainty how U.S. leaders would respond to the imminent collapse of a friendly regime in El Salvador, the Philippines, or some other embattled nation. But insofar as the LIC literature provides an insight into official thinking, we can detect a pronounced inclination toward direct U.S. intervention in future crises of this sort. "[Military] assistance should be a major aspect of our strategy for counterinsurgency," Volume II of the *JLICP Final Report* notes, "but we must not limit our assistance to training and material resources." Indeed, "Counterinsurgency strategy should also provide for direct support and intervention. It should identify the types of forces most appropriate to assist or intervene at each level of involvement. . . ."[50]

On this basis, a great deal of the JLICP report is devoted to a discussion of the preparatory steps needed to ready U.S. forces for possible employment in such situations. Most of this is of a highly technical nature—the need for lightweight radios suitable for tropical environment, the need for a low-cost, lightly armed surveillance plane for remote-area operations, the need for greater proficiency in certain Third World languages, and so forth. The underlying message, however, is clear: existing counterinsurgency efforts by friendly regimes may prove inadequate, and thus U.S. forces must again, as in Vietnam, be prepared to assume primary responsibility for combating a hostile guerrilla army.

PROINSURGENCY

Proinsurgency, or the sponsorship and support of anti-Communist guerrillas in the Third World, lies on the flip side of the counterinsurgency coin: while foreign internal defense is intended to prevent hostile guerrilla movements from seizing control of Third World countries, proinsurgency is intended to topple those revolutionary governments that have actually succeeded in assuming power. The tactics employed in these two missions may vary—in one case, Washington seeks to suppress an insurgent upheaval, while in the other it seeks to enhance the effectiveness of rebel operations—but the political impulse underlying both activities is essentially identical.

The overthrow of radical Third World regimes first emerged as a major U.S. policy objective during President Reagan's second term. In his 1985 State of the Union address, Mr. Reagan pledged to aid anti-Communist forces that are fighting pro-Soviet regimes "on every continent, from Afghanistan to Nicaragua." This theme was repeated in subsequent remarks by the president and other administration officials, thus endowing the policy with the name by which it is most widely known: the "Reagan Doctrine."[51]

The Reagan Doctrine has its origins, of course, in an earlier administration initiative—the concerted U.S. effort to topple the revolutionary government in Nicaragua by organizing and financing an army of anti-Sandinista insurgents, or *contrarevolucionarios* ("contras"). Originally portrayed as a modest paramilitary force whose principal mission was to intercept Nicaraguan arms being sent to leftist guerrillas in El Salvador, the contras were later described in more grandiose terms when Congress balked at supporting the lesser cause. These forces "are on the front line in the struggle for progress, security, and freedom in Central America," Secretary of State Schultz declared in 1985, and those in Congress who would deny funding to these "freedom fighters" are, "in effect, consigning Nicaragua to the endless darkness of communist tyranny."[52]

With the introduction of the Reagan Doctrine, this idealized portrait of the contras was extended to other anti-Communist forces—notably the *mujahidin* in Afghanistan, the non-Communist resistance in Cambodia, and the fighting units of UNITA (the National Union for the Total Independence of Angola). These forces, Secretary Schultz declared, are part of a "democratic revolution" that is "sweeping the world today."[53] To support and encourage this "revolution," the administration has provided overt or covert aid to the rebels in Nicaragua, Afghanistan, Cambodia, and Angola, and possibly to anti-Communist insurgents in other Third World countries.[54]

In justifying such assistance, administration officials are quick to affirm that support for anti-Communist insurgencies is as much a strategic objective as it is a moral imperative. Arguing that Soviet backing for Communist insurgencies in the Third World has eroded the geostrategic interests of the West, these officials suggest that the weakening or, better yet, the removal of pro-Soviet regimes would produce a corresponding improvement in the West's global power position. "When the United States supports those resisting totalitarianism," Shultz asserted in 1985, "we do so not only out of our historical sympathy for democracy and freedom but also, in many cases, in the interests of national security."[55]

For Shultz and other Reagan loyalists, the Reagan Doctrine represents the cutting edge of an administration drive to shift the "correlation of forces" between East and West back in America's favor. According to this view, the major international power shifts of the 1970s—the U.S. failure in Vietnam, the fall of the shah of Iran, and the rise of leftist regimes in Angola, Mozambique, and Nicaragua—favored the Soviet Union. Today, however, "the United States is restoring its military strength and economic vigor," while the Soviets are experiencing severe economic difficulties and "their clients are on the defensive in many parts of the world." For these reasons, Shultz avows, "the 'correlation of forces' is shifting back in our favor."[56]

For some U.S. analysts, Shultz's rhetoric hints of an administration plan to engineer the "rollback" of Soviet gains in the Third World. "The principal message that the Reagan Doctrine conveys to the Russians," Professor Robert W. Tucker wrote in 1986, is that "they have few, if indeed any, legitimate interests in the third world and that they must reconcile themselves to giving up their recently acquired positions."[57] This interpretation of the Reagan Doctrine is given added credibility by the emphasis placed by the administration on covert military operations and the acknowledged provision of assistance to rebel forces in Afghanistan, Angola, Cambodia, and Nicaragua; such aid reportedly has also been given to antigovernment forces in other Third World countries, including Libya and Ethiopia.[58]

The high degree of White House reliance on covert operations to implement the Reagan Doctrine was dramatically revealed by the Iran-contra arms scandal of 1986–87. As documented in the Tower Commission Report of March 1987, officials of the National Security Council organized an elaborate network of Swiss bank accounts, secret arms depots, hidden airfields, and proprietary airlines to supply the anti-Sandinista rebels in defiance of U.S. laws and regulations.[59] It is also likely that this clandestine apparatus was used to funnel arms and equipment to the UNITA forces in Angola and possibly to other anti-Communist rebel groupings in the Third World.[60]

Given the emphasis on secrecy and covert activity in the implementation of the Reagan Doctrine, it is not surprising that proinsurgency has been accorded scant discussion in the formal LIC literature. In only one place—a short section on "unconventional warfare"—does FC 100-20 address this topic, noting that the Army may be called upon to engage in or support "a broad spectrum of military and paramilitary operations conducted in enemy-held, enemy-controlled, or politically sensitive territory." Such operations are said to include, but not be limited to, "the interrelated fields of guerrilla warfare, evasion and escape, subversion, sabotage, and other operations of a low-visibility, covert, or clandestine nature."[61]

Unconventional operations of this type fall within the traditional province of the Army's Special Forces (SF), and so receive somewhat greater attention in the specialized SF literature. In TRADOC Pamphlet 525-34, *US Army Operational Concept for Special Operations Forces*, it is noted that the Special Forces will sometimes be ordered to "provide support and advice to indigenous resistance forces" in order to "exploit military, political, economic, or psychological vulnerabilities of an enemy."[62] SF activities, in such cases, will normally entail guerrilla warfare and subversion. These functions are described in Pamphlet 525-34 as follows:

☐ *Guerrilla warfare:* military operations conducted in enemy-held or hostile territory "by irregular, predominantly indigenous forces." Such operations are intended to "wear down and inflict casualties upon the enemy, damage supplies and facilities, and hinder and delay enemy operations." When successful, guerrilla warfare "lowers enemy morale and prestige; disrupts the economy, politics, and industry in enemy occupied areas; and maintains . . . the will to resist within the native population."[63]

☐ *Subversion:* politicomilitary operations whereby "resistance elements use force, violence, or penetration by a series of planned political actions to undermine, overthrow, or affect the decisions or actions of an incumbent government or occupying power." Such operations may entail the extensive use of sabotage: "SF are capable of advising and assisting resistance forces in the conduct of sabotage which contributes to both resistance and U.S. objectives."[64]

These methods and tactics were originally developed in the early Cold War period when it was thought that U.S. forces might be called on to organize anti-Soviet partisan movements in Eastern Europe during the course of a major East-West conflict in Europe. Although of little relevance to a contemporary conflict in Europe (which presumably would be decided in a matter of days or weeks either by massive conventional engagements or through the use of tactical nuclear weapons), these tactics have—as events in Nicaragua have shown—been revived and updated for use in a Third World context (see Chapter 6).

As with counterinsurgency, proinsurgency entails a significant risk of escalation. By sponsoring insurgent attacks on a sovereign government, the United States automatically becomes a party to the conflict, thereby inviting retaliation by the target regime. Even more worrisome, a number of U.S.-sponsored insurgent groups may face catastrophic defeat at some future date, thereby forcing U.S. leaders to choose between humiliation and the direct use of American forces in what could become a full-scale conflict—a choice that could arise in Nicaragua at almost any time.

At this point, proinsurgency remains a relatively underdeveloped concept from the doctrinal point of view. The Iran-contra arms scandal of 1986–87 could also produce a temporary slowdown in the conduct of such operations. Proinsurgency does, however, enjoy widespread support in Washington—among many Democrats as well as Republicans—and thus is likely to remain an important feature of the Pentagon's LIC agenda.

PEACETIME CONTINGENCY OPERATIONS
On many occasions since the end of World War II, U.S. military forces have been employed in limited, episodic fashion to supress civil disorders, to rescue American civilians from overseas conflict zones, to intimidate hostile governments, or to otherwise "project power" in the pursuit of U.S. foreign policy. Such activities, which are generally

confined to Third World areas, are termed "peacetime contingency operations"—"peacetime" in the sense that they fall short of an all-out global conflagration on the scale of World Wars I and II, and "contingency" in the sense that they represent a sudden, ad hoc response to an unforeseen event. Military activity of this sort is expected to increase in the years ahead, and is accorded an important role in LIC doctrine.

According to Army doctrine, peacetime contingency operations "are politically sensitive military operations . . . characterized by the short-term rapid projection or employment of forces in conditions short of conventional war." Such operations supposedly "become necessary when diplomatic initiatives are ineffective in achieving extremely time-sensitive, high-value objectives, or when unexpected threats to US interests materialize that require a rapid response."[65]

Implicit in this view of contingency operations is the belief that much of the world (and especially the Third World) is threatened by endemic violence, and that it may be necessary therefore for the United States to employ military force to protect its vital overseas interests against multiple and sudden disorders. Such views are not unique to the current era—one recalls, for instance, the "big stick" approach of Theodore Roosevelt—but seem to resonate strongly in the views of many Reagan administration officials. "We and our allies have come to be critically dependent on places in the world which are subject to great instability," Defense Secretary Weinberger declared in 1981, "and in those areas, some nations are both strongly armed and hostile to us." To protect critical Western interests in these areas, we must develop "a better ability to respond to crises far from our shores, and to stay there as long as necessary."[66]

All of this seems to suggest a renewed U.S. commitment to serve as a global gendarme—a role that American leaders firmly repudiated in the aftermath of Vietnam. Nowhere in the official LIC literature is there a formal acknowledgment of this sort of role, but current doctrine for contingency operations certainly comes close to embracing such a posture. According to the *JLICP Final Report*, "diplomatic failure to influence a belligerent may require the immediate use of military forces to protect national interests, to rescue United States citizens, or to defend United States assets."[67] Further confirmation of the "police" nature of contingency operations is given by the Army's discussion of the major categories into which such actions fall:

□   *Show of force:* the conspicuous deployment and exercise of U.S. forces in the vicinity of a potential belligerent, in order to demonstrate America's willingness to employ force against that country if it persists in behavior considered inimical to vital U.S. interests. Such deployments "lend credibility to a nation's promises and commitments . . . and demonstrate the viability of military force as an instrument of national power."[68] Typically, show-of-force operations entail the deployment of U.S. warships off the coast of a hostile power, the introduction of U.S. air and ground forces into neighboring countries, or the holding of military "exercises" in contested or sensitive areas (of the sort conducted on a regular basis in recent years in areas bordering on Libya and Nicaragua).

□   *Strike operations:* short-term military actions that are undertaken to "recover United States personnel and property or [to] conduct punitive action in support of political and diplomatic measures."[69] Such attacks usually entail a brief, rapid, and forceful response to some overseas threat or challenge, and are often intended as a warning of further military action. Typically, such operations involve some use of America's rapid-response capabilities: carrier-based strike aircraft, Marine Corps amphibious forces, the Army's airborne, airmobile, and Ranger units, and the "special" forces of all four services.[70] Examples of such actions include the October 1983 invasion of Grenada and the 1986 air strikes on missile batteries in Libya. Strike operations can also include punitive raids against nations charged with supporting terrorism (see below).

□   *Peacemaking:* the use of U.S. military forces "to ensure the maintenance of civil law and order" in troubled foreign countries. The United States may be called upon to conduct such functions "in support of a threatened host government," or following the overthrow of a hostile regime.[71] Conspicuous examples include the 1965 U.S. intervention in the Dominican Republic and the 1983 U.S. Marine deployment in Beirut. Peacemaking operations involve the use of military forces in an internal security capacity, usually within the confines of a single country; they must be distinguished from "peacekeeping" operations, which entail the use of American forces to enforce a cease-fire or to provide a buffer between two hostile nations.

Once viewed as a relatively trivial function, contingency operations of these types are now viewed as a major "peacetime" activity of the U.S. armed forces. In accordance with this outlook, the Reagan administration has authorized a significant expansion of America's quick-strike forces (carrier battle groups, amphibious assault forces, Ranger battalions, and so forth) and its long-range mobility assets (intercontinental transport planes, rapid sealift vessels). In addition, the Army has introduced an entirely new type of combat unit—the ten-thousand-man "light infantry division"—specifically configured for rapid delivery to Third World combat zones (see Chapter 4).

TERRORISM COUNTERACTION

"Terrorism counteraction" is the Army's term for all measures undertaken for the prevention, defense against, and punishment of terrorist activities. Such measures, once considered a distinctly subordinate activity, are now seen as a major military responsibility. Under current doctrine, terrorism counteraction is broken down into two basic functions: *antiterrorism,* or defensive actions taken to deter terrorist attacks and to reduce the vulnerability of potential terrorist targets; and *counterterrorism,* or offensive actions taken to combat terrorist groups or to punish those governments that harbor, train, or otherwise aid terrorist organizations.[72]

Terrorism, according to the Army, is "the calculated use of violence or threat of violence to attain goals that are political, religious, or ideological in nature. This is done through intimidation, coercion, or instilling fear."[73] Clearly, this definition could apply to the activities of a wide assortment of extremist groups. In practice, however, the Reagan administration has tended to view terrorism as an essentially leftist, anti-Western phenomenon, presumed to be inspired or fostered by the Soviet Union and its allies.

In shaping the administration's view on terrorism, no voice has been more persistent than that of Secretary of State Shultz. "Terrorism . . . is neither random nor without political purpose," he declared in 1984; rather, it is intended "to achieve distinctly political aims." Though often employed by autonomous groups, terrorism has been "co-opted" by hostile states "that support and sponsor terrorist actions . . . in pursuit of their own strategic goals." Such states—he specifically names Cuba, Iran, Libya, and the Soviet Union—are using terrorism "as a modern tool of warfare" against the United States and its allies.[74]

For Shultz, terrorism and terrorism counteraction are an important part of the LIC landscape—a "gray area" of intermediate conflict falling between all-out combat and untroubled peace. Because these "gray area" challenges are directed at our strategic interests, "we must be willing to use military force" in responding to them.[75] In consonance with this outlook, terrorism counteraction has been designated a major Pentagon responsibility, and a number of special units have been created for antiterrorist activities (see Chapter 4). Moreover, a new body of doctrine has been developed for the use of military forces undertaking preemptive or retaliatory strikes against terrorist organizations and their alleged supporters.

The core of the new doctrine is contained in National Security Decision Directive No. 138 (NSDD-138), signed by President Reagan on April 3, 1984. Although its text has never been made public, the broad outlines of NSDD-138 are widely known. In a 1985 article in the *Journal of Defense and Diplomacy,* then National Security Adviser Robert C. McFarlane indicated that the directive identified terrorism as "a threat to national security," and held that state-sponsored terrorist assaults constitute "hostile acts" and that their perpetrators "must be held accountable."[76]

Much of NSDD-138 reportedly concerned the protection of U.S. personnel and facilities abroad, and the improvement of U.S. and allied intelligence on terrorist organizations. However, key sections of the directive authorized the use of military force to conduct both preemptive and retaliatory strikes against terrorists. "The United States . . . will not use force indiscriminately," McFarlane avowed. "But we must be free to consider an armed strike against terrorists and those who support them, where elimination or moderation of the threat does not appear to be feasible by other means."[77]

In accordance with this principle, the Department of Defense has begun to establish policy for the use of military force in countering terrorism. At this point, doctrine for antiterrorism (that is, defensive operations) is far more developed than that for counterterrorism (offensive operations). Indeed, on the topic of counterterrorism, the Pentagon is quite circumspect—at least in its doctrinal statements. Given the inherently sensitive nature of such operations, supreme authority over their management is said to lie with the Department of State and not with the Department of Defense. It is further assumed that the host nation will assume primary responsibility for taking military action in response to terrorist attacks against U.S. facilities within its territory. Only when host-nation forces are unable to take such action will Washington consider unilateral military action, and then only under guidelines established by the president and the secretary of state.[78]

Clearly, in this particular area, doctrine has been developed more rapidly by the White House than by the Department of Defense. While Army documents appear to envision a very restrained use of military force in combating terrorism, the president and his advisers have been prepared to approve far more elaborate and forceful operations. Thus, on April 14, 1986, Mr. Reagan authorized a series of air strikes against government facilities in Tripoli (among them, the residence of Colonel Muammar Qaddafi) following terrorist activities in West Germany that were linked by Washington to Libyan authorities. These strikes, conducted by FB-111 bombers based in England and A-6 attack planes flown from U.S. aircraft carriers in the Mediterranean, were considerably more severe than any previous U.S. military action taken in response to terrorist activity.[79]

In the wake of the Libyan raids, U.S. officials made it clear that the administration was prepared to order similar actions in response to future incidents of terrorism. The April 14 attacks, President Reagan declared two days later, should be seen as "but a single engagement in a long battle against terrorism." A week later, he affirmed that the United States was prepared to "act again" against Libya or other nations deemed responsible for future terrorist attacks on U.S. citizens.[80]

In discussing military activity of this sort, American officials consistently stress the controlled and "surgical" nature of U.S. retaliation. Post-attack analysis of the April 1986 strike against Libya, however, suggests a rather more indiscriminate use of violence than the official rhetoric would suggest.[81] And while the raid on Tripoli provoked a relatively mild Libyan response, future attacks on Libya or other Middle Eastern countries could invite significant retaliation and thus ignite a major international conflict. Despite this risk, such action continues to enjoy strong support in Washington and is likely to remain an important component of the LIC repertoire.

ANTIDRUG OPERATIONS

Another LIC mission that is likely to witness considerable growth in the years ahead is the use of military resources to combat the flow of illegal drugs into the United States. While such activities have heretofore received only scant attention from Pentagon strategists, they have become a high priority for members of Congress and for administration officials who seek a more vigorous drive against narcotics-trafficking. Reflecting the views of many lawmakers, Senator Dennis DeConcini of Arizona declared in 1986 that "we must treat illegal drugs as a national security threat to the United States."[82] This view was subsequently affirmed by President Reagan, who in April 1986 signed a secret directive identifying the illegal drug traffic as a significant threat to national security, and authorizing the Department of Defense to engage in a wide range of antidrug activities.

At this point, primary responsibility for halting the drug traffic still remains with civilian agencies—notably the Justice Department and its Drug Enforcement Administration (DEA), the Coast Guard, and the Customs Service. Indeed, a number of century-old statutes have generally excluded the military from involvement in what has, until fairly recently, been considered a civil law-enforcement function. However, as a result of recent legislative and presidential decisions, the armed services are assuming an ever-expanding role in antidrug operations.

The first major initiative in this area was undertaken in 1981, when the armed services were authorized by Congress to share any intelligence on narcotics-trafficking obtained during the course of military operations with federal, state, and local law-enforcement officials. The secretary of defense was also granted the authority to make certain facilities and equipment available to such officials, and to allow military personnel (acting in a support capacity only) to be employed in antidrug operations conducted by civilian law-enforcement agencies.[83]

Since the adoption of these statutes, the armed services have provided substantial assistance to the DEA and other civilian agencies. Much of this includes the provision of intelligence data acquired by military aircraft during routine patrols in the Caribbean, the Gulf of Mexico, and along the Mexican border. During Fiscal 1985, for instance, U.S. Navy and Air Force patrol planes reportedly amassed over ten thousand hours of flight time while acquiring such data. The services have also provided ships and aircraft for large multiagency drug-interdiction operations such as "Hat Trick" in the Caribbean.[84]

President Reagan's April 1986 directive on narcotics control provided the armed services with even wider latitude in conducting antidrug operations. Specifically, the directive allows the Pentagon to help plan strike operations against drug laboratories and processing plants in foreign countries, to transport U.S. civilian agents and foreign police during these operations, and to conduct expanded intelligence activities.[85]

Under this authority, the Defense Department conducted its most elaborate antidrug operation to date in the summer and fall of 1986: a prolonged search-and-destroy mission in the coca-growing Chaparé region of Bolivia, during which U.S. Army Black Hawk helicopters ferried DEA agents and Bolivian police units to the site of suspected cocaine-processing facilities. This endeavor, known as Operation "Blast Furnace," was credited with temporarily halting the production of cocaine in Bolivia, and was cited by administration officials as the model for future operations in other drug-producing countries.[86]

Other activities that are being conducted in accordance with the 1986 presidential directive include the use of military aircraft and radar to detect low-flying planes crossing into the United States from Mexico; the use of Air Force special operations helicopters to transport Bahamian antidrug officers in the Bahamas and Turk islands; and the loan of helicopters and fixed-wing aircraft to civilian law-enforcement agencies in the United States.[87]

Even this is not sufficient for some U.S. lawmakers who want to employ the armed services in a more vigorous campaign against the narcotics trade. Several proposed statutes would oblige the Pentagon to assume responsibility for guarding U.S. coasts and borders against drug smugglers, and would empower military personnel to seize, search, and arrest suspected smugglers (an authority they are now denied under the Posse Comitatus Act). Although Congress has yet to adopt the most sweeping of these measures, pressure is building for a more vigorous Pentagon role in combating illegal drugs.[88]

Some advocates of an expanded U.S. role in low-intensity warfare also view the drug issue as a useful vehicle for mobilizing public support behind their interventionist policies. Without providing much evidence, these ideologues claim that leftist guerrillas in Latin America are cooperating with narcotics dealers in order to finance arms purchases. "There is an alliance between some drug traffickers and some insurgents," Colonel Waghelstein claimed in 1987, and "dollars accrued to the drug dealers find their way into some guerrilla coffers." By emphasizing this connection in official statements, he suggested, the Pentagon would obtain "the necessary support to counter the guerrilla/narcotics terrorists in this hemisphere." This approach, moreover, would provide the Pentagon with an "unassailable moral position" from which to oppose those "church and academic groups" that have resisted U.S. intervention in Central America.[89]

PEACEKEEPING OPERATIONS

Current doctrine envisions one additional role for U.S. forces in the low-intensity arena: international peacekeeping operations, or the insertion of U.S. troops into foreign conflict zones in order to safeguard a cease-fire agreement, or to separate warring parties. Such operations, according to the JLICP report, are "military operations conducted in support of diplomatic efforts to achieve, restore, or maintain peace in areas of potential or actual conflict."[90] Typically, such operations are sponsored by the United Nations or some other supranational agency, and are conducted by multinational forces of which the U.S. contingent is a part.

Military operations of this sort might seem to fall in quite a different category than those described earlier. In fact, the discrepancy is not all that great: for most LIC theorists, peacekeeping—like counterinsurgency and contingency operations—represents a legitimate means for protecting U.S. interests in turbulent Third World areas. "Increasing world tension, continuing conflicts, scarce resources, and general distrust have created environments" in which such operations may be required, the Army notes. "Given the worldwide nature of U.S. national interests, it is vital to U.S. security to maintain not only the capability to employ force, but also the ability to assist in the peaceful resolution of conflicts."[91]

Peacekeeping operations, then, can be viewed as a military action taken to contain or defuse an overseas conflict when it is not in America's interest to permit the prolongation of that conflict, or the defeat of one side or the other. Such a situation can arise when a local conflict threatens U.S. access to oil supplies or other strategic materials, or when both warring parties are allies of the United States. Examples include the U.N. peacekeeping mission on Cyprus (where both contending parties, Greece and Turkey, are U.S. allies as well as members of NATO), and the U.S. observer force in the Sinai (a role mandated by the Camp David accords).[92]

CONTINUITY AND CHANGE IN LIC DOCTRINE

Together, these six mission areas comprise the basic terrain of low-intensity conflict as perceived by American strategists. Clearly, it is a complex and varied terrain—but one in which, nonetheless, certain basic themes and assumptions stand out. First and foremost, we are made abundantly aware that it is Third World disorder—and, more precisely, Third World insurgency—that comprises the dominant feature of low-intensity warfare. Of equal importance, current doctrine emphasizes a vigorous U.S. response to threats arising in the LIC arena. Beyond these two key points, we can detect a number of other basic themes that resonate throughout the LIC literature.

In seeking to identify these themes, we are inevitably driven to make comparisons with U.S. doctrine of the Kennedy era. Some current precepts are, in fact, updated variants of the original counterinsurgency formula; others, however, represent innovations of the post-Vietnam period. By identifying and classifying these two types of presumptions, we arrive at a full appreciation of LIC doctrine in all its complexity.

First, those themes that bear the greatest resemblance to earlier doctrine:

1. *Low-intensity conflict is generally characterized by a clash between revolutionary and counterrevolutionary processes.* Given the Third World locus of low-intensity warfare, it is not surprising that such conflicts tend to involve a struggle between proponents of radical change and the guardians of the prevailing order. "The substantive dimensions of [low-intensity] conflicts evolve primarily from revolutionary and counterrevolutionary strategies and causes," LIC theorist Sam C. Sarkesian declared in 1985.[93] For the most part, current U.S. strategy is intended to help existing, status quo regimes to defend themselves against revolutionary upheavals. In the case of proinsurgency, however, the United States seeks to engineer the collapse of revolutionary governments that have actually come to power. Similarly, in contingency operations and counterterrorism, LIC doctrine envisions the use of military forces to intimidate, coerce, or punish left-leaning Third World regimes.

2. Given the sociopolitical character of revolutionary and counterrevolutionary conflict, *low-intensity operations must incorporate both nonmilitary and military modes of combat.* Because insurgency is bred in a climate of social malaise, U.S.-backed counterinsurgency campaigns must seek to neutralize public disaffection areas through social, political, and economic initiatives aimed at "winning hearts and minds" for the prevailing regime. Similarly, in cases of proinsurgency, the United States must seek to exploit political divisions within the target society. "The struggle between the insurgent and the incumbent," the *JLICP Final*

Report notes, "is over political legitimacy—who should govern and how they should govern." Accordingly, "one of the principal elements in this struggle is the effort to mobilize popular support. Whoever succeeds at this will ultimately prevail."[94]

3. *The U.S. military commitment to future LIC engagements should consist primarily of highly trained, "special" formations that can operate successfully in a demanding Third World environment.* Given the socio-political context of LIC combat, participating U.S. forces must be skilled in political, economic, and psychological operations as well as in conventional military operations. "Success in revolutionary and counter-revolutionary conflicts is not necessarily contingent upon sophisticated weaponry or those with the biggest battalions," Sarkesian avowed in 1986. Rather, "success depends on the quality and dedication of individuals on the ground, who can blend the military with the political and social, and function as skilled political mobilizers and teachers, as well as efficient soldiers."[95]

These three precepts, and much of the doctrinal material in the current LIC literature, would not appear novel to most counterinsurgency experts of the Kennedy period. Indeed, one is continually struck by the affinity between much of current doctrine and such earlier statements as the *U.S. Overseas Internal Defense Policy* of 1962—an affinity derived from the abiding characteristics of revolutionary and counter-revolutionary warfare. But there are other strands of current thinking that are not quite so derivative. These precepts appear to reflect some of the major global transformations that have occurred since 1965:

4. *Low-intensity warfare encompasses a broad spectrum of military operations, and thus U.S. forces must be prepared to shift rapidly from one type of LIC activity to another.* In the 1960s, low-intensity conflict was largely equated with counterinsurgency—an outlook that tended to circumscribe the training and equipment provided to the LIC forces of the time. Under current doctrine, however, U.S. forces may be required to perform low-key advisory functions one day, and rather intense contingency operations the next. As a result, U.S. strategists argue that present-day LIC forces should be trained and equipped for a wide variety of military operations, and be provided with the mobility to move rapidly from one combat zone to another. "The low-intensity battlefield of the future," Colonel Motley averred in 1985, "will require strategically

responsive and flexible forces organized to respond to a broad spectrum of combat operations and a wide variety of contingencies."[96]

While this outlook clearly derives from the very practical problem of having to configure U.S. combat forces for a varied and unpredictable set of military demands, it also suggests a rather laissez-faire approach to low-intensity conflict and its various components. One senses, in fact, that U.S. leaders are not overwhelmingly committed to any single aspect of LIC but rather are prepared to move from one to the other as opportunity and circumstances demand. If a counterinsurgency campaign is bogging down in one place, then *bam!* let's try proinsurgency and antidrug operations somewhere else; better yet, let's move on all fronts at once and see what produces the optimum results. This free-wheeling, aggressive posture is plainly evident in the military behavior of the Reagan administration—with the invasion of Grenada coinciding with peacekeeping in Beirut, with counterinsurgency in El Salvador proceeding alongside proinsurgency in Nicargua and Angola—as well as in the establishment by the Army of four rapidly deployable, multipurpose light infantry divisions. The great danger with such a posture, of course, is that this predisposition to move from one LIC arena to another will someday lead to precipitous intervention in an overseas conflict that cannot be controlled or brought to a favorable resolution.

5. *When regular U.S. forces are committed to LIC operations abroad, they should seek to achieve a rapid victory through overwhelming strength and firepower.* This dictum arises from the experience of Vietnam, where the gradual buildup of U.S. troops permitted the North Vietnamese to infiltrate sufficient forces to offset U.S. strength in the South—causing a stalemate that produced massive public opposition in the United States. To prevent such an outcome in the future, American strategists now stress the *rapid* introduction of U.S. forces (hence, "Rapid Deployment Force") plus the application of superior firepower to overcome enemy resistance. "While the American people are not particularly antiwar," Captain Ralph Peters wrote in *Military Review,* "they are absolutely antistalemate." Accordingly, the United States should avoid direct military involvement in LIC operations "unless [it] opts for the approach that delivers overwhelming combat power in a swift and violent manner," shattering enemy forces and "thus getting the thing over with." This, he said, "is the fundamental *military* lesson of US involvement in Vietnam."[97]

This lesson was clearly applied in Grenada, where the United States employed a force of seven thousand troops—backed up by an aircraft carrier and ten warships—to overcome a ragtag group of Cuban and Grenadian defenders. Similarly, U.S. naval maneuvers in the Gulf of Sidra (claimed as territorial waters by Libya) have also been characterized by a massive show of strength. Most analysts believe, moreover, that any direct U.S. military action in Nicaragua—should such ever occur—will entail a swift and violent assault by powerful air, ground, and naval forces.[98] Such an encounter would, in the eyes of U.S. strategists, remain in the domain of low-intensity combat, but would actually comprise something much closer to a *high*-intensity conflict; and while a Central American engagement of this sort is not likely to trigger a global conflict, it certainly would result in considerable death and destruction in Central America itself; moreover, any attempt to follow this scenario in South Asia or the Middle East could result in a major regional conflagration of unforeseeable scope and intensity.

6. Given continuing public resistance to direct U.S. involvement in protracted Third World conflicts, *the continuing development and application of LIC doctrine abroad requires sustained political intervention at home.* For many LIC proponents, the "homefront"—that is, the domestic political environment in the United States—is as much a target for political and psychological warfare as is the population of overseas LIC battlefields. "A hard-hitting, sophisticated information campaign [is] required," Kupperman affirmed in 1983, "to convert the public and policy attitudes away from the conventional wisdom" of focusing on Europe and to adopt "the new philosophy" of seeing military power "as the political instrument of choice" in combating low-intensity threats in the Third World.[99]

Such education is essential, in the view of many American strategists, because the particular nature of low-intensity warfare—the prevalence of civilian casualties and the U.S. tendency to side with brutal dictators against popular opposition forces—entails a clash with basic American values. "The American view of war is generally incompatible with the characteristics and demands of counterrevolution," Sarkesian noted in 1985. A counterinsurgency strategy that entails the suppression of dissident organizations and the liquidation of revolutionary leaders "is not likely to be in accord with democratic norms"; accordingly, "support and assistance for the offensive phase of counterrevolution are likely to create political and moral dilemmas for Americans." To overcome these dilemmas, U.S. leaders must convince the public that "revolution and counterrevolution develop their own morality and ethics that *justify any means to achieve success.*"[100] (Emphasis added.)

These views are typical of those held by LIC strategists in Washington. Although we can expect continuing debate on the fine points of doctrine, these basic precepts are likely to govern the U.S. military response to future low-level engagements abroad.

While it is risky to make broad generalizations, there does appear in all of this to be a clear and consistent commitment to the use of military force in dealing with low-intensity challenges in the Third World. Such usage may begin as a relatively restrained and inconspicuous deployment of military advisers, but could escalate rapidly into something much greater. The distance between "low-" and "high-" intensity conflict may be much smaller that we would like to believe.

Clearly, the greatest risk we face from an aggressive policy of intervention is the danger that a small conflict will escalate rapidly into a large, uncontrollable conflagration. Such escalation is, in fact, the most likely scenario for the onset of World War III—and the nuclear peril such a conflict would entail. But even in the absence of such catastrophe, we face a significant threat to our rights and liberties at home. Although intended to free U.S. military personnel to operate as they see fit on foreign soil, the domestic political measures advocated by ardent LIC enthusiasts would inevitably erode the integrity of our democratic values and institutions. Once we surrender a free press and key democratic values to the exigencies of war, we may find that other barriers to authoritarianism will disappear as well.

LOW-INTENSITY WARFARE: THE WARRIORS AND THEIR WEAPONS

STEPHEN D. GOOSE

THE world is awash in "low-level" conflicts; today there are some forty wars going on around the globe, involving more than one-quarter of the world's nations.[1] U.S. strategists are convinced that the United States has "vital" interests—i.e., interests that might need to be defended through the use of military force—in nearly every one of these hot spots. The Reagan administration's "go anywhere, do anything" approach to military power, and its very broad conception of low-intensity conflict (LIC), has led to the mustering of numerous forces and weapons for engagement in the various categories of low-level combat. As a result, the United States is now engaged in a multibillion-dollar effort to create and equip an array of new forces for future deployment in every region of the Third World. In this chapter, we will examine those U.S. forces that are most attuned to the emerging LIC mission: the Special Operations Forces of all the military services; the Army's light infantry divisions (LIDs); and the Pentagon's so-called "power projection" forces. While almost any element of America's military could be used for combat in the Third World, these are the specialized forces that are being sized, equipped, and trained specifically for future American military intervention in the developing areas.

SPECIAL OPERATIONS FORCES

Special Operations Forces (SOF) are the principal U.S. military units for engagement in low-intensity warfare. They would be at the cutting edge of almost any American intervention anywhere in the Third World. Secretary of Defense Caspar Weinberger reaffirmed this unequivocally in 1986: "The particular skills and supporting capabilities which the military offers to the prosecution of low-intensity conflict are chiefly to be found in our Special Operations Forces."[2]

Special Operations Forces are best known for their attempted rescue of the American hostages in Iran in 1980, and for spearheading the U.S. invasion of Grenada in 1983. SOF are the U.S. military's elite, highly trained commando units. They are sometimes called America's "secret soldiers," and include hush-hush units such as the Delta Force that the Pentagon will not even acknowledge exist. Other elements of SOF include the U.S. Army Special Forces (the "Green Berets"), the Rangers, the 160th Army Aviation Battalion, psychological operations and civil affairs units, the Navy's sea-air-land (SEAL) commando forces, the Air Force Special Operations Wing, and special-operations-capable Marine amphibious units (MAUs).

Special Operations Forces are America's experts in guerrilla and antiguerrilla warfare, in sabotage, and in counterterrorism operations. SOF are also called on to do the "dirty jobs"—they are the forces that are usually ordered to carry out clandestine operations in foreign countries in peacetime. SOF learn to fight in any terrain, in any location in the world. SOF skills include parachuting, underwater demolition, scuba-diving, sabotage, pathfinder operations, camouflage, escape and evasion, aerial insertion and extraction, intelligence-gathering, and interrogation. They are expected to be experts in foreign languages and customs, and to be able to fight with foreign weaponry. There are also SOF experts in psychological operations and civil affairs—that is, specialists in "winning hearts and minds," as well as in killing and destroying.

Combating terrorism has been a major preoccupation of the Reagan administration, and SOF have been given the major responsibility for this role. The Delta Force, based at Fort Bragg, North Carolina, is the primary U.S. antiterrorist unit. Helicopter support for the Delta Force is provided by the Army's Task Force 160, located at Fort Campbell,

Kentucky. The crack counterterrorist personnel from the other services are in the Navy's SEAL Team 6, stationed at Dam Neck, Virginia, and in the Air Force's Special Operations Squadron 8, located at Hurlburt Field, Florida.[3] While the U.S. military has not attempted any hostage rescue missions since the debacle in the Iranian desert in 1980, these forces have reportedly assisted or observed up to fifty hostage situations around the world since 1980.[4]

THE REAGAN "REVITALIZATION" OF SOF

America's Special Operations Forces are now undergoing an unprecedented peacetime expansion, following a sharp decline after the Vietnam War. Secretary Weinberger has told Congress that SOF are "one of this Administration's highest priorities,"[5] and his words have been echoed by the Joint Chiefs of Staff and many other military and political leaders. Congress has enthusiastically approved and funded this buildup. Troop levels, annual spending, weapons inventories, and the *use* of SOF have all increased dramatically under a "revitalization" plan due to be completed in 1990.

In contrast to the concurrent buildup of nuclear arms and U.S. conventional forces in Europe—initiatives which are consistently justified in terms of enhancing "deterrence" (i.e., the prevention of war)—the expansion of Special Operations Forces has always been rationalized on the grounds that they are the units most likely to engage in actual combat operations. These are forces for *fighting*, not for deterring war. As Mr. Weinberger affirmed in 1984, "The high priority we have assigned to SOF revitalization reflects our recognition that low-level conflict—for which SOF are uniquely suited—will pose the threat we are most likely to encounter throughout the end of this century."[6]

From 1981 to 1985, active-duty SOF manpower increased about 30 percent, from 11,600 soldiers to 14,900. With reserves added in, total SOF strength now stands at about 32,000. By 1990, under the Reagan administration's revitalization plan, active-duty SOF manpower will rise to 20,900 (an 80 percent increase over 1981), and total SOF will number 38,400.[7] In conducting this troop buildup, the Army has added a fourth Special Forces group (and retains plans for a fifth), a third Ranger battalion, and a fourth psychological operations battalion. The Navy has added a sixth SEAL team (with plans for a seventh) and two new swimmer delivery vehicle teams. Moreover, a new bureaucracy for command, control, planning, and oversight of the SOF buildup has been established. This apparatus incorporates the Joint Special Operations Agency, the Army's 1st Special Operations Command, the Air Force's 1st Special Operations Wing, and, since 1987, a Unified Combatant Command for Special Operations.[8]

The SOF budget has risen at a much faster rate than the rest of the Pentagon budget during the Reagan years, and is continuing to grow while the rest of the budget is being held in check by a deficit-conscious Congress. Spending on SOF skyrocketed from $441 million in Fiscal Year (FY) 1981 to $1.7 billion in FY1987. Furthermore, the administration asked Congress for $2.5 billion for SOF in FY1988, and current Pentagon plans call for nearly $8 billion more for Fiscal 1989–92.[9] Even this is not enough for some congressional leaders, who have said that the administration's request may need to be doubled.[10]

Most of this money is being spent on new weapons designed expressly for SOF. Each branch of the armed services buys and maintains its own SOF weaponry and equipment—much of which is highly specialized, technologically advanced, and very expensive. By 1990, the Navy will have 54 special warfare craft, up from 8 in 1981, and 6 submarines converted to carry naval commandos and launch new minisubs known as swimmer delivery vehicles.[11] The Air Force's special operations aircraft inventory will expand from 42 units in 1981 to 129 in 1990, including 21 MC-130 "Combat Talon" transport aircraft costing nearly $57 million apiece.[12] The Army is developing two new types of helicopters, is fielding an engine-propelled parachute, and is acquiring laser weapons and other specialized types of ground weaponry.[13]

The actual use of SOF has also increased during the Reagan administration. The invasion of Grenada was led by SOF units from each of the armed services.[14] SOF have been especially active in Central America— in combat exercises, training activities, and, according to some sources, covert military operations.[15] In 1984, Noel Koch, then principal deputy assistant secretary of defense and the senior Pentagon official for SOF matters, told Congress that Special Operations Forces were "the most heavily used of our military forces today."[16]

On a day-to-day basis, the most extensive use of SOF capabilities is in U.S. military training teams (MTTs) sent to foreign countries. Today Special Operations Forces are active around the globe training military forces in Latin America, the Middle East, Asia, and Africa. Under the Reagan administration, the number of MTT man-weeks abroad has increased more than fivefold, from 1,161 in 1980 to an estimated 5,787 in 1984.[17] Special Operations Forces make up 25 to 35 percent of all MTTs, including virtually all of those employed in counterinsurgency training.[18] From 1981 to 1984, SOF training teams operated in over three dozen nations, including Grenada, Honduras, El Salvador, Costa Rica, Colombia, Lebanon, Saudi Arabia, Somalia, Tunisia, Morocco, Liberia, Zaire, the Philippines, and Thailand.[19]

Reflecting the high priority accorded these forces since 1981, sweeping organizational changes have been made in SOF and a new bureaucracy has sprung up to govern them. A key step was the establishment of the Joint Special Operations Agency (JSOA), reporting directly to the Joint Chiefs of Staff. It was approved in October 1983, just days before the Grenada invasion, and activated in January 1984. The JSOA mandate is to advise the JCS on all aspects of special operations, including strategy, planning, budget, resource development and allocation, doctrine, training, and employment of forces.[20]

The individual services have also established new SOF agencies. The Army created its 1st Special Operations Command (1st SOCOM) in 1982, uniting all Army SOF units under a single commander at Fort Bragg. In 1983, all Air Force search-and-rescue and SOF units were united in the newly created 23rd Air Force. Subsequently, the 1st Special Operations Wing of the 23rd Air Force was established at Hurlburt Field.[21]

A continuing perception in Congress that SOF are plagued by managerial problems has produced a variety of further reorganization proposals. One 1985 proposal went so far as to suggest the creation of a "sixth service" (in addition to Army, Navy, Air Force, Marine Corps, and Coast Guard) for Special Operations Forces.[22] In 1986, three different proposals—one offered in the Senate, one in the House, and one submitted by the Pentagon—were hotly debated on Capitol Hill; all reflected a perceived need to streamline the command and control of SOF capabilities and to develop a common doctrine and strategy for these disparate units.

The SOF reorganization debate culminated, on October 15, 1986, with the passage of the National Defense Authorization Bill for Fiscal Year 1987. Under this law, a Special Operations Forces Unified Combatant Command will be established at the Pentagon with a four-star general as officer in charge. Pursuant to this statute, in April 1987 the Defense Department established the U.S. Special Operations Command (USSOC) at MacDill Air Force Base, Florida, with General

James J. Lindsay of the Army serving as its first commander in chief. The Command will be responsible for developing doctrine, coordinating strategy, and training and equipping all SOF detachments. In addition, an assistant secretary of defense for special operations and low-intensity conflict, a deputy assistant to the president for low-intensity conflict, and a board for low-intensity conflict (to be housed in the National Security Council) will be named.[23]

This new bureaucracy will guide and supervise the individual SOF units, though they will remain under the operational control of their respective services. Each of these units is described briefly below.

ARMY SOF

The Army has by far the largest contingent of SOF, with more than 10,000 on active duty and over 13,600 in the reserves.[24] Army Special Operations Forces are divided into six groups:

☐ *Special Forces,* commonly known as the "Green Berets" and famous for their fighting prowess in Vietnam, now function mainly as military trainers and advisers in friendly Third World countries. They are organized into four Special Forces groups (SFGs), each of which is about 1,400 men strong. The 1st SFG, activated in 1984, is stationed at Fort Lewis, Washington. The 5th SFG, currently located at Fort Bragg, is moving to Fort Campbell. The 7th SFG is based at Fort Bragg, with one battalion (the 3rd) permanently stationed in Panama. The 10th SFG is based at Fort Devens, Massachusetts, with one battalion (the 1st) stationed in Bad Tölz, West Germany. Another active-duty group will be established in 1990–91. There are also four SFGs in the Army Reserve and National Guard. In addition, small Special Forces detachments are based in South Korea and Berlin. These supersecret units are thought to be "stay behind" forces, trained to go underground and create disruption behind enemy lines when and if Allied forces are overrun.[25]

Each Special Forces group is dedicated to a particular region and assigned to a geographic unified command: the 1st SFG is oriented to the Pacific and Southeast Asia (and assigned to the Pacific Command); the 5th SFG to Southwest Asia (Central Command); the 7th SFG to Central and South America (Southern Command); and the 10th SFG to Europe (European Command).[26] This specialization is desirable, Secretary Weinberger has said, because "our Special Operations Forces require thorough familiarity with the terrain, the social and religious mores, the ethnic composition, the political systems and infrastructure, and the climatic conditions of their potential areas of operation."[27]

The Special Forces are growing in size and becoming increasingly active around the globe. Green Berets make up the bulk of an ever-increasing number of military training teams sent abroad to teach counterinsurgency methods. Reagan administration officials have also indicated that Green Berets will soon begin teaching insurgency techniques to the Nicaraguan contras as part of the $100 million in aid approved by Congress in 1986.[28]

☐ The *Rangers* are a rapid-reaction force whose primary mission is combat behind enemy lines. The Rangers are known for their airborne assault skills; Ranger paratroopers made up the bulk of the initial attack force on Grenada.

The roughly two thousand U.S. Rangers are organized into the 75th Infantry Regiment (Rangers), which is divided into three battalions: the 1st at Hunter Army Airfield, Georgia; the 2nd at Fort Lewis, Washington; and the 3rd at Fort Benning, Georgia. The three battalions alternate responsibility for the Ranger Ready Force, which is supposed to be capable of deploying for combat anywhere in the world within eighteen hours of notice.[29] Like the Green Berets, the Rangers are also expanding: in 1984, the Fort Benning battalion was added and a new Ranger Regimental Headquarters was established.[30]

☐ The *Delta Force* is a formerly supersecret unit that was recently the subject of a major motion picture of the blood-and-guts fantasy variety. Still, the Defense Department refuses to comment on Delta, and little is really known about it. It was formed in the 1970s and constituted the core group of the force sent to Iran for the failed hostage-rescue attempt of April 1980.[31] Formally known as the 1st Special Forces Detachment–Delta, it is based at Fort Bragg and thought to number about three hundred soldiers.[32] The Delta Force is likely to be the first unit called on for highly specialized covert missions.

The Delta Force is the main element of America's counterterrorist force, and is reported to have been on the scene for numerous hostage situations around the globe since 1980. These include the rescue of General James Dozier in Italy in December 1982, the Venezuelan airliner hijacking in July 1984, the kidnapping of Western relief workers in the Sudan in 1983, the crisis at the Libyan embassy in London in 1984, and the hijacking of a Kuwaiti airliner in Iran in December 1984.

Delta was also reported to have been sent to Cyprus to prepare for a rescue attempt of passengers held captive aboard a TWA flight in Beirut in June 1985. Press accounts indicate a U.S. counterterrorist team, probably including members of Delta, was assembled to attempt an assault on the hijacked cruise ship *Achille Lauro* in October 1985. Elements of Delta were also reportedly deployed in reaction to the Pan Am Flight 73 hijacking in Pakistan in September 1986.[33]

Attention has been focused on Delta in recent years not only because of America's preoccupation with terrorism, but also because of charges of financial misconduct. An investigation is underway into an alleged $200,000 in double billings by Delta Force members for expenses incurred while traveling overseas to protect U.S. ambassadors. The Army has launched another investigation into alleged financial misconduct by SOF units in spending more than $150 million on classified paramilitary and intelligence missions. The investigation has resulted in indictments and court-martial proceedings against several Delta members.[34]

☐ *Task Force 160* (TF-160), formally the 160th Aviation Battalion (Assault Helicopter) of the 101st Army Air Assault Division, is a top secret unit formed in 1981 to provide helicopter transport and attack support to the Delta Force and other U.S. special units.[35] TF-160 is nicknamed the "Night Stalkers," and is known for its daredevil night-training exercises; its motto is "Death Waits in the Dark." Major General William Moore, a top Army SOF official, told Congress in 1984 that TF-160 has the most sophisticated aircraft in the Army and "probably the best helicopter pilots in the world today."[36]

While TF-160 is currently the only Army Special Operations Aviation unit, a significant expansion is underway. In the first quarter of fiscal 1987, a new Special Operations Aviation company was activated; in FY 1988, the National Guard's 45th Aviation Battalion will be converted to special operations, and in FY1989, another Special Operations Aviation company will be added.[37]

☐ *Civil affairs* (CA) personnel are employed to train and advise foreign military forces in civic action, which is defined by the Pentagon as "the use of . . . military forces on projects useful to the local population . . . contributing to economic and social development, which would also serve to improve the standing of the military forces with the population."[38] Such specialists now in the active-duty force structure are organized into the 96th CA Battalion, about six hundred strong, at Fort Bragg. Most CA specialists are in the reserves.[39]

☐   *Psychological operations* (PSYOP) personnel are propaganda specialists. The 1,100 active-duty PSYOP troops are organized into one psychological operations group with four battalions at Fort Bragg. Additional PSYOP personnel are in the reserves.[40] The fourth PSYOP battalion was added in 1985, and two new PSYOP companies will be activated in FY1988.[41] PSYOP troops make use of all forms of mass communication—television, radio, newspapers, posters, leaflets, and so forth. They possess special communications equipment, such as an air-transportable fifty-thousand-watt radio transmitter that can be moved anywhere in the world, as well as loudspeakers for use from vehicles, aircraft, naval vessels, or by a single person.[42]

Psychological operations are carried out before, during, and after combat operations. PSYOP personnel are also trained to conduct covert psychological operations in such a way that the U.S. government's responsibility is not evident or, if discovered, the White House can deny involvement.[43] Central America is being used as a crucible to test the effectiveness of CA and PSYOP troops. Numerous CA and PSYOP personnel have been sent to El Salvador in an attempt to "win hearts and minds" through the highly publicized provision of "humanitarian" assistance. Such PSYOP activities include medical aid, food distribution, construction projects, and numerous public relations efforts.[44]

ARMY SOF WEAPONRY

Army SOF are equipped with most of the latest infantry weaponry, ranging from pistols, rifles, and machine guns to mortars, recoilless rifles, rocket launchers, and antitank guns. Some weapons have been specially adapted for SOF, including the Colt Commando rifle (a variant of the M-16A1) and the M-21 sniper rifle.[45] The Army's 1st Special Operations Command states that "Special Forces weapons experts are capable of firing and maintaining all US Army weapons that might be used by friendly guerrilla forces." They are also familiar with foreign weapons, and "since sophisticated weapons may not always be available, Special Forces troopers are trained in the use of 'homemade' weapons."[46]

The Army is also developing some new systems for SOF. These include the "pursuit deterrent munition," which is basically a land mine adapted "to permit hand employment" and designed to "protect and warn troops involved in operations [and] to deter pursuing troops," and the "penetration augmentation munition," described as a "man-portable, one-step, multi-stage demolition munition which is used to crater roads or destroy bridge piers and abutments."[47] The Army is also developing a "para-plane" parachute (also called a "ram air" parachute), which is a parachute with an engine and propeller; a prototype was delivered in 1986, and initial operational use of the final system is scheduled for 1989.[48]

In 1984, the Army and Air Force chiefs of staff agreed to "Initiative 17," an interservice agreement whereby the Air Force will transfer its SOF helicopter transport mission to the Army—a step that was prompted by long-standing Army complaints over a lack of Air Force interest in special operations. With the adoption of Initiative 17, SOF aviation has become a major priority for the Army. Army Chief of Staff John Wickham told Congress in 1986 that the Army already had a force of 107 helicopters exclusively dedicated to special operations—mainly UH-1Hs, UH-60s, CH-47s, OH-6s, and Hughes 500 MDs—and that new SOF helicopters are presently in development. The Army has $25 million in its fiscal 1987 research-and-development (R&D) budget for enhanced SOF aviation, specifically for "the development, modification and testing of aircraft and aviation systems suitable for support of Special Operations Forces."[49]

The Army is developing two new helicopters for special operations: the MH-60X and the MH-47E. Both are scheduled to be delivered between 1989 and 1991. The MH-60X will be a modification of, and will replace, Army UH-60 helicopters in the SOF inventory. Improvements include upgraded engine and transmission, precision navigation equipment, special radars, aerial refueling, and other items. The MH-47E, which will be a modification of existing CH-47Ds, is described as "the most sophisticated aircraft in the Army inventory." It is being designed specifically for special operations "conducted at tactical altitudes, over unfamiliar mountainous terrain, in [bad] weather [or] at night, for extended ranges."[50]

NAVY SOF

Navy Special Operations Forces, called sea-air-land troops, or SEALs, are direct descendants of the "frogmen" of World War II. Currently numbering about seventeen hundred, they are divided into two Naval special warfare groups, which are further broken down into six SEAL teams, two SEAL delivery vehicle teams, two special boat squadrons, two special boat units, and three special warfare units.[51]

SEALs are trained to conduct beach, coastal, and riverine reconnaissance prior to combat, to clear beaches and harbors, to destroy enemy harbor facilities and other installations in maritime areas, to disrupt enemy shipping, and to infiltrate clandestinely into enemy territory. Of all the services, Navy SOF are generally considered the toughest and best trained.[52] The SEALs have also been widely employed in combat operations. As avowed by Commander R. M. Rieve, commanding officer of SEAL Team 2, "SEALs have been involved in virtually all hostile incidents in which a US-backed contingency response has been required."[53]

SEAL teams number about 175 men. Teams 1, 3, and 5 are based at Coronado, California; Teams 2 and 4 are based at Little Creek, Virginia; and Team 6 is based at Dam Neck, Virginia.[54] Teams 1 and 2 were formed in 1962 and saw extensive action in Vietnam. Teams 4 and 5 were formed as underwater demolition teams in 1946 and converted to SEAL teams in 1983. Team 3 was added in 1983, specifically for action in Southwest Asia.[55] The very existence of SEAL Team 6, which is specially trained for counterterrorism, is rarely acknowledged; formed in November 1980, it was reportedly mobilized to attempt an assault on the terrorist-held *Achille Lauro* in 1985, but did not arrive on the scene in time due to transportation difficulties.[56]

The three special warfare units, each with seventeen members, are stationed at Subic Bay Naval Base in the Philippines, at Roosevelt Roads Naval Station in Puerto Rico, and at Machrihanish airfield in Scotland. These units reportedly specialize in clandestine activities; their assumed wartime mission would be to sow confusion and disruption behind enemy lines.[57]

The Navy is regarded as the service most enthusiastic about the SOF revitalization. Since 1980, two new SEAL teams have been added and two others converted (producing a total of six teams), the two swimmer delivery vehicle teams were created, and twenty-one SEAL platoons were formed (for a total of forty-one).[58] A seventh SEAL team will be established between 1988 and 1990 and assigned to the European Command.[59] The Navy is also seeking new special operations craft and weaponry; special operations procurement initiatives from 1986 to 1991 are expected to total $1.1 billion, plus another $342 million for maintenance costs.[60]

NAVY SOF VESSELS AND WEAPONRY

Special equipment provided to the SEALs includes scuba equipment which leaves no bubbles in the water, the latest in rubber inflatable craft, hand-held sonar gear, two-man swimmer-portable sounding equipment for hydrographic surveys, special communications equipment, and the hand- and waterborne sensors of the Battle Area Surveillance System (BASS).[61] The SEALs also have a variety of surface and subsurface vessels designed for special operations. The Navy is very secretive about the subsurface systems, which include swimmer delivery vehicles, swimmer weapons systems, and dry deck shelters for submarines. Swimmer delivery vehicles (SDVs) are small, submersible, James Bond–type craft. They can be launched from surface ships or submarines (on top of or under the water), and can then "proceed submerged to the target beach area, conduct their reconnaissance mission, and return to the parent ship all undetected." SDVs reportedly carry "a range of ordnance . . . capable of doing extreme damage."[62] The Mark-VII SDV carries four men, the Mark-VIII six men, and the Mark-IX two men. Apparently, a Mark-X SDV is under consideration.[63] In 1981, when the Navy began adding Mark-IX SDVs, they had a total of twelve SDVs;[64] the number today is unknown.

To carry SEALs and their SDVs to combat areas, the Navy is building dry deck shelters (DDS) for six submarines. A dry deck shelter is basically a pod attached to the deck of a submarine that will permit combat swimmers and SDVs to leave and reenter a submerged sub; each DDS is able to carry one SDV.[65] The Navy currently has three dry deck shelter submarines. Two are former Polaris nuclear missile submarines: the *Sam Houston* and the *John Marshall.* These vessels were converted to attack subs in 1980–81, and then reconverted in 1983–85 at a cost of $16 million to carry two dry deck shelters each. The subs will each be able to carry two SDVs and about fifty combat swimmers. The other DDS sub is the *Cavalla,* a Sturgeon-class, nuclear-powered attack sub; it is believed to have joined the fleet with its DDS in 1983.[66] The Navy plans to convert three more Sturgeon-class subs to DDS configuration, for a total of six—three assigned to the Atlantic Fleet and three to the Pacific Fleet.[67]

Surface vessels employed by Navy SOF include several types of patrol boats that are designed to be faster, quieter, and more maneuverable than regular U.S. Navy boats. They are used for surveillance, for insertion and extraction of SEALs, and for interdiction. One such vessel is the Seafox, which is thirty-six feet long, can carry ten SEALs at speeds over thirty knots, and has many features designed to reduce its visibility and audibility.[68] Since 1981, the Navy has added twenty-eight Seafox craft for a total of thirty-six.[69] The Navy is also buying eighteen heavier special warfare craft, named Sea Viking, for an estimated $235 million. These will be surface effects ships, meaning that they ride over the water on a cushion of air. The 110-ton, seventy-nine-foot Sea Viking will be able to travel at high speeds in rough, open-ocean conditions and to operate from the well-decks of amphibious transport ships. Delivery of the lead craft was made in November 1985, and all eighteen are expected to be operational by April 1987.[70]

AIR FORCE SOF AND AIRCRAFT

The Air Force has forty-one hundred SOF troops organized under the 23rd Air Force 1st Special Operations Wing (1st SOW), which was established in 1983 at Hurlburt Field, Eglin Air Force Base, Florida.[71] In addition, there are five special operations squadrons (SOS)—three at Eglin, one in the Philippines, and one in West Germany—plus one special operations helicopter detachment in Panama. There are also two SOS in the reserves and one in the National Guard.[72] Air Force SOF are responsible for long-range infiltration and exfiltration of SOF ground forces, and for rescue operations.

As noted above, the Air Force is transferring its helicopter lift mission to the Army in accordance with Initiative 17. Until that process is completed, however, the Air Force will maintain a large inventory of helicopters and other aircraft for special operations—more than 135 fixed-wing planes and helicopters with the active forces, the reserves, and the National Guard.[73]

There are fifty-five "core aircraft" in the Air Force's SOF inventory, of which thirty-five are in the active force structure: fourteen MC-130E "Combat Talon" transport planes, ten AC-130H "Spectre" gunships, seven HH-53H "Pave Low" helicopters, and four UH-1N helicopters. Four of the MC-130s are in West Germany and four are in the Philippines; the UH-1Ns are in Panama. The rest of the aircraft are based at Hurlburt Field, except for four UH-1Ns transferred in 1985 to Homestead Air Force Base, Florida, to support drug traffic surveillance.[74] More than eighty other aircraft in the active SOF are classified as "augmenting forces," meaning they are earmarked for missions such as search and rescue, but could be called on for special operations.

The two most important Air Force SOF aircraft are the HH-53 helicopter and the MC-130 transport aircraft. The HH-53H Pave Low III is a long-range, low-level rescue helicopter designed for incursions into hostile territory and for night and adverse weather operations. Sophisticated avionics allow operations in almost total darkness, and as low as a hundred feet with no visual outside reference. In addition to the seven HH-53H Pave Low helicopters now in the active core inventory, twelve of the HH-53s in augmenting forces are being upgraded to MH-53J Pave Low III configuration—two in FY1986 and ten more by FY1988—for a total of nineteen.[75]

The MC-130 Combat Talon provides the aerial backbone for special operations. A Lockheed C-130 transport aircraft adapted for special operations with the addition of precision navigation, terrain-following radar, electronic countermeasures systems, and in-flight refueling, the Combat Talon can carry twenty-six troops, has a range of forty-two hundred nautical miles, and operates at up to thirty-five thousand feet. It is used to deliver, resupply, and recover men and equipment behind enemy lines during daytime or at night, and also for reconnaissance. In Grenada, Combat Talon aircraft from the 1st SOW ferried the first Ranger units to the island for the invasion. Nine MC-130Es are fitted with the Fulton Recovery System, a surface-to-air recovery system: a person on the ground is attached to a floating balloon that the Combat Talon snatches with "whiskers" on its nose and then "reels in" its catch. It can handle two people and up to five hundred pounds. A six-man system is also being developed.[76]

By 1990, the Air Force will add twenty-one MC-130H Combat Talon IIs to its inventory, in the biggest single program in the SOF revitalization effort. The H version will have better avionics and communications systems than the existing E version. Delivery of the first seven MC-130Hs is expected during FY1987, and all twenty-one will be funded by FY1989. Total program cost will be nearly $1.2 billion, or nearly $57 million per aircraft—making the MC-130H one of the costliest aircraft in the world.[77]

The Air Force is also working with the Navy and Marine Corps in developing the V-22 Osprey (JVX) tilt-rotor aircraft. The Air Force will use it for special operations, the Navy for search and rescue, and the

Marine Corps for airborne assault. The V-22 is an airplane/helicopter hybrid that, because of the rotors on its wings, can take off and land vertically like a helicopter but flies like a plane in the air. It will be able to transport twelve troops, with a range of over 500 nautical miles and a cruising speed of 250 knots.[78] The Air Force is expected to buy eighty of the aircraft for special operations, at a cost of over $30 million each.[79] The Air Force anticipates delivery of the first V-22 in FY1993 and of the last in FY1997.

MARINE CORPS SOF

Marine Corps units are technically not part of the Special Operations Forces. However, in 1985 the Corps started a program specifically intended to enhance the special operations capability of forward-deployed Marine amphibious units (MAUs). An MAU consists of an infantry battalion (about two thousand men) and its helicopters. Marine Corps Commandant General P. X. Kelley signed a memorandum in June 1985 which called for MAU improvements in sabotage, subversion, counterterrorism, psychological operations, and escape-and-evasion skills.[80]

Under current Marine Corps plans, the MAUs assigned to the Mediterranean area (the 22nd, 24th, and 26th) are to be used as a test program for this enhancement effort. They will be designated Marine amphibious units (special operations capable), or MAU(SOC)s, and their primary mission will be "the amphibious raid and the ability to conduct this complex operation on short notice, at night and at extended ranges."[81]

SOF AND NUCLEAR WEAPONS

Although the primary SOF mission is to provide a spearhead for low-intensity warfare in the Third World, they are also trained to use nuclear weapons in larger conflicts. Specifically, SOF have the responsibility for emplacing nuclear land mines known as special atomic demolition munitions (SADMs). Indeed, a 1st Special Operations Command briefing paper stated that "SADM capability is considered to be an important mission of Special Forces."[82] Moreover, a staff manual for the Naval Special Warfare Group 1 refers to a nuclear safety officer whose job is to monitor the nuclear-training program of nuclear-capable SOF units.[83]

U.S. Army field manuals say that Special Operations Forces would use SADMs primarily to block enemy advances and destroy key structures and installations. Potential uses might include blocking or destroying tunnels, bridges, and canal locks; severing communications routes; and creating water barriers by destroying dams or reservoirs.[84] SADMs can be used on the surface, underground, or underwater. According to an Army briefing paper, SADMs might be falling out of the sky or rising out of the ocean: "The device can be deployed either by static line [parachute], military free fall, or by scuba."[85]

The SADM is the smaller of the two types of nuclear land mines in the U.S. arsenal. It weighs only about sixty pounds and can be carried by a single soldier, hence the nickname "backpack nuke." Its explosive power is estimated between .01 and .1 kiloton (the Hiroshima bomb was 12.5 kilotons).[86] Of the 260 SADMs in the U.S. arsenal, about 100 are believed to be in West Germany and 20 in South Korea.[87]

SOF AND COVERT OPERATIONS

One of the most disturbing aspects of the Reagan administration's concept of low-intensity conflict is a renewed emphasis on covert operations as a means for pursuing U.S. goals and interests abroad. Mr. Reagan wants to move beyond "containment" of the Soviet Union to attempt the "rollback" of the Communist "empire," and his chosen method is covert operations intended to facilitate the overthrow of Communist-backed Third World governments—a policy often dubbed the "Reagan Doctrine." (See Chapter 3.) With the firm belief that democracy can be promoted through such means, the administration views covert operations not as exceptional, last-ditch emergency measures, but rather as a key instrument of foreign policy. Since 1980, the number of covert operations undertaken by the United States and the number of covert operatives employed by the CIA have more than tripled.[88]

The revitalization of the CIA—and especially of its covert action branch—has occurred even more rapidly than the revitalization of the Pentagon's Special Operations Forces. In the past decade, the U.S. intelligence budget (covering the CIA, the National Security Agency, and other components of the intelligence community) has tripled to about $25 billion.[89] The CIA work force grew from about fourteen thousand people in 1980 to over nineteen thousand in 1986, and the number of covert CIA operatives rose from approximately three hundred under President Carter to over a thousand in the second year of the Reagan presidency.[90] By 1983, the resurgence of the CIA was making headlines around the country. "Clearly the cloaks and daggers have come out of cold storage at CIA headquarters in Langley, Virginia," reported *Newsweek*. "For better or worse, the Company [i.e., the CIA] is back in the business of covert action—with a global scope and an intensity of resources unmatched since its heyday twenty years ago."[91]

At the end of the Carter administration, the CIA was engaged in about a dozen covert operations, almost all of them small in scale. Today the United States is engaged in more than forty covert operations, many of them large-scale.[92] The Reagan administration has at least five major covert paramilitary operations underway: in Afghanistan, Nicaragua, Angola, Cambodia, and Ethiopia. CIA operations have also been reported in Turkey (providing support for exiled Iranian rebels), Chad, Sudan, and elsewhere.[93]

The revival of CIA covert operations has raised suspicions of a return to the cooperation between the CIA and the Special Operations Forces that prevailed during the Vietnam War. Indeed, the CIA reportedly has applied strong pressure for an increase of the Army's Special Forces.[94] In 1984, Senator Jim Sasser of Tennessee warned, "There's a real danger that these Special Forces could be used by CIA programs and thus skirt Congressional review."[95] The infamous CIA manual for the Nicaraguan contras, *Psychological Operations in Guerrilla Warfare*, was taken from a Vietnam-era Green Beret manual.[96] Other traces of CIA-SOF collaboration came to light in September 1984, when two Americans, members of a "private," paramilitary, anti-Communist group, were shot down in a CIA-supplied helicopter over Nicaragua. One, a detective with the Huntsville, Alabama, police force, was also a captain in the Special Forces Group of the Alabama National Guard.[97]

CIA-SOF cooperation appears especially close in Central America. Army Special Forces began training anti-Sandinista contras in October 1986 as part of the $100 million in military and economic aid approved by Congress in 1986. Army SOF troops will reportedly provide both military training and training in civic action. All of these training operations will come under the supervision of the CIA.[98]

It is still not widely realized how little control is exercised by Congress over the intelligence community. Special House and Senate oversight committees were set up in the mid-1970s following revelations about CIA abuses, but the committees cannot veto covert actions. The president can unilaterally initiate a covert action and is merely required to *notify* the Senate and House intelligence committees. To stop an operation, the entire Congress must pass legislation specifically blocking funds for it, which has only been done rarely (most notably with regard to Angola in 1975).[99]

Oversight of covert actions by uniformed SOF personnel is even less rigorous than that of the CIA. The Pentagon is careful to assure Congress that it will, as required by law, report SOF involvement in covert operations. But SOF covert activity could go largely unsupervised by Congress because the oversight mechanism is not as entrenched and well-established as for the CIA. The reporting requirements and expectations about prior notification are not routine. The Pentagon does not regularly report details of specific SOF activities to the Congress, so some covert actions could go unnoticed. A 1984 Congressional Research Service report concluded: "Special operations have not been the subject of regularized congressional oversight, and could well fall between the jurisdiction of those who oversee intelligence operations and those who oversee military operations."[100]

Even before the Iran-contra arms scandal, Representative Lee Hamilton of Indiana, chairman of the House Permanent Select Committee on Intelligence, wrote a critique of the Reagan administration's covert programs in which he stated, "The need for accountability is acute today because of the growing prominence of paramilitary and military covert action in US foreign policy." Certainly, the revelations of the Iran-contra arms scandal have made Hamilton's words seem particularly prescient. According to Hamilton:

> [Covert action] is too easy to initiate, requires the review of only a few people in the executive branch, and tempts policymakers to use it as a convenient tool to change policy without the approval of Congress. . . .
> This problem is especially serious in the case of large-scale military operations. Today the administration is seeking to combat communist and communist-supported governments around the world, and military covert action is the cutting edge of policy. The president can fund a war secretly, without public debate, deepening US involvement in what the administration calls "low-intensity" wars. . . .[101]

For those familiar with the origins of the U.S. involvement in Vietnam, Hamilton's remarks will also provide a reminder of how small-scale special operations can escalate into a full-scale U.S. military commitment.

A LOADED GUN?

As low-intensity conflict gains momentum, SOF activity is certain to increase substantially. Given the Reagan administration's determination to overthrow Communist and Communist-backed governments around the world, the SOF buildup could lead to a new wave of U.S. military operations—especially covert operations—in the Third World. The risks of U.S. involvement in a regional conflict, particularly a conflict in which the United States does not have clear political or military objectives, would increase greatly. Even more sobering is the prospect of SOF activities aimed at pro-Soviet regimes that could lead step-by-step to a conflict with the Soviet Union. As suggested in 1984 by Lieutenant General John T. Chain, then Air Force deputy chief of staff for plans and operations, maintaining SOF in volatile areas is "like carrying a loaded gun."[102] Capable, well-armed Special Operations Forces are needed for their original purpose—support for conventional forces during large-scale war—but not for a new flood of "peacetime" military actions, overt or covert.

LIGHT INFANTRY DIVISIONS

In the most far-reaching development in U.S. Army force structure since the end of the Vietnam War, the Defense Department is creating five new light infantry divisions (LIDs) for "quick reaction to low-intensity scenarios."[103] It is the first time in U.S. history that the Army is fielding divisions designed specifically for low-intensity combat. Like the SOF revitalization, the LID initiative reflects the Pentagon's belief that the most likely field of combat for U.S. forces in the foreseeable future will be in troubled areas of the Third World, and that the typical U.S. Army heavy division—the tank-laden force designed to fight in Europe—is poorly suited for most LIC operations. The light infantry divisions will be highly trained elite units, with special skills and equipment for fighting low-level conflicts. They will number 10,700 soldiers instead of the 15,000 to 18,000 in a standard Army division.[104] LIDs are supposed to be able to get anywhere in the world in six days or less, and will be among the first American troops to go to war in the Third World.

The Army has made it clear that LIDs are intended primarily for combat outside of Europe—forces whose explicit mission is to fight and deter conficts in the Third World. General Wallace H. Nutting, then commander in chief of the U.S. Readiness Command, told Congress in 1984 that the LID "is better suited to the low-to-mid intensity conflicts we see as threats to U.S. forces in the near-term, i.e., [in] Central-South America, Africa and Southwest Asia. . . . It is better suited for jungle, mountain and urban terrain. . . . "[105] In briefing reporters on hypothetical scenarios which might involve LIDs, Army spokesmen have mentioned El Salvador, Cuba, the Dominican Republic, Panama, Venezuela, Israel, Korea, Laos, Thailand, and Vietnam.[106]

The fundamental assumptions underlying formation of the LIDs are that the United States has a vital stake in nearly every trouble spot around the globe, and that it needs military forces to cope with them— military forces that can get there quickly. The Army's position on LID has been simply stated: "To deter war, Light Infantry Divisions must be able to fight anytime, anywhere and against any opponent."[107]

The first priority for the LID is to get there *fast.* Army officials proudly proclaim that, because of its small size and lighter equipment, an LID will be able to deploy worldwide in one-third the time and with one-third the airlift sorties of a standard division (a sortie is a one-way trip by one aircraft). An LID is designed to be airlifted with just five hundred sorties by C-141 transport aircraft; by comparison, an airborne division requires one thousand sorties, and a mechanized/armored division requires fifteen hundred.[108] All LID equipment and weapons will be transportable by C-141s, which can use more austere airfields than the larger C-5 transport aircraft—currently the backbone of U.S. airlift capabilities.[109]

Once on the scene, the LIDs are to seek victory through tactical mobility, rapid maneuver, and battlefield skills, rather than through massive use of firepower. Key tenets for the LIDs are usually described by such words as "offensiveness, initiative, surprise, improvisation, total self-reliance."[110] LID soldiers will fight primarily in small teams, most often on foot, carrying only weapons, ammunition, and whatever else can be stuffed in a rucksack. LIDs put a priority on "soldier power," employing a much higher percentage of combat troops (and hence fewer support troops) than a standard Army division. An average LID will have 32 percent fighters compared to 16 percent for a regular division.[111] In the military's jargon, an LID will thus have more "bite" because of a stronger "tooth-to-tail" ratio of combatants to support personnel. The LID concept stresses that leadership, training, and conditioning will make the difference on the battlefield.

CURRENT STATUS

The Army plans to establish five new LIDs—four active-duty divisions, plus one National Guard division. Two light divisions are now fully organized: the 7th LID at Fort Ord, California, and the 25th LID at Schofield Barracks, Hawaii. Both were existing regular divisions that were converted to light units. Two other active-duty LIDs are being created from scratch: the 10th LID was initially activated at Fort Drum, New York, in February 1985 and is scheduled to be fully organized in 1989; the 6th LID was formally activated in March 1986 and is slated for full activation at Fort Wainwright, Alaska, in late 1988 or early 1989. The 29th National Guard LID was formally activated in October 1985 at Fort Belvoir, Virginia, and is expected to be at full strength by the end of 1987.[112]

Even prior to the LID initiative, the Army had "lighter" divisions. The 101st Air Assault and 82nd Airborne divisions are smaller and much more mobile than regular divisions. They are slimming down to even lighter configurations, with the conversions to be completed sometime in FY1987.[113] Moreover, the 9th Infantry Division (Motorized), formerly known as the High Technology Test Bed Division, will also be configured as a lighter division in FY1987. When these plans are completed, the Army will have eight divisions that can be considered light and ten heavy divisions in the active force structure, plus another six light and four heavy divisions in the National Guard.[114]

The Army maintains that the LIDs will not have specific geographic responsibilities, and that each will be trained to operate under any conditions, in any terrain. Some of the LIDs, however, clearly are suited for special missions in particular regions of the world:

☐   The 7th LID at Fort Ord was officially designated the first operational LID on October 1, 1985, and subsequently completed a year-long "certification" process—primarily a series of field exercises to "validate operational concepts and organization."[115] The exercises culminated with Operation "Celtic Cross IV" in California in August 1986, when the 7th was tasked first with stamping out an internal insurgency in a fictional country, and then with stopping an invasion by one of its neighbors—a scenario clearly suggestive of Central America.[116] Because of its location, the 7th LID would be particularly useful for conflicts in Central America or Asia. It also undergoes extensive desert training and probably will have primary LID responsibility for the Middle East/ Persian Gulf region.

☐ The 25th LID in Hawaii became the second operational light infantry division when its conversion was completed in 1986. It seems logical to assume that the 25th will be primarily trained for missions in the Asian theater.

☐ The 10th LID at Fort Drum is officially designated the 10th Mountain Division (Light). While it will be specially trained and equipped for mountain fighting, its commander, Major General William S. Carpenter, has said that it will have a broad combat mission. Given its location and training, an orientation toward Southwest Asia appears likely. Currently, one brigade of the 10th is stationed at Fort Benning and will stay there until construction work at Fort Drum is completed around 1989. When at full strength, the 10th will consist of two brigades at Fort Drum and a "round out" brigade in the National Guard—the 27th Infantry Brigade headquartered in Syracuse, New York.[117]

☐ The 6th LID, based in Alaska, will specialize in cold-weather operations. During wartime, the highly famed Eskimo Scouts will serve with the 6th. It is presently headquartered at Fort Richardson, near Anchorage, but will move to Fort Wainwright, near Fairbanks, when construction is completed there in 1989. Special requirements for soldiers of this division include cross-country skiing, maneuvering on snowshoes, survival in −40°F temperatures, and mountain-climbing. The soldiers of the 6th will be outfitted with special winter clothing, as well as Arctic tents, skis, snowshoes, snowmobiles, and ahkios (toboggans). While the Army says that the primary mission of the LID is the defense of Alaska, it also maintains that from Alaska the 6th can deploy anywhere in the world in less than six days.[118]

WEAPONS AND EQUIPMENT

Light infantry divisions will be outfitted primarily with basic Army gear, but the weapons-and-equipment inventory of an LID will be very different from that of a standard division. In keeping with the emphasis on speed and mobility, the LID will have no tanks or armored personnel carriers, and, except for the 7th LID, no heavy artillery. The main armament for an LID will be small howitzers and mortars, TOW and Dragon antitank weapons, Stinger and Vulcan antiaircraft weapons, rocket and grenade launchers, machine guns, and rifles. It will travel by helicopter, small armored vehicle, motorcycle, and truck. The combat aviation brigade in each LID will have about one hundred helicopters, including AH-1S Cobra gunships for attack, UH-60 Black Hawks for transport, and OH-58C Kiowas for reconnaissance.[119]

The LID will also use some of the latest Army equipment rolling off the production lines, such as the high-mobility multipurpose wheeled vehicle (HMMWV, or "Hummer"), improved 81-mm mortars, squad automatic weapons, Stinger shoulder-fired antiaircraft missiles, remotely piloted vehicles, remotely monitored battlefield sensor systems, and new night vision equipment.

The 1¼-ton Hummer will be the key vehicle for the LID. In 1983, the Army awarded a $1.2 billion contract for production of 55,000 Hummers. The vehicle can serve as a cargo or troop transport, a TOW missile carrier, an armaments carrier (with variants for a 40-mm grenade launcher and 7.62-mm and .50-caliber machine guns), a communications platform, or an ambulance. New versions are being developed for carrying Stinger missiles, remotely piloted vehicles, and a 25-mm chain gun.[120] While its proponents call it "the ultimate off-road vehicle,"[121] it has been plagued with quality control problems, which at one point resulted in suspended production.[122] Each LID will receive 694 Hummers, except the 6th, which will get 850 small-unit support vehicles (SUSVs) instead. [123] The SUSV, which can carry seventeen soldiers, is better suited for snow travel.

LIDs will use the Army's latest, sophisticated remotely piloted vehicles (RPVs)—small, pilotless, remote-controlled, propeller-driven aircraft that fly into hostile territory and provide real-time intelligence on enemy activities. The R4E-40 "Skyeye" RPV has been used by the Army for several years, mainly in Central America. It has a small TV and forward-looking infrared (FLIR) night-vision sensors that can spot targets, conduct reconnaissance and damage assessment, and perform other functions. The RPV's signals are projected on a TV screen monitored by controllers, and the precise information on target locations can be transmitted to artillery units in order to obtain pinpoint accuracy.[124]

LIDs will be the first Army units to receive REMBASS (REmotely Monitored BAttlefied Sensor Systems), a collection of seismic, acoustic, magnetic, and infrared sensors that detect the movement of people and vehicles. REMBASS utilizes a new generation of sensors that can not only detect, but also classify, sounds; it can differentiate between wheeled and tracked vehicles; it can calculate the speed and direction of movement; and it can detect body heat. First deliveries of operational REMBASS units were scheduled for the end of 1986; preproduction models were used in the Grenada invasion.[125] And because night operations are to be a forte of LIDs, each combat soldier in an LID will have night-vision goggles and weapons sights that convert infrared radiation into easily recognizable images.[126]

Although Army officials have said that the LID initiative "does not require appreciable new equipment," some new weapons are being developed primarily for LIDs. There is a crash program to develop an extremely light howitzer; the objective is a howitzer with the range and lethality of the M198 155-mm howitzer, but weighing a maximum of 9,000 pounds instead of the M198's 15,780 pounds.[127] A significant research program is also underway on the Advanced Antitank Weapons System–Medium (AAWS-M) to replace the Dragon antitank missile. The AAWS-M will be a man-portable system with a special night sight; it will be fielded in the mid-1990s.[128]

A CRITICAL DEBATE

There is a heated debate being carried out in the Pentagon and in professional military journals over what the LID is supposed to do and what it will be capable of doing. Some see it as designed strictly for low-intensity warfare; others see it as an all-purpose force for low-, mid-, and high-intensity conflict. Some see it as a substitute, in certain situations, for heavy divisions; others see it as simply a "time buyer" to hold the line until heavy divisions arrive. The predominant official view, however, is that LIDs will be most useful if deployed *before* hostilities begin.

The reasons for this are both pragmatic—an LID is not equipped to land in the middle of a fight—and theoretical. According to the Army, "their rapid deployability will enable them to arrive in a crisis area before a conflict begins. . . ." And, "by demonstrating U.S. resolve and capability, they may well prevent the outbreak of war."[129] Elaborating on this precept, Army Chief of Staff General John Wickham stated, "The basic goal in this design is to defuze [*sic*] a crisis prior to hostilities, and provide a capable, coherent combat force early, should hostilities ensue." He spoke of "designing it light enough to deploy with speed and agility in a *pre-crisis* or low-intensity setting," and of reducing the probability of mid- to high-intensity action through effective "*pre-crisis* and low-intensity actions."[130] (Emphasis added.)

Presumably, the idea here is that an LID could act as a sort of peacekeeper, like a referee trying to keep two fighters apart. This sounds attractive, but it is important to remember that the concept did not work in Lebanon, but instead served to exacerbate tensions and to create resentment of U.S. forces. In fact, the key notion to grasp is that offensive—indeed, *preemptive*—action is crucial to the success of the LID. As an Army major put it in *Military Intelligence* magazine: "Of great significance is the fact that the employment of the light divisions can be a proactive rather than a reactive sword. . . ."[131] Seeking out and destroying the enemy at the onset of battle is a central element of LID doctrine.

A wide range of criticism has been leveled at the LIDs by professional military people: criticism of its mission (too broad, too narrow, duplicative); criticism of the force structure (too light, not sustainable, lacking in transportation-and-support structure); and criticism of the locations of the LIDs (Alaska and New York State being rather far from, and quite unlike, the most probable Third World battlefields). The most frequent criticism among military professionals is that LIDs will be too light, too weak, and too lacking in the necessary firepower and sustainability to prevail in the most likely situations in which they will be committed. Given the increasingly large and sophisticated arsenals in many Third World countries, the LID simply may not be able to cope without armor and heavier artillery; conceivably it could be overwhelmed by Syrian or Iranian or even Nicaraguan divisions, not to mention Cuban or Soviet forces.

In the final analysis, however, the major problem with LIDs may be simply the fact that they *exist*. Once the United States has rapid-reaction forces of this sort in place, the temptation to use them without taking sufficient time to consider the appropriateness or the potential negative repercussions will be great. The Army's approach to LIDs seems to be: let's get there fast and ask questions later. Once these "hair trigger" intervention forces are employed, the probability of any conflict remaining low-intensity for long is very low. The United States may find itself embroiled in a conflict it cannot extricate itself from easily.

POWER PROJECTION FORCES

The SOF revitalization program and the creation of light infantry divisions are part of the overall effort to boost U.S. "power projection" capabilities. While such expeditionary forces could be used anywhere in the world, "power projection" is largely a euphemism for fighting in the Third World. Aside from SOF and LIDs, the main elements of the current buildup of power projection capabilities have been enhancements to the Rapid Deployment Force (specifically formation of the Central Command, maritime prepositioning, and airlift and sealift programs) and acquisition of new naval forces (notably aircraft carriers, battleships, and amphibious assault forces).

RAPID DEPLOYMENT FORCE AND CENTCOM

In 1979, following the Iranian Revolution and the Mideast oil crisis, President Carter announced the establishment of the Rapid Deployment Force (RDF). The RDF concept was intended to enhance America's capabilities for fighting in distant areas in the Third World, particularly in the Persian Gulf region. Although the term "Rapid Deployment Force" is no longer used by the Department of Defense, the key elements of the program have continued apace, most notably the expansion of U.S. airlift and sealift assets and the creation of maritime prepositioning ship squadrons. Referring to advances in those areas, Secretary of Defense Weinberger reported in 1986 that "FY1986 and FY1987 will mark the full achievement of major improvements in our force projection capabilities."[132] As a result of this effort, U.S. airlift capabilities will increase by 80 percent in the 1980s, sealift capabilities by 110 percent, and matériel prepositioning by 150 percent.[133]

The RDF was originally conceived as a small, flexible, quick-strike force designed to protect U.S. interests in the Persian Gulf region or elsewhere in the Third World. Within a few years, however, it was transformed into a new unified command—the Central Command, or CENTCOM—with responsibility for what the Pentagon calls "Southwest Asia" (an area stretching from the Horn of Africa and the Arabian Peninsula to Pakistan) and with over two hundred thousand U.S. military personnel at its disposal.

The new command was not built up from new fighting units; instead, CENTCOM was given the authority to call on forces earmarked for other combat theaters (particularly in Europe). These forces include roughly one-fourth of America's active Army and Marine Corps divisions, Navy aircraft carrier battle groups, and Air Force tactical fighter wings. Specifically, the forces designated for CENTCOM include:

- 4⅔ Army divisions (1st Mechanized, 7th Light Infantry, 101st Air Assault, 82nd Airborne, plus one mechanized brigade and one air-assault cavalry brigade)
- 7 tactical fighter wings (about 500 aircraft)
- 2 strategic bomber squadrons (28 B-52s)
- 3 aircraft-carrier battle groups
- 1 surface action group (spearheaded by a battleship)
- 1⅓ Marine divisions and air wings

In addition, CENTCOM has access to the SOF assets described above.[134]

To ensure the effectiveness of any CENTCOM forces sent to battle in Southwest Asia, the United States has acquired access to military facilities in the area. According to Secretary Weinberger, "We have reached formal agreement with several nations, and are seeking permission from others, to preposition matériel and conduct routine training exercises during peacetime, and to use their facilities during crises."[135] The Defense Department has also built up major naval facilities and stationed maritime prepositioning ships at Diego Garcia, an island archipelago in the Indian Ocean belonging to the United Kingdom. Written or verbal agreements regarding access for U.S. forces have also been reached with Oman, Somalia, Kenya, Egypt, Morocco, and Portugal (regarding the Azores), and the United States has spent about $1.1 billion improving ports and airfields in those nations and Diego Garcia so that they can better serve Rapid Deployment Forces.[136]

MARITIME PREPOSITIONING

In 1985 and 1986, the United States deployed thirteen maritime prepositioning ships (MPS) around the globe.[137] These are basically huge floating warehouses stuffed with everything from tanks to toilet paper. Secretary Weinberger has said that the MPS program "provides for one of the most dramatic improvements in rapid force projection." He noted that MPS "will make it possible to deploy an operational force to remote regions much faster than was previously possible."[138] From their forward deployed locations, the ships would be quickly dispatched to trouble spots where airlifted American troops would meet them and pick up their combat gear.

The MPS vessels are divided into three squadrons, each of which has enough weapons, equipment, and supplies to keep a Marine brigade

(16,500 men) fighting for thirty days. The ships are being leased from private owners at a cost of eighty thousand dollars per day, based on a five-year lease.[139]

A Marine brigade is assigned to each squadron of MPS vessels. The 6th Brigade in North Carolina is assigned to the 1st Squadron, which went on station in the eastern Atlantic in 1985. The 7th Brigade in California is assigned to the 2nd Squadron, based at Diego Garcia since late 1985. The 1st Brigade in Hawaii is assigned to the 3rd Squadron, stationed near Guam in 1986. The five ships of the 2nd Squadron are to replace the eleven smaller "Near-Term" prepositioning ships which have been at Diego Garcia for several years.[140]

AIRLIFT AND SEALIFT

The Department of Defense has undertaken a massive effort to expand its long-range airlift capabilities, spending more than $11 billion during FY1981–86 on this undertaking. As a result, U.S. airlift capacity has reportedly increased by 50 percent since 1981.[141] Major airlift programs include:[142]

☐ Purchase of 50 new C-5B jumbo transport aircraft at a cost of $7.9 billion.

☐ Purchase of 60 KC-10 tanker/transport aircraft at a cost of $3.8 billion.

☐ Modification of 77 existing C-5A aircraft (entailing the repair of structural weaknesses in the wings) so as to enhance their payload and durability.

☐ Modification of 19 wide-bodied passenger aircraft in the Civilian Reserve Air Fleet (CRAF) so that they can carry military cargo in an emergency.

☐ Purchase of 211 C-17 transport aircraft, starting in 1988, at a cost of almost $35 billion.[143] The C-17 will be smaller than the C-5, and therefore able to use the more austere airfields and shorter runways likely to be found in the Third World, while still being able to carry the full range of Army weapons and equipment.

A similiar effort to improve U.S. sealift capabilities is also underway. The Department of Defense spent $1.7 billion on sealift improvements during FY1981–86. Admiral James Watkins, chief of naval operations, told Congress in 1986 that U.S. sealift capacity had grown 30 percent

108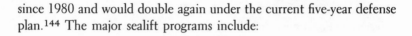

since 1980 and would double again under the current five-year defense plan.[144] The major sealift programs include:

☐ *Fast sealift ships:* eight SL-7 container ships that were purchased in FY1981 and 1982 and then converted to "roll on/roll off" configuration (for easier, faster unloading) by the end of FY1986. Able to travel at thirty knots, these are the fastest cargo ships available, and, in the words of the Defense Department, provide an "early sealift surge capacity not previously available."[145]

☐ *The Ready Reserve Force:* a part of the National Defense Reserve Fleet that is being expanded from 77 ships to 119 by the early 1990s.[146]

☐ *Sealift Discharge:* a series of programs to enable U.S. forces to unload in austere ports or in areas lacking port facilities, consisting of auxiliary crane ships, transportable barges, mobile piers, portable ramps, unloading facilities, etc.[147]

☐ *Containership utilization:* modifications to U.S. containerships to provide a break-bulk capability, again with the goal of permitting unloading without modern ports.[148]

NAVAL FORCES

Generally ignored in the reams of publicity devoted to former Navy Secretary John Lehman's drive for a "600-ship navy" is the degree to which the buildup is aimed at improving America's capability to intervene in the Third World, rather than its ability to engage and defeat the Soviet Navy on the high seas. In his Annual Report to Congress for FY1986, Defense Secretary Weinberger affirmed that the principal objective of the Navy's Five-Year Plan (FY1986–90) is to expand and improve U.S. power projection forces.[149] The most important elements of the naval buildup that are applicable to U.S. intervention in Third World conflicts are aircraft carriers, battleships, and amphibious assault forces.

The most powerful element of America's power projection capability is its aircraft carriers. These giant vessels will be of little use for attacks against the Soviet Union in any future superpower conflict because of their vulnerability to precision-guided antiship missiles. The Reagan administration has clearly shown, however, that carriers are the weapon of choice for fighting in the Third World, as witnessed in Lebanon, Grenada, and Libya. From January 1976 to July 1985, American aircraft carriers responded to thirty-five international incidents; of those, twenty-two were ordered by President Reagan from 1981 through 1985.[150] Carriers have also been used as instruments of diplomacy and coercion in Central America, the Middle East, North Africa, the Persian Gulf, and the Far East.

Currently, the United States has fifteen aircraft carriers, fourteen of which are "deployable" (one of the carriers is always undergoing a major three-year-long overhaul known as the Service Life Extension Program [SLEP]); another carrier, the *Lexington,* is used for training only. Construction of two more carriers was approved by Congress in FY1983: the *Abraham Lincoln,* to be delivered in 1989, and the *George Washington,* scheduled for delivery in 1991.[151] The initial procurement cost for the *Lincoln* and *Washington* will be $3.3 billion each, but that is only the tip of the iceberg. The thirty-year-life-cycle cost of an entire aircraft carrier battle group, including operating and maintenance costs, escort and supply vessels, midlife conversions, and multiple buys of aircraft and ordnance, can total nearly $50 billion.[152]

The U.S. is also taking four World War II–vintage battleships out of mothballs and refurbishing them at a cost of more than $1.8 billion.[153] Three battleships have already been reactivated: the *New Jersey,* the *Iowa,* and the *Missouri.* A fourth vessel, the *Wisconsin,* is scheduled for delivery in January 1989. These ships will be the centerpieces of four new "surface action groups" (SAGs) which are to be home-ported in different locations around the United States as part of the Navy's strategic dispersal plan.

Battleships, like carriers, would be of little value against the sophisticated ships, aircraft, and weapons of the Soviet Navy, but could prove very useful in Third World settings. Thus far, the battleships have been used primarily for gunboat diplomacy, and for the bombardment of shore positions—the *New Jersey* earned a good deal of notoriety for the alleged inaccuracy of the hundreds of shells its 16-inch guns lobbed into Lebanon in February 1984. Commander R. James Abbott, a surface force officer involved in developing policy on battleship deployments, said in 1986 that battleship groups will be most useful for "significant presence operations and port visits." Compared to an aircraft carrier, which has to sit thirty to forty miles offshore in order to get the winds and sea room it needs to operate, "a battleship can sit there on the horizon where everyone can see it."[154]

In addition to procuring carriers and battleships, the Navy is also engaged in what it calls a "major and long-needed modernization and expansion" of its amphibious assault forces. By the mid-1990s, the Defense Department plans to have increased its amphibious assault capabilities by one-third. A key aspect of the buildup will be the capability to launch attacks from over the horizon (i.e., out of sight beyond the curve of the earth), thus gaining the benefits of increased surprise and less vulnerability.[155]

Three new classes of amphibious assault ships are being built—the LHD-1 amphibious assault ship, the LSD-41 landing ship, and a new LSD variant, along with a new air-cushioned landing craft, the LCAC. Current Navy plans call for five LHD-1s, eight LSD-41s, six LSD variants, and sixty-nine LCACs by the year 1996. The LHD-1s, LSD-41s, and LCACs are already under construction; the LSD variant is still being designed.[156] Of the $11 billion estimated cost for the LHD, LSD, and LCAC programs, $6.3 billion had been spent as of mid-1986.[157] These ships will allow the United States to move a Marine amphibious force (MAF) and a Marine amphibious brigade (MAB) simultaneously, with the ships carrying 15,600 troops, 210 helicopters, and 59 new LCAC landing craft.[158]

CONCLUSION

In spite of the tendency of both proponents and critics of the Pentagon's increasing emphasis on low-intensity warfare to focus on its so-called "nonmilitary" components—i.e., doctrine and policy considerations—the most important aspect of the LIC phenomenon may prove to be America's buildup of a wide range of forces for combat in the Third World. The United States is spending billions of dollars to restructure and equip its armed forces so that they can intervene more effectively in the Third World, and yet there has been little debate about the implications of those actions.

Many of the specific objectives for the new LIC forces remain unclear. The most basic questions of what interests these forces are supposed to protect, and how they are supposed to protect them, have not been adequately answered. What does seem clear, however, is that the new emphasis on countering the threats posed by low-intensity warfare, combined with a vastly expanded U.S. capability for rapid military action in distant areas, is likely to result in increased U.S. military involvement in regional Third World conflicts. The likelihood of a heavier U.S. reliance on military operations—both covert and overt—to achieve U.S. goals in the Third World, and the attendant dangers of full-scale U.S. involvement in overseas conflict, grow with each new "improvement" in Special Operations Forces, light infantry divisions, and the other power projection forces described above.

EL SALVADOR: COUNTERINSURGENCY REVISITED

DANIEL SIEGEL AND JOY HACKEL

THE United States's first major counterinsurgency effort since the Vietnam War is being waged in the tiny Central American republic of El Salvador. That is where President Reagan first vowed to "draw the line" against revolution in the Third World, and where Washington is implementing its post-Vietnam strategy for combating insurgencies. El Salvador, according to U.S. strategists, "is an ideal testing ground" for modern low-intensity conflict doctrine.[1] What happens in the Salvadoran laboratory, suggests Colonel John Waghelstein, former head of the U.S. military group in El Salvador, may "be useful to the next generation of security and advisory assistance practitioners in the Third World."[2]

"There are many, many wars going on in El Salvador," as General John Galvin, the commander of the Pentagon's Southern Command (SouthCom) told a conference on low-intensity conflict in March 1987, "and we want to be fighting all of them."[3] Indeed, since 1981, Washington has engaged in "many wars" to keep the left out of power in El Salvador. The administration's counterinsurgency strategy involves three interrelated projects: first, to fashion the Salvadoran military into a powerful counterinsurgency force (to defeat the armed/political revolutionary alliance, known as the FDR-FMLN [the Revolutionary Democratic Front and the Farabundo Martí National Liberation Front]);

112

second, to implement "hearts-and-minds" programs to win civilian support along with efforts to underwrite the Salvadoran economy; and, finally, to replace formal military rule with a "third force" civilian government that captures support at home and abroad.

These three projects comprise a massive "nation-building" program similar to the one undertaken by the United States in South Vietnam. But, as in that war, U.S. policy has failed in its avowed objectives of bringing development, democracy, and peace to El Salvador while defeating the leftist opposition. Instead, it has fostered a weak client state that grows increasingly dependent and militarized, facing endless warfare through the 1980s and beyond.

THE BATTLEGROUND

U.S. counterinsurgency doctrine was first exported to El Salvador in the 1960s, following the Cuban revolution, when there was no armed insurgency to counter.[4] For over a hundred years, Salvadorans had endured almost ceaseless military rule at the behest of the country's small, landed elite, the so-called "fourteen families" who dominated El Salvador's underdeveloped agricultural economy. A peasant uprising in 1932, led by Communist Party leader Agustín Farabundo Martí, was crushed when government forces massacred approximately thirty thousand Salvadorans in three weeks—an infamous episode known as the *matanza*. In the decades that followed, reformist political parties were blocked from achieving change at the ballot box by a de facto alliance of the armed forces and the landed oligarchy who were determined to maintain total power.

An intricate paramilitary network, organized by the U.S. Central Intelligence Agency (CIA), the Green Berets, and the State Department during the Kennedy-inspired Alliance for Progress, helped sustain this status quo by assassinating anyone who opposed the regime.[5] Two organizations, ORDEN (Democratic Nationalist Organization), a rural death squad group composed of grass-roots informants and assassins, and ANSESAL (National Security Agency), an elite presidential agency that coordinated nationwide intelligence, dominated this network. According to José Alberto "Chele" Medrano, a CIA asset who originally set up ANSESAL in 1961, "the State Department and AID's Public Safety office in El Salvador had administrative responsibility for establishing the ANSESAL network . . . but the substantive day-to-day intelligence work was coordinated by the CIA."[6] Green Beret advisers, according to Medrano, also helped "plan the structure and ideology of ORDEN."[7] These organizations enabled Salvadoran security officials to identify, track down, and eliminate virtually all opponents of the government.

In the 1970s, however, cracks in El Salvador's economic, political, and military power structure began to emerge. Presidential elections in 1972 saw the Christian Democratic candidate, José Napoleón Duarte, defeat the Army's choice, Colonel Arturo Armando Molina, only to have the military intervene on Molina's behalf. Unmitigated repression and mounting economic inequities among an expanding population— between 1961 and 1980 the number of landless peasants rose from 12 percent to 65 percent—led popular church, labor, peasant, and student organizations to begin unifying their efforts for structural change. By 1980, five guerrilla groups united to form the Farabundo Martí National Liberation Front, which stepped up insurgent operations in the cities and countryside. That same year, the Revolutionary Democratic Front (FDR) was formed and became allied with the FMLN as the political arm of the FDR-FMLN revolutionary movement.

In the wake of the Sandinista revolution in Nicaragua in July 1979, the Carter administration decided that El Salvador's iron-fisted ruler, General Carlos Humberto Romero, like Somoza in Nicaragua, was a political liability. On October 15, 1979, Washington sanctioned a re-formist coup by young Salvadoran officers and fashioned a new military-civilian junta. However, divisions between reformers, who called for purging the corrupt and repressive generals, and right-wing military officials who had long controlled the Salvadoran armed forces and who still held ultimate power, soon became apparent. Increased paramilitary repression and the government's inability to implement reforms called for by the October 1979 coup led to the collapse of the first junta, and then a second, in early 1980 as civilian members resigned in fear and disgust. In their place, Washington engineered the appointment of Christian Democratic leader José Napoleón Duarte to a third junta dominated by old-guard military officials. At this pivotal juncture in Salvadoran history, the Carter administration sided with the most militarist sectors of the junta against the reformists to create a "friendly" military corps and, in the words of then U.S. Ambassador Robert White, "preserve the military as an institution."[8]

Following the October 15, 1979, coup, Carter and then Reagan began modernizing the Salvadoran armed forces to contain, control, and crush the opposition. As U.S. low-level military strategy evolved, it emphasized three distinct elements: control of the paramilitary war; retraining and reequipping the Salvadoran military; and an escalating air war to contain the mounting insurgency.

FROM DIRTY WAR TO COUNTERINSURGENCY

In 1980, U.S. counterinsurgency strategy relied on a "dirty war" waged by the broad paramilitary network organized by Washington almost twenty years before. At that time, death squad operations, which every morning littered tortured bodies in gutters and town squares, constituted the main activity of the Salvadoran national security apparatus to check the organization of a viable opposition. While U.S. officials claimed the *esquadrones de la muerte* were ad hoc groupings of rightwing vigilantes "who are taking the law into their own hands," former Salvadoran Army Captain Ricardo Fiallos admitted that they were "made up of members of the security forces" and that acts of terrorism were "planned by high-ranking military officers."[9]

"The target," as one U.S. diplomat described death squad operations in 1984, "is anybody with an idea in his head."[10] Between 1979 and 1983, this paramilitary system eliminated or forced underground a growing mass opposition movement. All actual or potential opponents of the government—priests, professors, students, union leaders, lawyers, dissident Christian Democrats—became victims. Death squad–style killings accounted for a substantial share of the thirty-eight thousand political murders during this period—a stage of U.S. strategy described by FMLN commander Joaquin Villalobos as "necessary genocide."[11]

Yet, even as the death squads destroyed popular urban and peasant organizations, their massive repression became increasingly counterproductive to Washington's low-intensity warfare strategy. Gratuitous paramilitary killings swelled the ranks of the armed opposition, violating a key tenet of low-intensity conflict—not to create more enemies than already exist. Perhaps even more important politically, public revulsion inside the United States over death squad massacres contributed to congressional cutbacks in military aid.[12]

For these reasons, Reagan administration officials began to urge their Salvadoran counterparts to restrain this form of bloodshed. In late 1982, U.S. Ambassador Deane Hinton publically condemned what he dubbed "the gorillas of the right." In July 1983, a National Security Council strategy paper called for the "elimination of military participation in death squads"; later that year Vice President George Bush personally delivered this message to the country's top thirty-one military commanders during a high-profile trip to El Salvador.

After mid-1984, paramilitary killings dropped sharply. Widespread disappearances and killings by security personnel and unidentified men in urban areas gave way to less visible forms of abuse—imprisonment, temporary detention, psychological and physical torture.[13]

Aside from helping redirect state violence into more select forms, the Reagan administration had to restructure and retrain El Salvador's armed forces. As Pentagon analysts concluded in February 1981, the Salvadoran Army was "not organized to fight a counterinsurgency war," and had "no hope" of defeating the guerrillas with existing resources.[14] The Salvadoran military repeatedly violated the cardinal rule of counterinsurgency: the need to display a modicum of respect for the civilian population in order to isolate the guerrillas. The high command clung to an ineffective, conventional warfare strategy of indiscriminate air attacks and large periodic sweeps through guerrilla-controlled regions. The Army also suffered from command-and-control breakdowns, poor morale, widespread corruption, high rates of casualties and surrenders, and low reenlistment. The "major problem area facing us," as U.S. military group commander Colonel John Waghelstein observed in 1982, "was how to modernize, equip and train the Salvadoran Army to fight a successful counterinsurgency campaign."[15]

The Pentagon undertook the task of converting El Salvador's "9-to-5, five-day-a-week" garrison-bound Army into an unconventional and aggressive war-fighting machine. Tactically, this meant forcing the military to abandon ponderous, large-unit sweeps of the countryside in favor of mobile, small-unit, "search-and-destroy" operations. U.S. advisers encouraged their Salvadoran counterparts to mirror guerrilla-style warfare: surprise attacks, ambushes, night actions, and saturation patrolling in squads of five to ten men. "A change in approach was needed," as Waghelstein later wrote in a study for the Army War College. "This was achieved through a painstaking process involving a detailed analysis of guerrilla operations, constant discussions with the ESAF [Salvadoran Armed Forces] leadership, and the Socratic method."[16]

The change was also achieved through a massive influx of military aid. Between 1980 and 1987, the United States provided nearly a billion dollars to the Salvadoran Armed Forces. U.S. assistance expanded the combined size of military and security forces from twelve thousand to over fifty-three thousand men in those six years, many of whom were trained by U.S. advisers. The scale of this training program prompted one Pentagon official to boast in mid-1986 that "every soldier in [El Salvador's] army has been trained by us in one way or another. We have trained every infantry battalion in their army. We have trained every helicopter pilot in the Salvadoran air force."[17]

Washington also began grooming a younger generation of junior officers. Faced with the fact that El Salvador's Military Academy produced only twenty-five to forty officers a year in 1981, the U.S. immediately moved to train over a thousand officer candidates in 1982 and 1983 at the Infantry School at Fort Benning, Georgia. They became the mechanism through which U.S. advisers were able to begin pressuring the traditional Salvadoran military elite to dismantle the rigid *tanda* system in which seniority or political connections—rather than military performance—determined one's assignment in the field.

Beginning in 1979, a "55-man" U.S. advisory group—"probably twice" that number on a given day—provided the bulk of in-country training and direction of the war effort.[18] Pentagon advisers offered "observations and comment" to the Salvadoran high command "on the operations, planning, coordination, and control of major combat operations."[19] Five-man operations-planning and assistance teams (OPATs) worked with senior Army commanders in San Salvador and with the five outlying regional commands where they assisted in intelligence, logistics, communications, and administration.[20] These advisers were supplemented by at least 150 CIA agents who conducted a wide variety of intelligence and psychological operations.[21]

These U.S. programs were meant to modernize the ingrown nature of Salvadoran military politics, but, because of long-consolidated vested interests, the results were slow in coming. Until 1984, U.S. training programs, along with massive influxes of dollars, guns, and personnel, had failed to improve the military situation in El Salvador. Indeed, by the end of 1983, the Salvadoran Army was on the defensive against the guerrillas. "There's a fear that the army could be swept out," one administration official conceded. "It could all be over by Christmas."[22]

This crisis resulted in renewed U.S. pressure on the Salvadoran military command to redirect its overall approach to the insurgency. The Salvadoran military began implementing more sophisticated counterinsurgency practices only after the U.S. had once again engineered the shake-up of Army leadership. In April 1983, Defense Minister José Guillermo García, the last military remnant from the corrupt Romero era, was replaced by an advocate of a more modern approach to counterinsurgency, General Eugenio Vides Casanova, who oversaw a major reorganization of the high command late that year. Key field commands were stocked with young, "modern" rightist officers who adopted U.S.-devised tactics. Although the reorganization did not resolve all the strategic and tactical shortcomings of the military, one FMLN fighter admitted that government troops had "been forced into the field more often and with more effectiveness."[23]

Even more significantly, the reorganization resulted in an escalation of the regime's air war against the guerrillas. In 1984, the Salvadoran Air Force began an expanded and more sophisticated campaign of aerial bombing, strafing, aerial reconnaissance, and air mobile operations using a U.S.-exported helicopter fleet that more than doubled from nineteen to forty-six. By early 1987, the Salvadoran Air Force had approximately 175 aircraft, making it the largest air force in Central America.[24]

A sophisticated U.S. intelligence and reconnaissance network, operating from Palmerola Air Base in Honduras and from Panama, guided the Salvadoran air war.[25] With increasing accuracy, U.S.-trained pilots zeroed in on FMLN bases and their civilian sympathizers who provided the guerrillas food, clothing, shelter, medicine, and intelligence. These civilian groupings, or *masas,* are predominantly elderly people, women, and children living in the contested areas of northern Chalatenango, northern Morazán, parts of Usulután, and in the area near the Guazapa Volcano. The *masas* were described in a January 25, 1984, cable from the U.S. embassy in San Salvador as "something other than innocent civilian bystanders" since they "live in close proximity of" and are "intermingling with" the rebel army.[26] In the parlance of counterinsurgency theory, the *masas* represented a "strategic or logistical rearguard" of the guerrillas who must be either killed, terrorized into obedience, or forced to flee contested areas in order to "separate the fish from the water."

While the military's adoption of "air cavalry" techniques has limited the FMLN's ability to mount large-scale operations, the guerrillas have adapted by breaking down columns of one hundred to three hundred soldiers into small eight-to-twelve-person units. Even so, the FMLN maintains a unity of command that enables them to reconcentrate their forces for medium- and large-scale actions, such as the spectacular attacks at the military training center at La Unión in October 1985, the June 1986 raid on the San Miguel garrison, and the devastating blow against the El Paraiso Army garrison in April 1987, which killed sixty-nine government soldiers and a U.S. military adviser. And although aerial attacks weakened the FMLN's so-called "zones of control" in the northern and eastern parts of the country, by 1986 the guerrillas had expanded the war geographically into all fourteen provinces of the country, including San Salvador.

The U.S.-sponsored air war in El Salvador revealed the tensions of a carrot-and-stick approach to counterinsurgency that combined on-the-ground "hearts-and-minds" programs with more conventional ground sweeps and air-mobile operations. The inherently indiscriminate nature of aerial attacks undercut the Army's efforts to convince the Salvadoran peasantry that it was a benevolent protector of the people. "I've always had serious doubts about the role of airpower in this business," admitted one former high-level U.S. military adviser in El Salvador. "I think there's certain things airplanes can do, but there's no substitute for the soldier on the ground talking to a campesino."[27]

Fostering this "civic" vision of counterinsurgency among the Salvadoran military became critical to implementing U.S. low-intensity conflict doctrine in Central America. "This army," according to Colonel Waghelstein, "had no experience in what the French came to call the 'War on the Crowd'—the type of war in which the civilian population, or more precisely the support of the population, was the objective."[28] As opposed to conventional warfare involving large troop formations fighting set-piece battles in order to capture territory, U.S. advisers pressed the Salvadorans to focus on winning the allegiance of the populace. As Waghelstein described the concept, "the only territory you want to hold is the six inches between the ears of the campesino."[29]

THE NONMILITARY PROGRAM:
THE WAR ON THE CROWD

"The military is only one slice of the pie in this business," according to one Pentagon analyst. "The real war is the economic war, the political war, the social war."[30] Indeed, armed conflict on the battlefield has become only the most visible arena of Washington's larger nation-building project in El Salvador. While military operations have sought to physically eradicate the guerrillas, nonmilitary operations are aimed at weakening their social base by severing their links and appeal to the Salvadoran citizenry.

In an attempt to construct a "new El Salvador," Washington has designed and financed various "hearts-and-minds" pacification programs to be implemented by a civilian-military apparatus as well as right-wing private voluntary organizations. Loans and grants from the Agency for International Development (AID) have underwritten a variety of civic-action, civil defense, and psychological operations. Massive transfusions of U.S. economic aid have, in the meantime, offset the high cost of the military war and enabled the United States to keep El Salvador's flagging economy from collapsing under the strain of the protracted low-intensity campaign.

Pacification programs, modeled after the Civil Operations and Revolutionary Development Support (CORDS) project implemented in Vietnam, provided a bridge between direct military operations and civic action in El Salvador. In early 1983, U.S. counterinsurgency planners unveiled a "National Plan"—a coordinated set of military and civilian pacification strategies—with the claim that this would turn the tables on the FDR-FMLN. In March 1983, the provinces of San Vicente and Usulután were selected as a pilot region for the National Plan, according to a confidential cable, "because of its economic importance (cotton, sugar, coffee), its central position, its function as the highway, electric and communications link to the Eastern portion and its heavy concentration of displaced [persons]."[31]

El Salvador's military and government agencies jointly launched the AID-financed plan in June 1983. If successful, it would quietly militarize civilian life within the model provinces, ensuring government control without the constant presence of the armed forces.

By the year's end, however, it was evident that the civil defense units had failed miserably and the military could not prevent opposition forces from reinfiltrating the area. Reports surfaced in the U.S. press describing FMLN use of civic-action projects; the rebels were teaching in AID-funded schools and overseeing the implementation of certain projects.[32] The FMLN's Eastern Zone offensive, which began in September 1983 and lasted until January, proved to be the plan's most formidible obstacle. According to a State Department official, "The first two test cases— San Vicente and Usulután were clear failures. The military was operating under too many imperatives elsewhere in the country to clear an entire province. . . . [The National Plan] played into the guerrilla's tactical advantage—at that time, the strength of the insurgents was in their rural organizing and rural combat ability."[33]

In mid-1986 the Salvadoran Armed Forces advanced a second program for nation-building known as the "Counterinsurgency Campaign: United for Reconstruction" (UFR). Army Chief of Staff General Adolfo Blandón unveiled this revamped strategy for "conquering the minds and will of the population."[34] As stated in a secret government blueprint, UFR emphasized a four-phase approach of cleansing operations, consolidation, reconstruction, and construction.[35] Heavily funded by AID, UFR sought to incorporate every sector of Salvadoran society— private enterprise, the church, labor unions, civilians, and government ministries—in one pacification effort with the following specific goals:

1. To win the hearts and minds of the civilian population in order to mobilize its support for UFR and unite diverse sectors of the society to develop a solution to the crisis.

2. To create an atmosphere of peace and security for the people and protect their well-being in target regions with the goal of beginning a balanced development of the social, political, and economic sectors of society.

3. To destroy the tactical forces of the terrorists in selected regions and neutralize their zones of operations.

4. To isolate subversives politically, physically, and psychologically, neutralizing their influence over the civilian population.

5. To satisfy the aspirations of the civilian populace in selected areas.

6. To incrementally consolidate peace in the country.

7. [And] to fortify and consolidate the democratic process at a national level.[36]

UFR was distinct from the National Plan, since it granted greater control to local military commanders and strengthened the autonomy of the armed forces from civilian agencies. Yet both plans advanced nearly identical objectives. The UFR plan—as had the National Plan before it—attempted to refine previously unsuccessful "hearts-and-minds" programs. In particular, the UFR program called for "special importance" to be given to "Psychological Operations, the organization and training of Civil Defense Forces, Civic/Military Action and the active participation of the population of the area."[37]

PSYCHOLOGICAL OPERATIONS

Increasingly the Salvadoran military has relied upon psychological operations—PSYOP—as a primary component of the low-intensity war strategy in El Salvador. Descending upon remote villages with mariachi bands, multicolored leaflets, clowns and candies for children, and taped advertisements targeting their parents, the military engaged in a major public relations blitz across the country. As the Army official in charge of psychological operations boasted, the campaign used "the same techniques the Americans developed to sell Coca-Cola."[38]

PSYOP brought together the experience of the Pentagon, the CIA, the United States Information Agency, and Salvadoran and third-country military and government advisers in a concerted effort to undermine the image of the guerrillas while enhancing that of the government through various forms of media manipulation and propaganda.

"T.V., radio and newspapers must implement an information campaign supporting military operations," Colonel Waghelstein advised the Salvadoran chief of staff in June 1982.[39] Under U.S. tutelage, in 1983 the Salvadoran high command reorganized "Department 5," the psychological operations division of the military, increasing its funding and personnel, and its activities to influence public opinion. A Ministry of Communications and Culture was created in 1985. The Venezuelan Institute for Popular Education (IVEPO), with a staff of seventy-three employees in El Salvador, executed the media campaign.[40]

The CIA, which funneled $2 million to IVEPO in 1984 to assure the election of Napoleón Duarte, advised Congress that it was directing a covert "media relations" operation in El Salvador.[41] In 1985, the operation reportedly brought together the talents of the CIA and the National Security Council (NSC) in the effort to modify national and international press coverage of the war-torn country.[42] A three-year project by the NSC's Office of Public Diplomacy in the State Department involved "leaking" material on El Salvador to selected reporters.[43] A central goal of the program, according to congressional aides with access to classified information, was to change the country's image abroad and persuade the U.S. Congress to continue to supply aid.[44]

The PSYOP program received $1.5 million in U.S. appropriations in 1985 and was expected to receive more than $1 million in 1986.[45] The program included large-scale leaflet drops from airplanes, the opening of the armed forces' Radio Cuscatlán, and the distribution of flashy propaganda videos that government and private television and radio stations are required to air. Within El Salvador, the image of the war abroad was managed by dramatically increasing the volume of daily propaganda produced for international journalists while strictly limiting access to areas of conflict.

The PSYOP campaign polished the government's image at an international level and, of course, for a domestic audience in the United States. But in the Salvadoran countryside, the program hardly addressed the fundamental issues of concern to *campesinos*. For example, government leaflets dropped in a rural hamlet featured cartoon images of people imagining a picnic by the side of a stream, an image wholly unfamiliar to the dirt-poor residents.[46] Most of the impact of the psychological operations in rural areas appeared to dissipate when the clowns and mariachi bands boarded the helicopters and headed back to San Salvador.

CIVIL DEFENSE

Like PSYOP, El Salvador's civil defense program attempted to blur the distinction between civilian and military functions. While the civil defense units were said to protect Salvadoran civilians, their primary purpose involved establishing an informal intelligence network and guarding vital infrastructure against FMLN attacks. The chief of Salvadoran Territorial Services admitted that civil defense patrols were not actually defending themselves but served essentially as human antennas and buffers for the Army by attracting attacks by the enemy.[47]

Although El Salvador formally inaugurated its civil defense project in 1981, the effort rehabilitated the preexisting, tainted network of paramilitary forces known as ORDEN. Under the National Plan in 1983, direct and overt U.S. training of the units began and U.S. advisers urged the Army to integrate into local communities and work in closer coordination with local right-wing paramilitary groups.[48]

Although civil defense patrols were slated to play a central role in the UFR campaign, they proved to be a broken link in the government's counterinsurgency project. The Army had maintained that 90 percent of Salvador's towns would have civilian units by the end of 1985, but by August patrols were active in only 52 of El Salvador's 262 municipalities.[49] While the Army claimed the patrols were voluntary, many communities that refused to form paramilitary units were denied access to U.S. food aid and other forms of economic assistance.[50]

Salvadoran civilians had good reason to refuse participation in the civil defense network. The patrols were extremely dangerous for poorly armed civilians—the FMLN targeted some of the units for attack—leading some to label service as "municipal suicide."[51] The armed forces were notoriously late in responding to calls for support from the patrols. Payment for service was low, and usually only the most disadvantaged members of the community enlisted, since wealthier villagers could hire replacements or bribe the local commander to allow them to abandon their post. Perhaps most importantly, villagers were wary about the prospect of serving alongside former ORDEN members, known for their brutality and abuse of civilians. By 1986, the Army began experimenting with mixed units of civilians and soldiers but was unable to create a viable, national civil defense force.

CIVIC ACTION AND "HUMANITARIAN AID":
BARTERING FOR A SOCIAL BASE

Beyond psychological operations, the Salvadoran military has attempted to enhance its image through civic-action programs—an integral component of the Salvadoran government's efforts to fight and win on an unconventional battlefield. Assisted by U.S. technicians, Salvadoran troops began distributing food and medicine and building roads and schools. Such operations, according to Captain Robert Perry of the U.S. Southern Command, "undermine guerrilla efforts to build a manpower and resource base among the indigenous population . . . and pave the way for a durable partnership between civilian and military counterparts."[52] Thus, a "Civic Action Department" was created within the military high command, and Army field commanders received humanitarian aid directly from the government agencies for civic-action projects in the field. Civic-action operations were intended to give the armed forces a benevolent image even though villagers were apt to remember that the same soldiers who distributed food had previously destroyed the villagers' crops.[53]

More often than not, civic-action projects came with strings attached. Aid was used as bait to lure the population away from the guerrillas before a military sweep, and civic-action materials—food, clothing, medical supplies, and even propaganda—were dispensed only after efforts were made to categorize the population in a "divide-and-conquer" approach. One AID desk officer defined civic action as "services to the population for the purposes of obtaining intelligence . . . then you throw in a generous lump of humanitarian aid."[54]

The Pentagon encouraged and facilitated private U.S. "humanitarian" agencies, including relief organizations, churches, and corporations, to participate in joint civic-action efforts. In an era of fiscal austerity, when numerous "low-intensity conflicts" bid for U.S. federal funding, "humanitarian" efforts that could bypass congressional debate constituted a pragmatic, low-profile option for the Reagan administration. The joint effort was "all part of the low intensity conflict arena . . . [and] a tool in helping people feel better about the U.S. military presence and local military forces," according to Robert Wolthuis, director of the Pentagon's Humanitarian Assistance Office.[55] Between October 1984 and May 1987, El Salvador was the third-largest recipient of aid donated by private groups and transported by Pentagon aircraft and ships.[56]

By 1983, over eighty national and international private voluntary organizations (PVOs) were operating in El Salvador.[57] As a 1984 Pentagon Task Force Report on Humanitarian Assistance suggested, "a more cooperative effort with private relief organizations could enhance U.S. prestige abroad and promote the foreign policy objectives of the U.S. government."[58]

NATION-BUILDING AND THE
PRECARIOUS ECONOMY OF WAR

Notwithstanding PSYOP and civic-action operations or PVO support, the ability of the government to enhance its image with its own citizenry rested, in the final analysis, on its ability to manage El Salvador's gross social inequities and keep its impoverished, fragile economy afloat. El Salvador was already reeling from a global recession that struck many Third World nations in the late 1970s. Moreover, its economic crisis was exacerbated by the destructive effects of civil war. The Waghelstein study calculated the direct costs of the war from 1979 to 1983 at $596.8 million dollars.[59] The indirect costs of the war, such as increased capital flight, overall contraction of economic activity, and cutbacks in foreign commercial credits, were incalculable. As the economy edged toward the brink of collapse, the Reagan administration pushed through Congress massive doses of economic aid, providing over $1.4 billion from 1980 to 1986, and making El Salvador the third-largest recipient of U.S. economic aid.[60]

AID PROGRAMS: INSIDE THE TROJAN HORSE

Such U.S. economic aid has been guided by a political agenda designed to "stabilize" or underwrite a bankrupt economy with U.S. dollars; to "pacify" the populace by promoting rural development and "democratization" projects to undercut more far-reaching reforms proposed by the opposition coalition; and to "support private sector initiatives" through U.S. investment and trade policies.[61]

Although administration officials have repeatedly argued that U.S. social and economic development aid to El Salvador outstrips military aid by a three-to-one margin, one congressional study concluded that between 1980 and 1985, only 15 percent of total U.S. economic assistance addressed reform-and-development problems. In contrast, 30 percent was allotted for direct war-related aid, and 44 percent indirectly assisted the direct prosecution of the war.[62] According to a former Salvadoran minister of the economy, in the eight-year period between 1980 and 1987, the U.S. government provided more than $3.2 billion dollars in overall aid, "an equivalent of 6,700 dollars per inhabitant, or more than six times the country's current per-capita income."[63] In 1985, AID's allotments totaled $424 million, well over $1 million per day. Yet, in 1986, the Salvadoran government was spending less, taking inflation into account, on social programs such as health and education than it had in 1978.[64]

Even U.S. aid that appeared to be straightforward economic assistance has, first and foremost, served to undermine the government's opposition by promising liberal reforms or, more recently, by advocating a "private sector solution" to El Salvador's woes. Beginning under the Carter administration, agrarian reform served as a cornerstone for U.S. assistance policy toward El Salvador. Although significant redistribution of land never occurred, the program did win points in Washington by bolstering the reformist image of the Christian Democrats and appearing to undercut a central FDR-FMLN demand for a change in the system of land tenure.

Had Washington's agrarian project even remotely resembled the broad land reform originally proposed by the progressive junta of 1979, it might have served genuine development ends rather than counterinsurgency. Instead, the program was revamped and cut back with the aid of Roy Prosterman, a U.S. pacification expert who designed a similar program for Vietnam. U.S. advisers understood from the start that the new program would, as a classified cable from the U.S. embassy in El Salvador advised, "prove illusory as a means either of producing greater national wealth or better distributing it."[65]

The land reform further militarized the Salvadoran countryside and subsidized repression by inserting government forces into strategic guerrilla-held zones and contested areas to supply a "security shield" for the projects. The American Institute for Free Labor Development (AIFLD) reported that in the eight months after the land-reform project was enacted, 184 individuals associated with the program were "killed violently."[66] "From the first moment that the implementation of the agrarian reform began," Deputy Agriculture Minister Jorge Villacorta explained in his letter of resignation shortly after the reforms were announced, "what we saw was a sharp increase in official violence against the very peasants who were the supposed 'beneficiaries' of the process."[67]

By mid-1982, implementation of the agrarian reform was largely in the hands of its bitterest enemies. The Nationalist Republican Alliance (ARENA)—the party of the extreme right represented at the time by Roberto D'Aubuisson—controlled the Constituent Assembly and obtained key positions in the land-reform agencies—the Salvadoran Institute for Agrarian Transformation (ISTA) and the National Finance Office for Agricultural Lands (FINATA). The traditional landed elite was able to block reform by denying credit and other resources to the project. Land-reform efforts ground to a halt in 1983 when the Salvadoran National Assembly voted to end transfers of land under Phases I and III and refused to approve Phase II.

After the Reagan administration allowed the liberal agrarian reform option to run its course, Washington spurned other land-tenure schemes and turned its attention to modernizing and co-opting El Salvador's middle- and upper-class private sectors. Beginning in 1983, AID's program focused on strengthening the private sector and attracting a sector of businessmen away from the traditional oligarchy in order to create a centrist base of support for U.S. policies and to revitalize the economy sufficiently to prosecute the war.

Washington's efforts to build a coalition of modern business elites led to the formation of several business groups, the most prominent of which was the Salvadoran Development Foundation (FUSADES), a think tank and money funnel for elements of the "modernizing" right such as the ARENA splinter group Patria Libre. FUSADES became a

major conduit for U.S. funds and received over $90 million from AID
in local currency and aid for the development of certain private ventures.[68] FUSADES supplied low-interest credit and lucrative subsidies
to businesses willing to invest in nontraditional industries—such as
seafood, textiles, and the assembly of micro-components—that exported
their wares to "extra-regional" markets—often in the United States.
FUSADES opened up the Salvadoran economy to foreign-owned corporations by supplying capital and tax breaks to projects such as the San
Bartolo Free Zone, which employed Salvadorans in low-wage, labor-
intensive assembly operations such as sewing. The Reagan administration's enthusiastic support for the "private sector initiative" in El
Salvador reflected its preference for wooing the business class rather
than banking on liberal reform as the best means for countering the
insurgency.

STAGING DEMOCRACY:
THE CENTER CANNOT HOLD

The third major component of Washington's counterinsurgency strategy in El Salvador has been to foster a political process that would
channel both right-wing extremism and armed revolutionary struggle
into a stable, mildly reformist governing system. U.S. backing of José
Napoleón Duarte and his Christian Democratic Party (PDC) is historically consistent with earlier "successful" counterinsurgency efforts that
elevated so-called "third force" leaders—Ramón Magsaysay in the Philippines and Romolo Betancourt in Venezuela—whose popularity
helped undercut support for armed insurgencies. Three electoral compe-
titions—first in 1982 to elect a Constituent Assembly, in 1984 to select
a president, and in 1985 to choose a legislature—have undergirded the
Reagan administration's attempt to steer El Salvador toward a limited
constitutional democracy, breaking a fifty-year military-oligarchic stran-
glehold over the formal reigns of state power.[69]

   Although Reagan officials were closer to the rabid anti-Communism
and free-market ideology of the far-right parties—ARENA, the National Conciliation Party (PCN), and Patria Libre—the administration
backed the Christian Democrats in order to foster a consensus in El
Salvador and the U.S. Congress that could sustain a protracted counterinsurgency war and nation-building project. The White House had
difficulty boosting assistance to a junta that murdered American nuns

and killed eight hundred civilians a month in 1980–81.[70] Between mid-1981 and mid-1983, Congress required the Reagan administration to certify in hearings every six months that reforms on human rights and land tenure had been achieved. While the conditionality proved toothless for advancing reform, Congress did deny the White House portions of its funding requests during this period.[71]

The Reagan administration intervened during the 1982 elections after an alliance of rightist parties captured the Constituent Assembly, and threatened to make death squad leader Major Roberto D'Aubuisson the country's provisional president.[72] Fearing a tightening of congressional purse strings from the electoral result, the State Department dispatched special envoy Vernon Walters to pressure the Salvadoran military to prevent a D'Aubuisson presidency. The military complied, and presented the Assembly with a list of three "acceptable" candidates, from which it chose Álvaro Magaña, a conservative banker.

The 1982 vote was designed by Reagan officials to win over the hearts and minds of an American audience weary of supporting a pariah state. To be sure, the elections resulted in a president handpicked by Washington and the military, and led to a dismantling of the land reform by the ARENA-dominated Assembly. Nevertheless, the televised images of Salvadorans lining up to vote inspired Congress to increase total aid to El Salvador by nearly 100 percent.[73] Moreover, the elections created a new dynamic, a sideshow set apart from the civil war, of viewing Salvadoran politics as an intriguing electoral fight pitting the PDC against ARENA, Duarte against D'Aubuisson, "centrist" against far rightist.

Reagan officials succeeded in forging a "National Unity" government after the 1982 elections that began to establish new "rules of the game" for Salvadoran politics. The August 1982 "Pact of Apaneca" reduced internecine fighting between the far right and the center right by dividing up political offices between the PDC, the PCN, and ARENA. More importantly, the pact called for writing a new constitution in 1983, and holding presidential elections in March 1984 and legislative elections a year later.

The White House went all-out to ensure a PDC victory in the 1984 presidential elections, spending $10 million on the vote. The CIA funneled nearly $1 million to the PDC, and subsidized trips to El Salvador by European and Latin journalists, providing them with derogatory information about D'Aubuisson. At the same time, AID, through its affiliate AIFLD, heavily subsidized Salvadoran trade unions whose grass-roots organizers worked full-time for Duarte. U.S. funding and diplomatic pressures paid off: Duarte defeated D'Aubuisson in a runoff vote.[74]

With Duarte's election, and the PDC's subsequent victory in the March 1985 congressional elections, El Salvador disappeared from the debate in Washington over U.S. policy toward Central America. Viewing Duarte as the John F. Kennedy of El Salvador, a bipartisan U.S. Congress subsequently appropriated half a billion dollars of military and economic assistance yearly, with little or no discussion.[75] The media also fell in line. A survey of the mainstream U.S. press after Duarte's election found "that the Salvador story was no longer being reported as one of repression, escalating war and massive human rights violations, but rather as one of hope for peace and democratic renaissance."[76]

While elections defused the Salvador debate in Washington, they were also used to deflect demands in and outside of El Salvador for some negotiated form of power-sharing between the government and the opposition. In early 1982, internal administration documents described "efforts to co-opt the negotiations issue."[77] Washington's political solution was elections that excluded the FDR-FMLN rather than negotiations that included them in a new coalition government. Since negotiations began at La Palma in October 1984, Duarte has echoed the position of U.S. officials and the Salvadoran high command that the 1983 constitution is unbreakable: "There's no question of my agreeing to power with the rebels. Power is not on the table."[78]

THE FAILURE OF THE
CHRISTIAN DEMOCRATIC PROJECT

While Duarte's election provided unquestioned U.S. backing for the Salvadoran government and military, the PDC victory simultaneously generated its own unexpected and contradictory dynamics inside El Salvador. Within the narrow political space opened by "democratization," a vibrant popular movement reemerged in El Salvador's urban centers.

After his electoral victory, Duarte failed to deliver on campaign promises to seriously negotiate with the FDR-FMLN, respect human rights, expand the agrarian reform, and reactivate the economy. The virtual collapse of the Salvadoran economy proved the most devastating blow to Duarte. The PDC implemented a U.S.-devised economic strategy that alienated the very social base that put Duarte into office—labor—by gearing the economy toward the interests of the private sector, particularly nontraditional exporters. Meanwhile, Duarte's refusal to negotiate anything but the surrender of the FDR-FMLN compounded the economic crisis as the war consumed 50 percent of the national budget.[79]

The imposition of a U.S.-promoted economic austerity package in early 1986 unified a broad antigovernment opposition and dissolved Duarte's "Social Pact" with powerful sectors of his mass base, particularly labor. In February 1986, the National Unity of Salvadoran Workers (UNTS) formed in opposition to the austerity plan, claiming to represent three hundred thousand workers. The UNTS platform converged with the demands of the FDR-FMLN in calling for renewed dialogue between the Duarte government and the opposition, along with a return to national sovereignty.[80]

Ironically, the very political opening created to win El Salvador a new image abroad made possible a resurgent protest movement in San Salvador. Restraining the death squads and reopening the National University allowed the heart of the popular movement—workers and students—to organize aboveground and hit the streets for mass demonstrations.

Military and government officials responded to the urban movement with an "antiterrorist and antisubversive" offensive against church, labor, and human rights workers that suggested the FDR-FMLN had infiltrated and gained control of all organizations critical of the government. Duarte's increased preference for repression over reform, coupled with his unresponsiveness following the October 10, 1986, earthquake, which caused more than $1 billion worth of damage, led to a rapid decline of his popularity inside El Salvador and throughout Latin America. Aside from alienating his own social base, Duarte drew increasing public criticism from the military and the private sector, who accused him and the PDC of being too incompetent to fight the war and manage the economy.

By early 1986, Washington began to back away from Duarte, as he was no longer the force of cohesion who could satisfy the demands of labor, the private sector, and the military.[81] The U.S. embassy began cleaning up the image of the rightist political parties—particularly the reconstituted ARENA, without D'Aubuisson, and Patria Libre, the so-called "civilized right." Anticipating the 1989 presidential elections, Washington groomed the right as a potential alternative to the Christian Democrats.

Meanwhile, the Salvadoran military, shielded from popular criticism by Duarte's presidency and bolstered by over a billion dollars of U.S. assistance, has become the only viable institution built by Washington—the ultimate guarantor of U.S. policy. While no longer a handmaiden of the oligarchy, the Army has emerged as an autonomous and powerful political actor, loyal only to itself and the Pentagon. For instance, the military, disgusted by PDC incompetence, began directing programs once headed by civilian agencies, such as United for Reconstruction. The military's growing role in the "national recovery" from war, economic collapse, and the 1986 earthquake belied the Reagan administration's claim to have "civilized" Salvadoran political life.[82]

Heading toward the end of José Napoleón Duarte's Christian Democratic government, it became increasingly clear that the Reagan administration's "third-force" strategy of creating a stable political center had failed. While Washington remained enamored with El Salvador's "budding democracy," public cynicism inside El Salvador toward the whole electoral process increased. Few Salvadorans believe either the Christian Democrats, the far right, or U.S. strategists are able or willing to end the war, open the political process, or resolve the deepening economic crisis.[83]

THE ENDLESS WAR?

By mid-1987, over sixty-two thousand Salvadorans had been killed in the conflict, most at the hands of government forces.[84] Nevertheless, Washington's counterinsurgency war grinds on without apparent end. The ultimate success or failure of the U.S. low-intensity war remains impossible to predict. It is possible, however, to evaluate the limits and possibilities of the U.S. counterinsurgency project.

The U.S. presence has fundamentally altered the Salvadoran revolutionary process because the Reagan administration has achieved its minimal objective of "drawing the line" against a guerrilla victory. If the conflict had been solely (or even largely) Salvadoran, the FDR-FMLN would certainly have triumphed in the early 1980s. Instead, the FMLN faces the prospect of a long war of attrition, one that could well extend through the remainder of the century. Outright military victory is rarely mentioned any longer by the guerrillas, who are pressing for a negotiated settlement that would include some form of power-sharing.

Through its political initiatives, the administration has also succeeded in turning El Salvador into a "forgotten war." Duarte's election in 1984 forged a bipartisan congressional consensus that leaves unquestioned massive yearly doses of American aid. By "Vietnamizing" the war early and not using U.S. combat troops, President Reagan has limited domestic debate and anxiety over Washington's destructive role in this tiny nation.

However, inside El Salvador—where the war will ultimately be won or lost—the three unstable pillars of the counterinsurgency effort reveal the limits of U.S. power. Militarily, the Reagan administration has vetoed a guerrilla victory for now, but the FMLN remains a potent force that has deepened and expanded the war throughout the country and remains capable of direct attacks on central military posts. While El Salvador is often touted at forums on low-intensity warfare as a case study of what LIC doctrine can achieve, a more sober military assessment concedes that Washington's counterinsurgency strategy "is not a success. . . . There have not been the significant guerrilla defeats, with heavy insurgent losses in men and arms, large-scale guerrilla defections, or the lessening of rural political support for the rebels, which would signal the insurgency's decline. . . ."[85]

The FDR-FMLN remains the most militarily and politically potent insurgency in all of Latin America because the United States and Salvadoran governments have not addressed the root causes of the rebellion: poverty and landlessness. U.S. programs designed to remedy these disparities—such as civic-action initiatives and United for Reconstruction—resemble little more than Big Brother welfare schemes in which security concerns override any interest in genuine development. Meanwhile, the economic model that Washington has exported to El Salvador—which favors strengthening the most dynamic sectors of the private sector at the expense of social reforms—has only produced joblessness, austerity, and increasing dependence on the Colossus to the North.

The twin miseries of endless warfare and economic decline have foiled Washington's third major counterinsurgency goal of creating a stable government in El Salvador. José Napoleón Duarte quickly discovered the difficulty of trying to implement reform while waging war and bowing to the private sector. By 1987, the only discernible "third force" in El Salvador was a loose grouping of trade unionists, university students, the displaced, and church sectors—some formerly Duarte supporters—who demanded an end to economic austerity and the civil war in order to solve the grave problems of the country's poor majority. President Duarte had failed to live up to his messianic vision of himself as the "savior" of El Salvador and to the Pentagon's ideal of a counter-revolutionary democrat.

Low-intensity warfare strategists like Sam Sarkesian believe that counterinsurgency can be successful if the client government can "take the revolution out of the hands of the revolutionaries." In El Salvador, that means imitating guerrilla tactics on the battlefield, giving handouts to peasants, and tolerating a civilian president. However, as the Vietnam experience should have taught Washington policy-makers, a made-in-the-U.S.A. counterinsurgency is unlikely to contain or roll back a genuine historical movement struggling for equity and independence. While the Salvadoran revolution does not have a historical tradition to match that of the Vietnamese, it is, on the other hand, more politically entrenched than Latin American *foquista* guerrilla bands easily routed by Green Beret advisers in the 1960s. It is, in fact, far more entrenched in the world of the Salvadoran peasant than it was in 1981 when the United States embarked upon its ambitious counterinsurgency program. What this means is that short of a full-scale military occupation of the country, there is unlikely to be a military solution to the Salvadoran conflict.

"War is not simply a conflict between armies; more and more it is a struggle between competing social systems incorporating the political, economic, and cultural institutions of all rivals," writes historian Gabriel Kolko. "The longer the war, the more likely that it will be determined outside the arena of guns and battles."[86] Both sides of the Salvadoran conflict say they understand the political nature of the war, that "nation-building" efforts to organize the civilian population must take precedence over battlefield victories. But ultimately, only one side can win the war for hearts and minds. As the war approaches the final years of its first decade, it becomes increasingly clear that the consequences of the U.S. counterinsurgency plan are broken hearts and battered minds.

That is the price of President Reagan's vow to keep the left out of power in El Salvador. The administration assumed that it could create a stable political economy behind the Pentagon's "military shield."

Instead, the long low-intensity war has sapped the nation's economy and undermined political stability.

A just and lasting end to this war can only come through a negotiated political solution, arising from Salvadorans demanding peace and U.S. policy-makers conceding that they can no longer dictate events in the region. Sadly, the war's sponsors in Washington seem content to watch the carnage continue, slowly destroying El Salvador in order to save it.

NICARAGUA: U.S. PROINSURGENCY WARFARE AGAINST THE SANDINISTAS

PETER KORNBLUH

This is a great moral challenge for the entire free world. Surely no issue is more important for peace in our own Hemisphere, the security of our frontiers, for the protection of our vital interests than . . . Nicaragua.

> President Reagan
> State of the Union Address
> February 4, 1986

Since 1981, when Ronald Reagan took office pledging to "project American power throughout the world," Nicaragua has become the principal battlefield for a global doctrine of "proactive" U.S. interventionism. No single foreign-policy objective has so dominated the political agenda in Washington as making the Sandinista government "say Uncle." In the mind-set of U.S. policy-makers, Nicaragua has no reality as a small, impoverished nation that emerged from under the boot of dynastic dictatorship in 1979; rather, it represents a test case of U.S. strategies to roll back revolution in Central America and around the world.

The basis for U.S. policy in Nicaragua is found in the "Reagan Doctrine" of taking the strategic offensive against revolutionary regimes perceived to be proxies for the Soviet Union in the struggle for global domination. Through its open and avid paramilitary support of anti-

Communist "contras" in Nicaragua, as well as in Angola, Cambodia, Afghanistan, and elsewhere, the Reagan administration has boldly attempted to revive and relegitimize John Foster Dulles's concept of "rollback." One victory against the forces of communism, Reagan officials believe, would alter the future of U.S.-USSR competition for influence in the Third World. The political objective, administration proponents argue, is to demonstrate the fallacy of the Brezhnev doctrine of Communist invincibility: "to demonstrate to communist and noncommunist nations alike that communism is not, as the Soviets propagate, the 'wave of the future,' and that Communist rule, once installed, is reversible."[1] "Communist subversion is not an irreversible tide," President Reagan suggested in his first public enunciation of his doctrine. "We have seen it rolled back. . . . All it takes is the will and resources to get the job done."[2]

To implement the Reagan Doctrine and "get the job done," the administration has relied upon the evolving politicomilitary doctrine of low-intensity warfare. That doctrine calls for a multidimensional, integrated approach—to use the jargon of the Pentagon, the "synergistic application of comprehensive political, social, economic and psychological efforts"—to waging Third World wars. Given the post-Vietnam domestic political constraints on the overt use of force in the Third World, covert intervention, economic destabilization, pyschological operations, and propaganda campaigns have emerged, over the last six years, as the major fronts in the Reagan administration's war on Nicaragua. The objective of a counterrevolutionary assault by proxy—a tactic frequently used by the CIA since the 1950s—supplemented by severe economic pressures and the constant threat of U.S. overt intervention—has been to ruin Nicaragua's revolutionary experiment and discredit the Sandinistas politically among their followers. The target of the propaganda campaigns, however, has been to convince the American public that a bloody war of attrition against a country the size of Iowa is, somehow, in the national interest.

THE COVERT WAR

From the earliest days of the administration, fostering a counterrevolutionary proxy force to spearhead the U.S. attack on Nicaragua became the main instrument of American policy. President Reagan originally approved covert support for the "contras," as this force came to be known, as Washington's answer to a series of leftist revolutions in the 1970s.[3] Although virtually no one believed the contras would win, they represented the most direct method of bleeding Nicaragua's fragile social, economic, and military institutions while avoiding the domestic political costs of open intervention. Moreover, working through a surrogate force enabled the administration to invoke a "plausible denial" of responsibility and to shield itself from accountability to Congress and the American people. As the violence escalated, U.S. officials would falsely portray the conflict as "Nicaraguans fighting against Nicaraguans."

Besides draining scarce economic and human resources, U.S. strategists believed, the contra war would force the Sandinistas to discredit themselves politically. At the CIA's headquarters in Langley, Virginia, according to David MacMichael,[4] an Agency national intelligence analyst on Central America from 1981 through 1983, officials expected that contra operations

> would provoke cross border attacks by Nicaraguan forces and thus serve to demonstrate Nicaragua's aggressive nature and possibly call into play the Organization of American States' provisions [for collective defense]. It was hoped that the Nicaraguan government would clamp down on civil liberties within Nicaragua itself, arresting its opposition, demonstrating its allegedly inherent totalitarian nature and thus increase domestic dissent within the country, and further that there would be reaction against United States citizens, particularly against United States diplomatic personnel within Nicaragua and thus serve to demonstrate the hostility of Nicaragua towards the United States.

Over time, the situation would deteriorate and Sandinista rule would become untenable, according to this scenario. "The secret to success will be a steady and sustained effort," a classified State Department memorandum noted in 1982. "Barring serious miscalculation by the other side, there will be no opportunities for quick decisive action to end the problem."[5]

THE WAR BEGINS

Plans to build a counterrevolutionary army in Central America were on the drawing board as early as March 1981 when CIA Director William Casey submitted a proposal to Reagan for backing pro-U.S. forces not only in Nicaragua but in Afghanistan, Laos, Cambodia, Grenada, Iran, Libya, and Cuba.[6] With a presidential green light, U.S. operatives then established contacts with incipient anti-Sandinista groups in Florida and Central America. By August, the Agency had united the first contra organizations, the September 15 Legion and the Nicaraguan Democratic Union, under the leadership of Somoza's former National Guard officials to form the Nicaraguan Democratic Force (FDN).

The national security bureaucracy also geared up for the war effort. A Restricted Interagency Group—also known as the "Core Group"— was established to coordinate a broad and protracted paramilitary campaign against Nicaragua. By November, when President Reagan signed National Security Decision Directive No. 17 authorizing $19.5 million in funding for the CIA to create a paramilitary commando squad to conduct attacks inside Nicaragua, the foundation for the covert war to follow had already been laid.

NSDD-17 went into effect immediately. Dozens of U.S. intelligence operatives arrived in Honduras to assume covert posts. By December 1981, American agents—some CIA, some U.S. Special Forces—were working through Argentine intermediaries to set up contra safe houses, training centers, and base camps along the Nicaraguan-Honduran border. The Argentine military regime, already organizing former National Guardsmen to fight against communism in Central America, received $15 million in 1981 and 1982 to arm and train the contras; eventually, U.S. operatives known to the contras as "Major West," "Colonel Raymond," "George," "Tomas Castillo," "Donald," and "Alex" assumed control of the administration, logistics, and tactical operations of the covert war.

With the influx of American funds, equipment, and personnel, the frequency and destructiveness of the contra attacks escalated rapidly. On March 14, CIA-trained and -equipped saboteurs blew up two major bridges in Chinandega and Nueva Segovia provinces—an unofficial declaration of the covert war. "In Nicaragua, the Sandinistas are under increased pressure as a result of our covert efforts," a classified National Security Planning Group "summary paper" declared in April.[7] "The anti-Sandinista insurgency has caused the junta increasing military, economic and political costs," stated a subsequent CIA assessment. "Large numbers of reservists have been called up to active duty, scarce resources have been diverted to military expenditures, and the population has become aware of significant armed opposition to the regime."[8]

THE CONTRAS: FROM PROXY FORCE
TO "NATIONAL LIBERATION FRONT"

In the name of the Reagan Doctrine's pledge that the United States would sponsor "revolutionary democracy"—that is, the "forces of freedom" against the "forces of totalitarianism"—the CIA pursued a political and paramilitary strategy of support for the contras. On the political side, the Agency sought to create a democratic image for a surrogate army that a CIA Intelligence Information Report in mid-1981 characterized as a "not particularly effective group of Nicaraguan dissidents."[9] To disguise the fact that the FDN, the dominant contra organization, was led by former Somoza National Guard officers, the CIA quietly recruited into its leadership six prominent Nicaraguan exiles with anti-Somoza credentials. Beginning in January 1983, the CIA retained a Miami-based public relations firm (at $600,000 a year) to, according to the contract, "project a positive image" and "publicize the FDN and the FDN Directorate in specific target countries through newspaper/ magazine articles explaining what the FDN stands for."[10] By May, President Reagan had publicly christened the contras "freedom fighters" and admitted for the first time that his administration was supporting them.

Far from living up to their billing in Washington as "the moral equivalent of our founding fathers," however, the contras quickly established a reputation for abject brutality and gross violations of human rights. As early as mid-1982, the U.S. Defense Intelligence Agency reported that contra troops were engaged in "the assassination of minor government officials."[11] By the end of 1985, the Nicaraguan Ministry of Health estimated that 3,652 civilians had been killed, 4,039 wounded, and 5,232 kidnapped during contra raids.[12] The human rights monitoring organization Americas Watch reported that FDN forces "systematically engaged in the killing of prisoners and the unarmed . . . and indiscriminate attacks, torture and other outrages against personal dignity."[13]

On the battlefield, the CIA attempted to advance the contras beyond indiscriminate acts of butchery and into a more advanced phase of guerrilla insurgency—the creation of a political base among the peasantry. The now-infamous CIA *Psychological Operations in Guerrilla Warfare* training manual was a manifestation of this effort. Translated virtually word for word from a Vietnam-era Fort Bragg PSYOP lesson plan, the manual presented a sophisticated low-intensity war-fighting strategy that included civic action, "armed propaganda," and "neutralization" of civilian officials—all aimed at fostering a popular movement inside Nicaragua.[14]

The manual instructed the contras to regulate their savagery, to use terrorism selectively against the citizenry in order to erode the Sandinista's popularity while enhancing the contras' appeal. "In a revolution individual lives are under the constant threat of physical damage," according to the handbook:[15]

> If the government police cannot put an end to the guerrilla activities, the population will lose confidence in the government which has the inherent mission of guaranteeing the safety of citizens. However, the guerrillas should be careful not to become an explicit terror, because this would result in a loss of popular support.

The contras were advised to win the hearts and minds of the Nicaraguan population through "political proselytism" and civic-action operations—"working side by side with peasants . . . building, fishing, repairing etc." By relying on such psychological operations, the manual stressed, the contras could foster the social infrastructure necessary to advance their low-intensity campaign.

These operations would be coupled with what the manual called "the selective use of violence." The handbook contained explicit instructions for how contra provocateurs "armed with clubs, iron rods, placards, and if possible small fire arms" could instigate mob riots in the cities. If the contras encountered hostile individuals in the countryside, the manual recommended "eliminating the enemy in a rapid and effective manner." Village authorities and anyone associated with the Sandinista government were particularly singled out. As the CIA book advised:

> It is possible to neutralize carefully selected and planned targets, such as court judges, magistrates, police and state security officials etc. For psychological purposes, it is necessary to gather together the population affected, so that they will be present, take part in the act, and formulate accusations against the oppressor.

In practice, this meant a conscious campaign of violence against any symbols of the Sandinista revolution. Rural health-care facilities and doctors, schools and educators, agricultural cooperatives and agronomists became the principal victims of contra attacks on Nicaragua's social and economic infrastructure. CIA officials not only knew of, but also condoned, such acts. In late 1983, Duane Clarridge, the agent in charge of the covert war, admitted in a closed briefing of the House Intelligence Committee staff that the contras had killed "civilians and Sandinista officials in the provinces, as well as heads of cooperatives, nurses, doctors, and judges." "After all," Clarridge reportedly reasoned, "this is a war."[16]

DIRECT CIA ATTACKS

To accelerate the deleterious impact of contra attacks, the CIA undertook its own war of attrition against Nicaragua's already fragile economic structures. Between September 1983 and April 1984, the Agency conducted at least twenty-two air, land, and sea raids on vital Nicaraguan installations—all missions deemed too sophisticated for the contras. CIA officials ordered the contras to take credit for these operations even though in reality the only role they played was as cover for direct U.S. aggression.

The CIA attempted to adhere to the maxim of LIC doctrine—no direct use of American personnel in combat roles—by deploying a specially trained force of "unilaterally controlled Latino assets" (UCLAs) to carry out these raids. While U.S. agents furnished backup and logistics and provided what a CIA combat summary called "suppressing rocket fire" in at least two helicopter attacks, it was Latin American contract agents who actually entered Nicaraguan territory.[17] "Our mission," according to one Honduran UCLA, was "to sabotage ports, refineries, boats, and bridges and try to make it appear that the contras had done it."

These attacks took a heavy toll on Nicaragua. On September 8, 1983, UCLA-manned speedboats launched from a CIA "mother ship" anchored twelve miles offshore struck the oil facilities at Puerto Sandino. On October 10, at Nicaragua's largest port of Corinto, CIA commandos firing mortars and grenades ignited five storage tanks filled with 3.4 million gallons of fuel. More than a hundred persons were injured in the attack and twenty-five thousand inhabitants of the city had to be evacuated while a fire raged out of control for two days. In January, February, March, and April 1984, CIA-UCLA teams conducted attacks on Nicaraguan oil tanks, port facilities, communications centers, and military positions.

Sowing mines in Nicaragua's harbors became an integral part of this sabotage program. Authorized by President Reagan in December 1983 as part of a National Security Council "harassment" plan, the underwater charges were designed to sink small fishing boats and damage larger vessels.[18] UCLA commando teams, operating once again from a CIA mother ship anchored offshore, deposited the mines in the shipping channels of Nicaragua's major Atlantic and Pacific coast ports in early 1984. By the first week of April, ten commercial vessels had struck CIA-sown mines; six were non-Nicaraguan.

Harbor warfare—like CIA raids on oil facilities and contra attacks on agricultural cooperatives—was part of the Reagan administration's war of sabotage. "Our intention is to severely disrupt the flow of shipping essential to Nicaraguan trade during the peak export period," Lieutenant Colonel Oliver North wrote in a "top secret" memorandum titled "Special Activities in Nicaragua" dated March 2, 1984. U.S. policymakers presumed that once the contras announced the harbors had been mined no cargo ship would risk docking at Nicaraguan ports, thereby severely disrupting commercial trade links with the outside world. "It is entirely likely," North noted, that "no insurers will cover ships calling in Nicaraguan ports. This will effectively limit their seaborne trade." In fact, the mines did impede both imports and exports by sea and forced the Sandinista government to take the expensive measure of having goods trucked to and from ports in neighboring Central American countries. According to Nicaraguan authorities, the net damage from the CIA mining surpassed $10 million.[19]

In Washington, however, the mines produced a major political scandal that resulted in a congressional cutoff of aid to the contras in October 1984. Although the Reagan administration maintained support of the contras via a National Security Council–run surrogate supply network until Congress reversed its decision in mid-1986, the hiatus resulted in the covert war's loss of momentum for two years.

ECONOMIC DESTABILIZATION

To supplement the CIA-contra attacks inside Nicaragua, the Reagan administration mounted a campaign of economic destabilization from abroad. Bilateral trade and multilateral aid effectively became weapons of war. By undermining Nicaragua's commercial relations and its access to international credit, U.S. officials hoped to provoke economic deprivation throughout the country. Widespread unemployment and acute shortages of basic commodities would erode popular support for the Sandinistas; civil unrest would, in turn, create a favorable climate for the counterrevolution.

Nicaragua was particularly susceptible to this form of pressure. The Sandinistas had inherited an economy devastated by war and corruption. By the time Somoza fled to Miami, commercial and industrial property worth $481 million had been destroyed and approximately six hundred thousand people had been displaced by National Guard air strikes. During the final weeks of fighting, Somoza and his followers had looted the Central Bank, leaving Nicaragua's financial system "completely decapitalized," according to the U.N. Economic Commission for Latin America.[20] To reconstruct its war-torn economy, World Bank analysts predicted in 1981, Nicaragua would need hundreds of millions of dollars of external assistance on concessional terms.[21]

The Reagan administration's strategy of economic warfare sought to block Nicaragua's access to external support on three fronts: by halting U.S. bilateral aid and trade; by impeding Sandinista economic relations with U.S. allies; and by blocking multilateral development-bank loans. Following the model of Nixon's successful effort to destabilize the Allende government in Chile, the administration fashioned a policy to "make the economy scream" in Nicaragua.

TERMINATING BILATERAL ECONOMIC RELATIONS

Upon taking office, President Reagan suspended the remaining $15 million of an economic assistance package passed under his predecessor and effectively halted all U.S. bilateral aid to Nicaragua. The Sandinistas were pointedly excluded from the $350 million Caribbean Basin Initiative announced by President Reagan in January 1982 as well as the $8 billion "Marshall Plan" for Central America recommended by the Kissinger Commission two years later.

The administration also began to incrementally curtail U.S.-Nicaraguan trade relations. First, Washington terminated Export-Import Bank guarantees to Nicaragua, making it all but impossible for Nicaraguan businessmen to purchase expensive U.S.-made merchandise on credit. In 1982, the U.S. Commerce Department placed prohibitions on exports of chemical feedstocks to Nicaragua because of their alleged use in Nicaraguan food products being sold to Cuba. In June 1983, President Reagan ordered that all Nicaraguan consulates be closed, further obstructing Nicaragua's ability to conduct normal commercial transactions with the United States.

On May 10, 1983, the White House imposed direct trade restrictions, announcing that the quota for Nicaraguan sugar exports to the United States would be slashed 90 percent. "By denying to Nicaragua a foreign exchange benefit resulting from the high U.S. sugar price," according to the president's rationale, "we hope to reduce the resources available to that country for financing its military build-up, and its support for subversion and extremist violence in the region."[22]

Cutting Nicaragua's sugar quota portended the imposition of a total trade embargo two years later. In his National Security Decision Directive No. 124, signed in February 1984, President Reagan ordered that "the Secretary of State in coordination with the Secretary of Defense and the Directors of Central Intelligence and Office of Management and Budget should . . . review and recommend such economic sanctions against Nicaragua that are likely to build pressure on the Sandinistas." After a lengthy internal debate, on May 1, 1985, Reagan issued an executive order banning "all imports . . . of Nicaraguan origin [and] all exports from the United States of goods or materials destined for Nicaragua, except those destined for the organized democratic resistance."[23]

The embargo immediately cut off $58 million in Nicaraguan exports—bananas, coffee, and shellfish—to the United States and $110 million in U.S. exports of fertilizer, insecticide, and industrial and agricultural equipment to Nicaragua. Although it failed to wreck the economy, the impact was nevertheless severe, particularly on the private-sector agriculture which depended on U.S. goods and spare parts for production and U.S. markets for profits.[24]

BLOCKING INTERNATIONAL ASSISTANCE

To isolate the Sandinistas internationally, Washington attempted to garner allied support for its policy of economic denial. U.S. allies resisted State Department entreaties that they join the embargo; indeed, many Western nations quickly offered new commercial markets to the Sandinistas. Nevertheless, the administration maintained constant pressure on its allies to reduce trade with, and aid to, Nicaragua.

U.S. pressure proved far more successful at the international monetary institutions where, between 1979 and 1982, Nicaragua obtained 34 percent of its external financial assistance. Since the largest lenders, the Inter-American Development Bank (IDB) and the World Bank (officially the International Bank for Reconstruction and Development [IBRD]), represented sources of millions of dollars in actual and potential credits for postrevolutionary Nicaragua, the Reagan administration focused its efforts to block credits on these two financial institutions.

"Project implementation has been extraordinarily successful in Nicaragua," one internal World Bank assessment from the office of the U.S. executive director stated, "better than anywhere else in the world."[25] Nevertheless, under U.S. pressure the World Bank suspended all lending to the Sandinistas in November 1982. At the IDB, Reagan officials managed to obstruct at least eight pending loans to Nicaragua after September 1983, using tactics that ranged from outright vetos to behind-the-scenes manipulation of the IDB's bureaucracy. In the case of a $58 million loan proposal to expand private-sector agricultural production, for example, the administration delayed consideration of the loan for three years and finally threatened to terminate IDB appropriations if the loan was approved. "Our joint long-term goal of strengthening the Inter-American Development Bank and expanding its resource base would be undercut by Board approval of this proposed loan," Secretary of State Shultz wrote to IDB President Antonio Ortiz Mena on January 30, 1985.[26] Subsequently, the loan was remanded to the IDB's technical committee, where U.S. officials engineered a negative assessment of its economic viability.[27] From 1984 through 1987, Nicaragua received no new credits from the IDB and was effectively cut off from access to desperately needed development capital.

MODERN GUNBOAT DIPLOMACY

Escalating U.S. aggression forced the Sandinistas to put Nicaragua's debilitated economy on a wartime footing. Not only were government coffers drained by the costly counterinsurgency campaign against the contras and by the U.S. economic blockade; the Sandinistas also readied themselves militarily to resist a U.S. invasion. Given Nicaragua's historical experience (U.S. Marines invaded ten times between 1850 and 1930 and occupied the country from 1912 to 1933), the invasion of Grenada, and repeated threats by U.S. officials to use overt military force in Nicaragua, it appeared reasonable to conclude that the "worst-case scenario" of an open incursion was inevitable.

The Reagan administration's low-intensity warfare strategy deliberately cultivated this anxiety. Using continuous, highly visible, military "war games" in Honduras, the United States sought to instill a permanent paranoia in Nicaragua's leadership. "One of the central purposes [of the joint U.S.-Honduran maneuvers] is to create fear of an invasion, to push very close to the border, deliberately, to set off all the alarms," one administration official told the *New York Times*. [28] "Let them worry," was the way U.N. Ambassador Vernon Walters summarized U.S. strategy. "We have found that constructive ambiguity is a very powerful weapon in American foreign policy." [29]

Beginning in August 1983 with the six-month-long "Big Pine II" exercises, U.S. military maneuvers in Honduras emerged as one of the largest and most expensive psychological operations in the history of unconventional warfare. These "extended exercises" constituted the primary component of a calculated, interagency program known in the Pentagon's Orwellian jargon as "perception management." [30]

What Robert Kupperman in his Army-commissioned study, *Low Intensity Conflict*, called "the threat of force to achieve political objectives without the full-scale commitment of resources" proved an effective method of destabilization against the Sandinistas. [31] As Big Pine II, which brought twelve thousand American soldiers and two Pacific battleship groups to Nicaragua's borders and coasts, was followed by ever more dramatic displays of U.S. military power—for example, "Grenadero I" (a name chosen to remind the Sandinistas of the invasion of Grenada), "Ocean Venture," "Big Pine III," and "Solid Shield" in March 1987 in which more than fifty thousand U.S. troops participated—the Nicaraguan regime reacted with predictable alarm.

More than once, the Sandinistas declared that U.S. military intervention was "imminent" and mobilized both the armed forces and the population at large. During U.S.-created war scares in November 1983—following the Grenada invasion, which had begun as a "routine" naval maneuver—and the "MIGs crisis" of November 1984, during which U.S. officials falsely accused the Sandinistas of receiving Soviet aircraft and threatened to retaliate—Nicaragua was paralyzed by full-scale preparations to defend the country. Scores of citizens were sent home from work to dig air-raid shelters in the backyards of factories, homes, and businesses. Economic production halted, cash crops went unharvested, tanks lined inactive streets. Without firing a shot, the administration managed to severely disrupt the normal political, economic, and social functions of an entire nation.

Such U.S. military maneuvers embody the LIC doctrine of using all available "assets" to simultaneously prepare the battlefield and wage the battle. Not only have they kept the government psychologically off-balance and advanced the goal of destabilizing Nicaragua's economy; the maneuvers have combined support for the contras with the creation of a sophisticated military infrastructure for staging low- or high-intensity operations in the region.

General Paul Gorman, a member of the Restricted Interagency Group that oversaw the covert war in 1981 and 1982 and director of the Pentagon's Southern Command (SouthCom) in Panama from 1983 through early 1985, is widely credited as the architect of this strategy. In the summer of 1983, the general briefed White House officials "on how a network of permanent bases could be built in Honduras for use by U.S. forces."[32] Low-intensity warfare, Gorman believed, was "the form of political violence most likely for USSOUTHCOM" to encounter, and during his tenure he transformed a once sleepy backwater command into the military nerve center for counterrevolutionary warfare in the region.[33]

Less than four months after Gorman took command, Deputy Secretary of Defense Paul Thayer signed a classified "program decision" memorandum ordering all military services to add funds for SouthCom activities and to plan for expanded operations in Central America.[34] In the following year, the number of U.S. military personnel stationed in Central America increased by 23 percent to 11,600. From the U.S. compound in Fort Gulick, Panama, SouthCom personnel coordinated training teams, supervised military assistance programs, drew up contingency plans, analyzed intelligence, and directed the war games that rotated thousands of American GIs and reserve National Guard units in and out of the region.

Under the guise of these maneuvers, General Gorman engineered the construction of an elaborate permanent network of military and intelligence facilities in Honduras. Big Pine II marked the beginning of this backdoor buildup. During the course of the exercise, according to the General Accounting Office,

> American units constructed one 3,500-foot dirt assault airstrip, expanded one 4,300-foot dirt airstrip to 8,000 feet, expanded a 3,000-foot asphalt airstrip to 3,500 feet, installed or constructed nearly 300 wooden huts to serve as barracks, dining and administrative facilities [and] deployed two radar stations.[35]

During the Grenadero I exercises, U.S. combat engineers constructed two more airstrips, one at Jamastrán near the Nicaraguan-Honduran border, and the other at Cucuyagua in northern Honduras. By mid-1985 the United States had built or modernized eight airstrips, two training centers, two radar stations, four military base camps, and a twelve-mile "tank trap" near the Nicaraguan frontier at a cost of more than $100 million.

The Department of Defense justified this work under "Operation and Management" (O&M) regulations that require all construction to be impermanent and directly related to the exercises. Accordingly, in presentations to Congress, DOD officials argued that "all engineering work" was "incidental to the exercise program" and "temporary in nature."[36]

A General Accounting Office investigation found, however, that the Pentagon had violated O&M regulations. The construction of exercise-related facilities was clearly not "of a temporary nature." The GAO concluded that "the majority of these facilities remain in good condition, and in fact continue to be used, both by U.S. and Honduran personnel."[37] In a classified appendix, the GAO disclosed that the Big Pine II exercises were "a significant departure from past practices." As the report observed, "Except for NATO exercises, the United States does not generally leave facilities, materials, or equipment behind after training exercises overseas."[38]

In fact, some of these facilities and materials were left behind for the contras as part of collaborative DOD-CIA planning for a continuing escalation of proinsurgency operations inside Nicaragua. Under the pretext of Big Pine II, the air base at El Aguacate, thirty-two kilometers from the Nicaraguan border, was modernized to be used as part of the infrastructure for the covert war. Although Deputy Assistant Secretary of Defense Nestor Sanchez testified before the House Subcommittee on Military Construction that "we have no plans for [El Aguacate's] future use," SouthCom officials told GAO investigators that "the austere base, 8,000 foot landing strip, and the water system, constructed by the 46th Combat Engineers at Aguacate will be left behind for use by CIA personnel."[39]

But the overriding purpose of the military maneuvers and the accompanying buildup was to develop a permanent capability for waging protracted unconventional warfare in the region while simultaneously preparing for the contingency of overt intervention. At Palmerola, the largest U.S. installation in Honduras, the Pentagon sought to build a "compound for use as a contingency facility . . . suitable for extended deployments of joint service units, military training teams, and civic action project teams." In 1984, U.S. military officials also requested authorization for a "Forward Munitions Storage Area" to pre-position bombs and rockets and "enhance capabilities to execute tactical air contingency operations in support of allies in the region." A "residual force" of fourteen hundred men—the Joint Task Force Alfa—was permanently stationed at Palmerola to, in General Gorman's words, "aid in the operational aspects" of future maneuvers. Drawn from the U.S. Readiness Command at Fort MacDill, Florida, and described as a "self-contained combat control team fully able to direct a battle force of tens of thousands of troops," the task force mission, as its commander, Colonel William Comee, informed a visiting Senate delegation in July 1986, was to "test and integrate Low Intensity Conflict Doctrine in the region."

Indeed, the war games also provided an on-site opportunity for thousands of Army, Navy, Air Force, Marine, and reserve personnel drawn from units likely to be deployed in any invasion scenario to acclimate themselves to the terrain and to tropical conditions during combat simulation. Among the types of LIC testing the task force oversaw was how U.S. troops could sustain themselves in isolated zones in Nicaragua during an occupation.[40] At the same time, military tacticians were able to evaluate how men and equipment performed in the Central American environment. "These exercises have been invaluable for training U.S. forces for low intensity conflict under real world conditions," General Gorman testified before the Senate Armed Services Committee.[41]

The success of the Pentagon's effort to create and test a sophisticated military apparatus in the region emboldened U.S. officials to declare that they could, if called upon, conduct successful military operations against the Sandinistas. The U.S. military was "now in the position to assume a combat role in Central America should President Reagan give the order," military officials suggested to the press.[42] Such announcements reflected a "perception management" program directed at the American public. In a classified April 1985 White House report to Congress, however, President Reagan signaled that an invasion scenario was not out of the question. Such a military gambit, the report stated, "must realistically be recognized as an eventual option in the region if other policy alternatives fail."[43]

THE PROPAGANDA WAR

To advance the covert, economic, and military components of the war in Nicaragua, the Reagan administration has been forced to wage an intense battle on another front: the home front. More than any other factor, domestic opposition to U.S. intervention in the post-Vietnam era has impeded the escalation of U.S. intervention in Central America—a reality recognized at the highest levels of the administration and explicitly addressed by LIC planners. "We continue to have serious difficulties with U.S. public and Congressional opinion, which jeopardizes our ability to stay the course," one secret National Security Planning Group report on the region noted as early as April 1982.[44] "The American public remains shaken and divided by the Vietnam experience, less willing to support the application of power abroad," advised a confidential Rand Corporation study prepared for the Kissinger Commission in 1983. "In order to restore U.S. involvement in [Central America] to its traditional levels the U.S. government will need greater public consensus on the importance of U.S. interests and the nature of the emerging threat."[45]

From the outset, low-intensity war strategists understood that the success of the Reagan Doctrine in Central America required purging the "Vietnam syndrome" from the American psyche. The issue was addressed at the first Pentagon LIC conference at Fort McNair in Washington, D.C., when ABC *Nightline* anchor Ted Koppel chaired a panel on "how the government can engage the support of both the public and the media in combating low-intensity warfare." The classified Volume II of the military's *Joint Low-Intensity Conflict Project Final Report* contains a chapter entitled "The Need to Use Media Coverage and the Free Press to Further United States Operational Objectives."

Indeed, engineering a public consensus on its policy—winning the hearts and minds of the American people—was a critical adjunct to the administration's policy. Through a "Public Diplomacy" program, which included establishing executive-branch information bureaus to disseminate administration views, and the orchestrated use of rhetoric, disinformation, media manipulation, and intimidation of policy critics, the administration embarked upon an unremitting effort, in Secretary Weinberger's words, "to make our case at the bar of public opinion abroad and at home."[46]

The administration's use of "Public Diplomacy" to garner support for intervention in Nicaragua was coordinated at the highest levels of the U.S. government. On January 14, 1983, President Reagan signed National Security Decision Directive No. 77—"Management of Public Diplomacy Relative to National Security." Classified "Secret," NSDD-77 determined that "it is necessary to strengthen the organization, planning and coordination of the various aspects of public diplomacy of the United States Government relative to national security." The directive defined "Public Diplomacy" as "those actions of the U.S. Government designed to generate support for our national security objectives."[47] In April, NSDD-77 was distributed to the State Department, the DOD, the CIA, and the USIA for implementation.

A succession of institutional and public relations events followed. On April 27, Reagan gave a televised speech to a rare joint session of Congress to present his policies on Central America to the nation. In late May, the White House Outreach Working Group on Central America began operations under the direction of the president's director of public liaison, Faith Whittlesey. In July, the Office of Public Diplomacy on Latin America and the Caribbean initiated its activities in the State Department. In addition, on July 23, the president announced the formation of the bipartisan "Kissinger Commission" on Central America in a grandiose effort to foster bipartisan congressional support for his program.

These executive-branch offices assumed a central role in the administration's propaganda offensive on Nicaragua. The White House Outreach Working Group on Central America was chartered to "mobilize public opinion" and rally a vocal constituency of conservative interest groups behind the president's view that the spread of Communist revolution in Central America threatened the American way of life.[48] The Office of Public Diplomacy officially functioned as a domestic information agency, producing and distributing a stream of vituperative white papers and pamphlets on Nicaragua and sending staff members around the country to present the Reagan administration's case before hundreds of civic groups, Rotary Clubs, and university audiences. The work of the Kissinger Commission, aimed at an elite audience on Capitol Hill, was expected, according to classified NSC strategy papers, to "help build support for our long-term regional policy."[49]

All three organizations provided the institutional foundation for the administration's vociferous war of words against Nicaragua. Led by the president, U.S. official propaganda advanced four general myths: (1)

Nicaragua was the source of subversion in the region; (2) Nicaragua's military buildup was offensive in nature and portended an invasion of its neighbors; (3) the Sandinistas had transformed Nicaragua, in Reagan's words, into a "totalitarian dungeon"; and (4) that the United States was the "peacemaker" in the region and supported a negotiated settlement to the crisis.

These assertions served as the pillars of the administration's propaganda war; yet the available evidence contradicted all of them. While Reagan and his subordinates repeatedly accused the Sandinistas of "exporting revolution" to El Salvador, the CIA analyst responsible for tracking the flow of weapons in Central America, David MacMichael, charged that the administration had "systematically misrepresented Nicaraguan involvement in the supply of arms to Salvadoran guerrillas" to justify its efforts to overthrow the Nicaraguan government.[50] The oft-heard charge, advanced in one administration white paper after another, that Nicaragua's acquisition of Soviet arms was part of a master plan to conquer the rest of the region by force, was equally unfounded, according to a November 1984 CIA assessment: "The overall military buildup is primarily defensive-oriented, and much of the recent effort has been devoted to improving counter-insurgency capabilities."[51]

Moreover, reputable human rights monitors, such as Amnesty International and Americas Watch, challenged the administration's depiction of postrevolutionary Nicaragua as a "Central American Gulag."[52] So did the U.S. embassy in Managua. Embassy reports, for example, contradicted the president's claims that the Sandinistas had committed "genocide" against the Miskito Indians.[53]

Similarly, on the issue of religious persecution in Nicaragua—widely invoked by U.S. officials to bolster their verbal attacks on the Sandinista National Liberation Front (FSLN)—U.S. Ambassador Anthony Quainton sent a "confidential" cable to Washington on July 16, 1983, stating that "the evidence fails to demonstrate that the Sandinistas have followed a policy of anti-Semitism or have persecuted Jews solely because of their religion." Yet, four days later, the president told a White House Outreach Working Group audience that "the Sandinistas seem always to have been anti-Semitic. . . . After the Sandinista takeover, the remaining Jews were terrorized into leaving."[54]

Finally, the administration's assertion that it supported a peaceful resolution of the conflict strained credulity. To be sure, the administration paid lip service to the Contadora peace process led by the major

Latin American nations. Behind the scenes, however, the administration
blocked any agreement that would legitimize the Sandinista government. "We have effectively blocked Contadora Group efforts to impose
the second draft of the revised Contadora Act," proclaimed a classified
NSC background paper after the most promising Contadora treaty
initiative fell through in October 1984. Another "secret" briefing paper
prepared for Assistant Secretary of State Elliott Abrams a year later
summed up Washington's attitude toward Contadora: "Our interests
continue to be served by the process. Nevertheless, its collapse wouldn't
be a total disaster for U.S. policy."[55]

Through sheer rhetorical domination—with little regard for the
truth—Reagan officials attempted to set the parameters of national
debate over U.S. intervention in Nicaragua. The administration also
engaged in other, less-than-public efforts to manipulate public perceptions of reality in Central America. Under the supervision of the National Security Council, the Office of Public Policy on Latin America
funneled selected tidbits of classified information to favored journalists—particularly television reporters—as part of what one official characterized as a "vast psychological warfare operation" to manage the
media.[56] In an effort to silence public dissenters, the NSC ordered the
FBI to interrogate and intimidate critics of U.S. policy; in 1984 and
1985, FBI agents visited more than a hundred citizens who had traveled
to Nicaragua or attended public forums critical of the administration.
Similarly, at Customs, Americans returning from travels to Nicaragua
faced the prospect of harassment and the confiscation of books, personal
papers, and research materials.[57]

LOBBYING THE ELITE

A grass-roots movement of church, labor, student, and other concerned
citizens against U.S. intervention in Nicaragua, coupled with an inherent fear that Central America could become another Vietnam quag-
mire, undermined Reagan's efforts to rally public support for his policy.
Indeed, opinion polls consistently showed that 60 to 73 percent of the
American people opposed the president's efforts to overthrow the Sandinista government. Even the Kissinger Commission report, released
with great fanfare in January 1984, failed to generate public sympathy.
A Louis Harris poll taken the week after the report was released demonstrated that the majority of Americans soundly rejected every recom-
mendation in the commission's report.

Nevertheless, through the use of McCarthyite Red-baiting and illicit lobbying, the Reagan administration was able to erode the consensus in Congress against the war in Nicaragua. In speech after speech, the president cast those legislators who opposed his policy as supporters of godless Communists against the benevolent "democratic resistance." To bolster the official portrait of the contras as freedom fighters and make them more palatable to Congress, in June 1985 the administration organized a new civilian facade for their surrogate force. Two former members of the Sandinista government, Arturo Cruz and Alfonso Robelo, were combined with FDN leader Adolfo Calero to form the United Nicaraguan Opposition (UNO). And in October, the NSC's Lieutenant Colonel Oliver North met with UNO leaders to work on a political manifesto. As North recalled: "I said, 'Here is the U.S. Constitution. Read it.' "[58]

The administration also turned to high-profile public relations firms to project the new image of the contras and to lobby Congress to restore funding for CIA operations. Although federal laws prohibit U.S. officials from engaging in illicit lobbying campaigns, Reagan administration officials played a key role in planning and financing these activities.

In October 1985 the State Department's Office of Public Diplomacy signed a classified $274,000 contract with a Washington-based firm, International Business Communications (IBC), for services that included "arranging media events, interviews, and public appearances" for the contras and providing them with "points of contact" in the media and conservative public interest groups.[59] White House officials also collaborated with Carl Channell, head of the National Endowment for the Preservation of Liberty (NEPL) to plan a multimillion-dollar series of procontra television advertisements that targeted swing voters in Congress. North and White House Communications Adviser Patrick Buchanan held strategy sessions with Channell to plan his "Central American Freedom Program." North provided video footage for the commercials and personally participated in the NEPL's fund-raising events by giving speeches, writing letters, and meeting with potential donors. For those funders who gave significant amounts, North arranged a private meeting with the president.

The NEPL's sophisticated lobbying—illegal since it is registered as a nonprofit "educational" organization—contributed to the restoration of official aid to the contras. In June 1985, Congress authorized $27 million in "humanitarian assistance" and a year later voted to appropriate $100 million for full-scale CIA operations against the Sandinistas. "Your paid advertising and support of the president's program was critical to our success," Lieutenant Colonel North wrote to Channell in a "confidential" letter on August 15, 1985. "Your Central American Freedom Program is a vital link in the effort to forge a democratic outcome in Nicaragua," President Reagan informed Channell in a note dated February 21, 1986.

ILLEGALLY ARMING THE CONTRAS

These public lobbying efforts disguised a far more covert role played by the NEPL and IBC as principal domestic conduits for weapons to the contras during the moratorium on official U.S. aid. More than $2.2 million dollars of the money that North and President Reagan helped Channell raise was funneled into the NEPL's "toys" account—a secret slush fund for contra arms.[60] Much of the money was transferred to IBC, which, in turn, wired the money to a Swiss bank account established by North to secretly finance the continued purchase of weapons through an NSC-organized surrogate supply network set up in 1984. Into this account also flowed monies from friendly third countries such as Saudi Arabia, and millions of dollars from diverted profits from the secret sale of missiles to Iran.

At the behest of Oliver North, CIA Director Casey and other U.S. officials, "retired" covert intermediaries such as Major General Richard Secord and Major General John Singlaub used this money to purchase armaments in Europe and resupply the contras after Congress terminated aid in 1984. Known within the White House as "Project Democracy," these activities constituted the real covert war against Nicaragua—an international operation wholly outside the law and designed to be "plausibly denied" by official Washington. Despite the congressional ban, between October 1984 and October 1986 more than $50 million worth of arms—including rifles, ammunition, Claymore mines, mortars, and rockets—flowed to the contras through this clandestine mechanism.

But when the surrogate network was exposed in November 1986, it became the focus of a massive scandal, paralyzing and discrediting the Reagan presidency at home and abroad. As Congress investigated the events during televised hearings in the summer of 1987, it was evident that the imperial politics of the United States had come home to roost.

REAGAN'S DANGEROUS DOCTRINE

As the Iran-contra affair reached Watergate proportions in 1987, the future of the administration's undeclared war against the Sandinistas was put in doubt. Even as $100 million approved by the U.S. Congress began to flow to the contras and CIA advisers and Pentagon trainers returned to Central America en masse to plan and supervise renewed contra attacks on Nicaraguan villages, the scandal in Washington placed further contra aid in jeopardy.

The other components of President Reagan's low-intensity war, however, remained unaffected. The policy of economic destabilization continued to take a toll on Nicaragua's increasingly deteriorating economy. U.S. military maneuvers in Honduras continued unabated. And in May 1987, the administration renewed its high-pitched propaganda campaign in an effort to garner public support for more aid to the contras and to offset the impact of congressional hearings on the Iran-contra scandal.

The scandal dramatically revealed the high costs of the administration's low-intensity war doctrine on the political, legal, and moral standards of American society. It underscored Senator William Fulbright's observation, made during the Vietnam War, that "neither constitutional government nor democratic freedoms can survive indefinitely in a country chronically at war." Yet the revelations of crimes of state also demonstrated the lengths to which the president and his men were prepared to go to make the Reagan Doctrine a reality regardless of the political repercussions and regardless of the escalating cost to life and property in Nicaragua. Despite the scandal, and despite the continuing bloodshed, that commitment remained intact. "This Administration's support for the Nicaraguan freedom fighters . . . will not change," as President Reagan vowed in May 1987, and his administration would not "leave this situation to our successor unresolved."[61]

7

COUNTERINSURGENCY'S PROVING GROUND: LOW-INTENSITY WARFARE IN THE PHILIPPINES

WALDEN BELLO

For nearly a century, the Philippines has enjoyed the dubious distinction of serving as America's principal proving ground for the development and testing of strategies and tactics for low-intensity warfare. America's first major overseas LIC engagement, the Philippine Insurrection of 1899–1902, allowed the U.S. Army free rein to develop and test a variety of counterinsurgency tactics that are still emulated today. Fifty years later, in the early 1950s, the United States again used the Philippines as a counterinsurgency laboratory while leading the fight against the Communist-led Hukbalahaps ("Huks"). Today, the Pentagon's emerging strategy of low-intensity conflict is being battle-tested in the U.S.-guided war against the New People's Army (NPA).

When the United States replaced Spain as the colonial power in the Philippines in 1898, it was immediately confronted by a vigorous independence movement led by Emilio Aguinaldo. In attempting to subdue the rebellion, the U.S. Army drew on experiences gained during the Indian Wars of the post–Civil War era. However, the Philippine campaign posed a military challenge of rather greater magnitude than the Indian Wars. Instead of fighting several isolated campaigns against

The author would like to thank Erik Guyot for his invaluable assistance in preparing this chapter.

158

individual tribes, in the Philippines the U.S. Army was confronted with a nationwide resistance struggle waged by a politically unified government and Army. Also significant was the fact that the Philippines, though smaller than the American West, was far more complex in terms of the social terrain: the war had to be waged amid thickly settled areas whose populations were sympathetic to Aguinaldo's rebel forces.

In response to this challenge, the U.S. Army fought a brutal counterinsurgency campaign that in many respects anticipated the tactics employed in Indochina. To erode the rebels' base of support, vast areas were stripped of food supplies and thousands of civilians were forcibly resettled in fortified villages not unlike the "strategic hamlets" of Vietnam fame. In three years of bloody combat, an estimated 220,000 Filipinos died of combat or starvation.[1]

Today, nearly a century later, U.S. counterinsurgency experts are still studying the Philippine Insurrection for lessons that can be applied on the LIC battlefields of tomorrow. Thus, in a section on "populace and resources control" (PRC), the Army–Air Force Joint Low-Intensity Conflict Project (JLICP) concluded that brute force and calculated starvation can prove the cornerstones of an effective LIC strategy if one has the "political will" to employ them. As noted in the *JLICP Final Report*,

> The lesson learned from this experience is that military power can be effective against a guerrilla force which has the support of the population. Victory, however, required the political will to employ total control over the population and the government. This early American experience dramatically demonstrated a classic example of security/PRC. The insurgents were first separated from the population by strict security measures including resettlement, curfews, and an early forerunner of "free-fire" zones. The relocation of the populace, combined with food denial operations, resulted in defeat of the insurgency.[2]

PRC techniques of this sort were later employed in the Vietnam conflict, and can be seen today in U.S.-backed efforts to depopulate rebel-held areas of El Salvador (see Chapter 5).

In the Philippines, however, the emphasis has switched in recent years from an essentially military effort to one that stresses the primacy of political initiatives. This approach was first employed in the anti-Huk campaign of the 1950s, which now serves as a model for the struggle against the NPA. As suggested by Paul Wolfowitz of the U.S. Department of State in 1985: "An effective effort against the [NPA] insurgency requires far more than military means. The Philippine Armed Forces do not need any lectures from us on that score. In fact, one could say that they wrote the book on how to fight an insurgency successfully against the Huks in the 1950's."[3]

LESSONS FROM THE HUK CAMPAIGN

The "book" on counterinsurgency that Wolfowitz claims the Filipinos wrote was actually written, in large part, by Colonel Edward Geary Lansdale, a CIA operative with U.S. Air Force cover. Lansdale's mission was later described by former CIA Director Allen Dulles as "one of the first major attempts at secret warfare by the agency's covert operations department."[4] Colonel Lansdale arrived in the Philippines in September 1950. Less than two years later, the Huks had been subdued—not principally by decisive battlefield action, but rather by a strategy that combined the promise of political and economic reform with an elaborate intelligence and psychological warfare operation.

Coming on the scene at the high tide of the insurgency, when a rebel army of fifteen thousand had the U.S.-trained Armed Forces of the Philippines (AFP) on the run, Lansdale concluded that the "most urgent need was to construct a political base for supporting the fight. Without it, the Philippine Armed Forces would be model examples of applied military doctrine, but would go on losing."[5] Once a viable "political base" was established in Manila, it could be used "to mount a bold, imaginative, and popular campaign against the Huk guerrillas."[6] Reversing the traditional approach of using the military to protect civilian institutions, a "legitimate" government would in effect provide a shield behind which the military could be refashioned and sharpened. In line with this approach, Lansdale worked with his principal Filipino protégé—Secretary of National Defense Ramón Magsaysay—to build an effective political base. Their efforts ultimately met with success through two key initiatives: the "clean" congressional elections of 1951, and Magsaysay's program of "free land."

Under Lansdale's guidance, Magsaysay fielded Army and ROTC (Reserve Officers' Training Corps) units to patrol the polling booths in the 1951 voting, ensuring relatively honest elections (compared to the rigged and corrupt election of 1949). These elections helped restore the reputation of the Manila government, and also invested the military with a new image as the "defender" of democracy.

Magsaysay followed up this success with a promise of free land to Huk guerrillas who surrendered to the government, thus defusing the issue of land reform upon which the Huks' popularity had rested. By creating the impression that even dedicated Huks were abandoning the struggle and enlisting in the government effort, Magsaysay and Lansdale successfully eroded popular support for the rebels. In the face of a sophisticated and energetic public relations campaign offering the tantalizing prospect of government-donated land in Mindanao while also projecting a new image of the military as a defender of the democratic process against corrupt politicians, the Huks' ideological and political scaffolding—which rested largely on land hunger and antigovernment sentiment—soon fell apart. It was, in fact, a cheap victory, as only about five thousand Huks and their dependents (out of an estimated mass base of one million) were eventually settled in Mindanao.[7] As noted by David Sturtevant, an expert on peasant movements, "The [Huk] movement was not shattered by reforms; rather, it was shattered by the *promise* of reforms. That was enough."[8]

With the rebel base demoralized and the political initiative passing to the government, the reorganized Philippine military could seize the initiative on the battlefield. Indeed, under the strategy developed by Lansdale and the Joint U.S. Military Advisory Group (JUSMAG), political and ideological manipulation was given priority but was never meant to be a substitute for the purely military component of counterinsurgency. Following the capture of the Manila section of the Communist Party political bureau in October 1950, U.S.-advised intelligence officers conducted an aggressive effort to recruit informers, plant agents, and use defectors to penetrate and break the rest of the party structure and its military hierarchy. When the reformed Philippine Army launched its counteroffensive in 1951, large concentrations of Huks "became easy prey for encirclement and suppression" by newly formed, highly mobile battalion combat teams.[9] Those Huks who managed to retreat into the Sierra Madre mountain range subsequently found themselves hunted down by mobile units of the recently created Philippine Scout Rangers. By 1954, very little remained of the once formidable Huk insurgency.

In looking back at the anti-Huk campaign, U.S. counterinsurgency theorists point to two key lessons: the primacy of political initiatives to win popular support for the established government, and the use of aggressive small-unit tactics to engage and defeat the guerrillas on their own terrain (see Chapter 2). These techniques were soon to be applied in Vietnam, where Lansdale was posted in 1956. But while Lansdale's attempt to reproduce his successful Philippines strategy in Vietnam ultimately fell victim to the superior political and organizational capabilities of the National Liberation Front, U.S. strategists continue to extol the "lessons" of the anti-Huk campaign.

COPING WITH THE "MARCOS PROBLEM"

Thirty years after the defeat of the Huks, American officials concluded that the New People's Army—founded in 1969 to supplant the vanquished Huks—had developed into a formidable guerrilla threat. By the early 1980s, it was obvious that the brutal and corrupt dictatorship of Ferdinand Marcos was driving people into the hands of the NPA. Many U.S. analysts concluded from this that no real progress could be made in fighting the guerrillas so long as Marcos remained in power. But the situation was complicated by the fact that Marcos was a staunch U.S. ally, with strong support in both the White House and the Department of Defense.

In many ways, the relationship between Marcos and the United States resembled that between Washington and President Ngo Dinh Diem of South Vietnam. Though both strongmen were avowed allies of the United States and had an insatiable appetite for American military aid, they strongly resisted U.S. efforts to assume direct control of their armies—correctly sensing that this would result in a diminution of their hold over the officer corps. In both countries, the United States, swayed by the strong anti-Communist rhetoric of its clients, tolerated widespread corruption and inefficiency in the military until it became crystal clear that the insurgents were gaining the upper hand.

Following the imposition of martial law in 1972, the Nixon administration committed itself to the continued support of Marcos. Determined to retain U.S. possession of the key American military installations at Subic Bay and Clark Air Base, Nixon was unwilling to challenge Marcos so long as he regularly reassured Washington about continuing U.S. occupation of the bases. Thus, periodic U.S. endorsements of Marcos were accompanied by a 100 percent increase in military aid in 1972–75.[10] This stance was not fundamentally altered during the Carter administration: although the State Department issued some mild criticisms of human rights abuses in the Philippines, President Carter signed a new basing agreement that guaranteed Marcos $300 million in military aid and $200 million in economic support funds (ESF) for 1979–84. When President Reagan assumed the presidency, the human rights criticisms disappeared and an even more lucrative basing agreement was signed in 1983—one that provided Manila with $425 million in military aid and $475 million in ESF over five years.

By the early 1980s, the Armed Forces of the Philippines had become heavily dependent on U.S. military assistance. Thus, in 1984, U.S. aid represented up to 10.5 percent of the total defense budget. Indeed, the Pentagon claimed that U.S. assistance "provided funds for most of the force modernization programs [undertaken by the Philippines] over the past several years."[11] This provided Washington with a great potential for leverage in Manila, but this potential was not utilized until after the assassination of Benigno Aquino in 1983. That event shocked the world, but what was more shocking to the Reagan administration was the realization that the Marcos regime had lost what little political legitimacy it might once have possessed. The administration began a major reevaluation of American support for Manila, and one of the first manifestations of a more critical U.S. stance was a new assessment of the state of the insurgency.

Prior to the Aquino assassination, Pentagon officials had routinely accepted the Marcos regime's severely understated figures on NPA strength and popularity. In February 1984, however, a Defense Department official sounded the alarm bells in testimony before a congressional subcommittee. Using figures much closer to those employed by the NPA than those provided by Manila, James Kelly, deputy assistant secretary of defense for East Asian and Pacific affairs, informed the Asia–Pacific Affairs Subcommittee of the House Foreign Affairs Committee that ten thousand NPA guerrillas were active "in nearly all areas of the country," and that about one-fourth of all Philippine villages were "affected" by guerrilla activity. "We do not know how many noncombatant NPA supporters there are among the Filipino people," Kelly testified, "but NPA efforts to build more support in the countryside have been impressive."[12] By late 1985, the Pentagon was prepared to accept the accuracy of claims by the National Democratic Front (NDF)—the leftist political coalition to which the NPA belongs—that it had "influence" over 10 million of the Philippines' 55 million people.[13]

Marcos's severely underestimated estimates of NPA strength appalled U.S. officials, and, in a confidential policy paper issued later in 1984, it was suggested that:

> To impress upon President Marcos the seriousness with which we view the insurgency and the deplorable state of the Armed Forces to deal with it, we may need to provide private briefings for Marcos by a U.S. military intelligence team. This would be a sensitive undertaking. Marcos is not uninformed about the NPA threat or the deficiency of the AFP to deal with them. However, he is probably unwilling to admit either fully to the NPA threat or to the deficiencies of the AFP because to do so would be an indictment of his nearly twenty years of rule.[14]

At this point, it was clear to U.S. leaders that reform in Manila was essential. For the Pentagon, the reforms considered most essential were military, not political, in nature. The State Department, on the other hand, advocated a bolder, more overtly political strategy aimed at distancing the United States from Marcos and compelling him to make significant concessions to the elite Filipino opposition.

The massive urban demonstrations of 1983 and 1984—reflecting some degree of cooperation between the leftist, centrist, and rightist segments of the opposition—enabled a group of "pragmatists" at the State Department to come to the fore and exert considerable influence over the direction of U.S. policy. The leader of this group was Michael Armacost, who was appointed undersecretary of state for political affairs in the spring of 1984, following a stint in Manila as U.S. ambassador to the Philippines.

The pragmatists' strategy was not thought out in advance and then imposed on events, but instead was developed in response to the fluid situation in Manila. Nor was the overthrow of Marcos the immediate goal of their endeavors. Rather, it was to pressure him to open up the political system—to force him to share power with moderate elements of the opposition. "Ultimately," Armacost later explained, "our role was one of helping Marcos reach the right conclusions from events and developments."[15]

In essence, the State Department strategy represented a return to the policies of the anti-Huk campaign. For Edward Lansdale, the key U.S. objective at that time was a political one—the creation and deployment of a moderate "third force" between the corrupt Quirino administration and the Communist Huks. In 1984 and 1985, the State Department was groping toward a similar formula, hoping to outflank the left by creating a viable non-Communist opposition and then forcing Marcos to share power with it. The military dimension of counterinsurgency was not absent from the pragmatists' calculations, but political decompression was seen as a necessary condition for an effective military effort. As Wolfowitz explained in his congressional testimony, elections "can serve as the cornerstone of an effective counterinsurgency campaign by demonstrating the government's commitment to meeting the people's aspiration for a responsive leadership of their choice."[16]

The third-force strategy, however, did not receive active backing from other sectors of the U.S. government until a point of irreversible crisis was perceived in late 1985. Throughout 1984 and most of 1985, Washington's management of the "Marcos problem" evinced some of the same bureaucratic tensions that had plagued U.S. policy toward Diem. The State Department and the CIA had wanted to remove Diem, but the Defense Department—fearful of the destabilizing impact of such a development—was initially opposed to the power-sharing formula. The Pentagon was also reluctant to move decisively against Marcos. The Pentagon position was supported, moreover, by the president, who was reluctant to dump an old, trusted ally. Indeed, during an October 1984 preelection debate with Walter Mondale, Reagan strongly endorsed Marcos's rule, alleging that the alternative was "a large communist movement to take over the Philippines."[17]

But pressures to do something about the Marcos problem were growing too strong for even the president to resist. A loose "Inter-Agency Group" was set up in 1984 to review and modify U.S. strategy after Admiral William Crowe, Jr., the chief of the U.S. Pacific Command, returned from a visit to Manila with alarming information on the growth of the insurgency.[18] The result of this review was a new National Security Study Directive (NSSD) on U.S. policy toward the Philippines that was completed in November 1984 and adopted as policy in January 1985.[19] In many respects, this document represents a definitive expression of the emerging U.S. strategy for low-intensity warfare.

The NSSD was, in fact, an amalgam of prevailing U.S. views on the Philippines. Two key points were highlighted in the document. First, reflecting the position of the State Department, political reforms were described as urgently necessary. Most critical was "a more open political system that would offer a credible promise of democratic reform." Also vital were "a more open economic system that ends or substantially alters 'crony capitalism' and agricultural monopolies," along with "an effective military capable of carrying the fight to the communist insurgency while controlling abuses of its own power."[20] The NSSD's second key point reflected the president's and the Pentagon's reluctance to dump Marcos by affirming that the aforementioned reforms had to be implemented with Marcos in place. "The U.S.," it declared, "does not want to remove Marcos from power or to destabilize the GOP [Government of the Philippines]."[21] In the directive's now classic formulation of the "Marcos problem":

> While President Marcos at this stage is part of the problem, he is also necessarily part of the solution. We need to be able to work with him and to try to influence him through a well-orchestrated policy of incentives and disincentives to set the stage for a peaceful and eventual transition to a successor government.[22]

While reform at the top was the primary goal of the NSSD, the document also placed great emphasis on reform of the AFP. The specific reforms advocated by the Pentagon were designed to make the Philippine military a more effective counterinsurgency force. This process could not commence, however, without the "restoration of professional, apolitical leadership" at the highest levels of AFP management.[23] "It is obvious to all of us," said Richard Armitage, assistant secretary of defense for international security affairs, "that the people at the top have to be the ones that those down below can emulate. They can't be affected by habits of corruption."[24] In other words, Chief of Staff General Fabian C. Ver (who was indicted for allegedly planning the Aquino murder by a special investigating commission) and his clique of overstaying generals had to be removed.

The second major reform demanded by the Pentagon was a curb on the abuse of civilians by the military—a common practice that was seen in Washington as one of the main causes of the NPA's popularity. According to the NSSD, this was to be achieved both by tightening up on military discipline and by providing better pay to recruits so as to diminish the incentive to steal food and property from villagers. To further improve the image of the military, the NSSD called for stepped-up U.S. assistance to the AFP's civic action programs.[25]

Third, the Pentagon sought to reform the AFP's arms acquisition program. The Philippine government was to be discouraged from further purchases of jet fighters and other high-tech items for external defense, and encouraged instead to acquire practical counterinsurgency equipment. Armitage called the latter "move, shoot, and communicate items"—trucks, armored personnel carriers, helicopter spare parts, and field radios.[26] To cut down on corruption, U.S. aid would be transformed from commercial arms purchases financed through the Pentagon's Foreign Military Sales credit program to direct grants of equipment through the Military Assistance Program.

Fourth, and perhaps most critical, the Pentagon sought greater influence on the officer corps through a more active U.S. training program. Following a period of "neglect" during the 1970s, the Defense Department doubled the Philippines' allocation under the International Military Education and Training Program (IMET) to nearly $1.1 million in 1982. By 1986, the program had again doubled to $2.2 million, and entailed the training of about 460 Philippine personnel annually—most of whom were brought to military schools in the United States for instruction in civil-military operations, psychological warfare, and counterinsurgency. The NSSD envisioned an even more ambitious program, proposing to "assist in reestablishing training programs throughout the AFP, ranging from basic to advanced courses."[27]

Essentially, the Pentagon sought through this expanded training program to re-create the close intermilitary ties of the 1950s, which allowed Colonel Lansdale and other U.S. advisers to intervene in the day-to-day management of the anti-Huk counterinsurgency campaign. As one key Defense official noted:

> Most importantly, the program promotes rapport with the younger AFP officers who will be its future leaders. . . . If we are to have such special relationships among the future American and Philippine military leaders, we must invest in them now by providing opportunities for them to train and associate together.[28]

The Marcos military was not, of course, unaware of the strategic agenda of the training program. As a staff report evaluating IMET for the Philippine Command and General Staff College put it: "It is apparent that other than providing security assistance, IMET/P[hilippines] aims at gaining allies for the host country [i.e., the United States] in the guise of education and training packages."[29]

No neophtye in these matters, Marcos knew that acceding to the

Pentagon's proposed reforms would mean handing over substantial power to the United States—which would, in effect, be tantamount to digging his own grave. He was well aware of what had happened to President Diem after he gave the Americans a free hand in reorganizing the Vietnamese military. That such an Americanization of the AFP was the intended result of U.S.-sponsored reforms was also evident in the statements of Pentagon officials who often lapsed into the collective "we" when discussing the Philippine military, as in "We need more troop rotations." Or, as Armitage expressed it in his congressional testimony, "There is a certain frustration that we're not omnipotent and we can't do things our way."[30]

Pentagon pressure on the regime was incessant throughout 1984 and 1985, but, true to form, Marcos made promises of reform and never delivered on them. Instead, after engineering a whitewash in the Aquino murder trial, Marcos reinstated General Ver in early December 1985. Ver then proceeded to extend the terms of many retirable loyalist generals, offering the rationale that "the insurgency problem 'is so serious' that the expertise of older and mature generals are needed by the military establishment."[31]

The Pentagon's pressure for reforms did, however, have the effect of encouraging the emergence of the Reform the Armed Forces Movement (RAM), a network of disgruntled colonels and junior officers that spread throughout 1984 and 1985. The movement surfaced dramatically in the spring of 1985, when officers on review at the Philippine Military Academy stunned Marcos and the high command by distributing leaflets critical of the regime. These manifestos asserted that 70 percent of the officer corps backed RAM, whose objectives were described as the elimination of "boot-licking incompetents," the restoration of professionalism and esprit de corps, and the development of a "stronger, more motivated counterinsurgency force."

RAM members who were eventually to instigate the military revolt that ousted Marcos could only be encouraged by U.S. statements praising "a solid cadre of competent, patriotic officers in the AFP who have the determination to institute the necessary reforms and turn the NPA tide." Once RAM surfaced in 1985, Pentagon officials stepped up their public encouragement of the military reform movement. Overstaying generals were RAM's *bête noire,* and the movement's young officers could only take heart from Armitage's words of November 15, 1985:

Even the most brilliant operational plan is bound to fail without competent and credible leadership at all levels of the command structure. Now, more than ever, the Armed Forces must be led by officers of the highest professional standard and of the deepest loyalty to their country. Overstaying generals, who do not meet this criteria [sic], will stifle the emergence of new vigorous leadership and stifle the positive contributions of our security assistance program.[32]

SHOWDOWN

By mid-1985, with growing polarization between Marcos and the opposition and almost daily reports of NPA assaults on AFP units, the Reagan administration had passed from a period of uncertainty on how to resolve the Marcos problem to one of greater resolve. At a large interagency gathering at the National Defense University in late July, officials from the State Department, the Defense Department, and the intelligence agencies heard a panel recommend that "while the U.S. should not work for the overthrow of Marcos, it should take an open view about his removal from office."[33]

In October 1985, Senator Paul Laxalt of Nevada undertook his crucial journey to Manila as Reagan's emissary, carrying a toughly worded message for Marcos warning him to stop "screwing up" the counterinsurgency effort. On November 3, in response to mounting pressure from Washington, Marcos announced that he would hold presidential elections in early 1986 rather than in 1987, when the vote had originally been scheduled. Three days later, during a visit by former Assistant Secretary of State Richard Holbrooke, U.S. embassy Chargé d'Affaires Philip Kaplan assembled key leaders of the anti-Marcos political parties and, according to a confidential embassy cable, "emphasized the need for the opposition to get its act together given the limited time left before a campaign starts." Kaplan also noted that while the United States could not influence the date of voting, "what we can do—and are doing—is to press for free and fair elections."[34]

Such moves must be seen in the context of a concerted U.S. effort to prevent Marcos from conducting a blatantly fraudulent election. Given the widespread expectation that Marcos would use the AFP to steal the February 7 elections, Armitage's appeal of December 18, 1985, must have come across as virtually a call to the Philippine officer corps to disobey their commander in chief:

> The AFP would be faced with a supreme challenge during the electoral process. At stake would be nothing less than the credibility of the AFP and, in particular, the honor of its officer corps. The conduct of the Philippine military during this critical period would determine whether the AFP is, in fact, loyal to the constitution and a true pillar of support for the democratic process or whether the AFP is a more perverse entity, bent on a course which will accelerate the spiral of instability.[35]

By that point RAM members were "meeting with other sectors of the military, printing and distributing leaflets, and organizing 'prayer rallies' for soldiers to gather together and pray for clean elections."[36]

Despite considerable U.S. pressure, Marcos used his powers as supreme commander to prevent the victory of Corazon C. Aquino. But while millions of Filipinos took to the streets in protest, Mr. Reagan—still undecided on Marcos's fate—continued to hesitate, remarking that the elections had been marked by "fraud on both sides." Veteran diplomat Philip Habib was sent on a last-ditch effort to set up a "power-sharing arrangement" between Marcos and Aquino, but events in the Philippines could no longer be contained within the State Department formula of gradual political decompression.

On February 22, 1986, Defense Minister Juan Ponce Enrile, AFP Vice Chief of Staff Fidel Ramos, and two hundred officers and enlisted men belonging to RAM staged their daring mutiny in Manila. Hundreds of thousands of civilians, heeding the plea of Cardinal Jaime Sin, rushed to Camp Aguinaldo to protect the vastly outnumbered rebels. On February 23, the White House sent a decisive warning to Marcos not to use U.S.-supplied equipment to crush the rebels. Then, on February 24, Reagan finally decided to abandon his trusted ally and asked Marcos to step down. The next day, under cover of darkness, Marcos and his entourage were ferried by U.S. Air Force helicopters to Clark Air Base, and from there to exile in Hawaii.

Despite the bad feeling among Aquino forces created by Mr. Reagan's unwillingness to abandon Marcos until the eleventh hour, the State Department pragmatists knew that their full-court press on the regime for fair elections had contributed to a major tactical victory over the insurgents. Ironically, this had come about with the unexpected assistance of the left, which had frozen itself out of the anti-Marcos process by boycotting the 1986 elections. For some U.S. officials, it was 1951 all over again, when the AFP's presence had assured relatively clean elections and salvaged the legitimacy of the political system in the face of the advancing Huk insurgency. As one senior State Department witness summed it up in congressional hearings shortly after the political transition in Manila,

> The coming to power of the Aquino government constitutes a setback for the insurgency because:
> —The new government, in contrast to the previous government, enjoys widespread popular support.
> —The principal propaganda target of the communists, the Marcos regime, is gone.
> —The communist election boycott was repudiated by the majority of Filipinos by an even greater margin than during the 1984 national assembly elections.[37]

The third-force strategy had worked, at least temporarily. As a triumphant Armacost put it before foreign-service officers on April 23, 1986, "Our objective was . . . to encourage the democratic forces of the center, then consolidate the control by the middle and also win away the soft support of the NPA. So far, so good."[38]

A NEW BEGINNING?

As the dust settled, however, it gradually became clear that the situation was more complicated than such euphoric statements indicated. A government dominated by centrist elements had come to power and had seized the political initiative vis-à-vis the left. Yet, as events quickly made clear, there were two developments that could derail the U.S. stabilization plan: the presidential aspirations of Defense Minister Enrile, and President Aquino's declared policy of seeking "reconciliation" with the insurgents.

The most explosive issue in the immediate post-Marcos period was the conflict between Aquino and Enrile. Enrile, called an "old friend" by U.S. Secretary of Defense Caspar Weinberger, was regarded in Washington as an important asset in the U.S. effort to unite the still fragmented Philippine elite into a cohesive anti-insurgent bloc. As Armacost put it in 1986, "Enrile and [Fidel] Ramos are important as a bridge between the old regime and the new to help contain excessive zeal in dealing with the past."[39] Even more important, however, was Enrile's insistence on a hard-line approach to the insurgency—an outlook that accorded far more closely with Pentagon views than Aquino's more tolerant approach.

Enrile's presidential ambitions, however, prevented the new government from achieving a degree of political stability—Washington's principal goal at the time. While the United States was attempting to buttress the Aquino government, Enrile cultivated the support of conservative landowners and businessmen, and adroitly maneuvered himself to become a rallying point for elements of the old Marcos coalition that were in disarray following the February uprising. Enrile also stood in the way of a major Pentagon objective: the Philippine military's withdrawal from active politics in Manila, accompanied by a renewed commitment to the antiguerrilla struggle in the countryside. Following Marcos's departure, Enrile became the voice within the cabinet for officers who had been used to wielding great influence under the old regime and who were unwilling to surrender their political and economic advantages.

After months of debilitating conflict and persistent rumors of a coup, Aquino finally fired Enrile as defense minister in late November 1986. Although reluctant to see Enrile go, Washington expressed its "full support" for President Aquino throughout the crisis. Aquino was again given strong U.S. support two months later, during a military mutiny which resulted in the takeover of a Manila radio station by a few hundred soldiers. To warn the faction-ridden AFP against further attempts at destabilization, Armitage declared on March 17, 1987:

> Over the past year disaffected elements of the AFP disrupted the stability of the country by perpetrating a series of plots aimed at destabilizing the Aquino government. . . . Whatever their intentions, their actions threatened Philippine democracy and, to the extent that their actions added to the sense of instability, they unwittingly furthered the cause of their communist rivals. We categorically condemn any and all attempts to destabilize the legitimate government of the Republic of the Philippines.[40]

Yet the Reagan administration could not have been entirely displeased with the outcome of the Aquino-AFP tensions. For one thing, it provided Washington with greater leverage over Aquino—and thus

greater influence over the conduct of the counterinsurgency program—because she had sought, and received, explicit American backing during the showdown with Enrile. Equally positive from the
American point of view was the appointment of retired General Rafael
Ileto as defense minister to replace Enrile—a move that brought to
the top of the nation's military hierarchy a professional counterinsurgency expert who had founded the Philippine Scout Rangers and
worked with Colonel Lansdale to suppress the Huks in the early 1950s.
With Ileto as defense minister and Ramos as chief of staff, the military finally had the perfect team for a U.S.-directed counterinsurgency
campaign, since both were American-trained professionals with a reputation for incorruptibility.

More troublesome than the Aquino-AFP conflict from the Pentagon
point of view was the president's stated goal of seeking a peaceful
political settlement with the insurgents. Like her slain husband, Aquino
believed that by bringing the left into the parliamentary process she
could ultimately tame it. Pentagon officials, however, saw nothing but
danger and self-delusion in such arrangements. Thus, skepticism—if not
outright disagreement—marked the public U.S. response to Aquino's
peace initiative. "As a general proposition," Armitage declared,

> we support any program that would reduce bloodshed and eliminate the
> prospect of Filipinos killing each other. However, the continuing brutal
> attacks by the NPA and the [Communist Party's] continuing adherence to
> the doctrine of armed struggle leaves little doubt that, at the end of the day,
> military action will be required to defeat the insurgency.[41]

In less diplomatic terms, another U.S. official asserted shortly after the
preliminary negotiations with the rebels had commenced in August
1986, "She had to make the [peace] effort and she has made it and now
it's time to move to the next step."[42]

In this instance, the Pentagon found itself backing the hard-liners
within the military and opposing key civilian officials in the Aquino
cabinet. With such powerful forces arrayed against a cease-fire, it was
surprising that even a sixty-day temporary cessation of hostilities was
negotiated in November 1986. What was not surprising, however, was
that the cease-fire was abandoned after the sixty-day period. More than
a month after the collapse of the cease-fire, Armitage issued his strongest
attack yet on the proponents of a peaceful settlement:

As with the Marcos regime before it, the Aquino government has also regrettably failed to develop a comprehensive counterinsurgency plan that integrates military, political, economic, and social programs. Marcos erroneously relied exclusively on military action. Some members of the Aquino administration believe that they can rely almost exclusively on symbolic political acts to cure the insurgency. They continue to cling to the forlorn hope that the insurgents will fade from the scene and that coordinated civil and military action will not be necessary.[43]

A week later, perhaps not coincidentally, President Aquino beat the drums of war at a speech at the Philippine Military Academy. "The answer to the terrorism of the left and the right," she avowed, "is not social and economic reform but police and military action." Aquino concluded her talk with a plea for "a string of honorable military victories."[44]

The government's affirmation of the military option and the installation of key professionals in the AFP leadership could not, however, disguise the fact that significant obstacles still stood in the way of the U.S. plan to convert the Philippine military—now known as the New Armed Forces of the Philippines (NAFP)—into an efficient counterinsurgency force.

To begin with, pro-Marcos or pro-Enrile officers remained in key positions, unreconciled to the new politics and hardly satisfied with Aquino's concessions. To maintain the military's fragile unity, NAFP chief of staff Ramos jettisoned many proposed reforms that would have threatened the interests of influential military sectors. Thus, no effort was made to cut down the bloated size of the armed forces in order to make them an effective counterinsurgency force, as the United States desired. Moreover, mutinous troops were generally treated with kid gloves; for instance, the rebel troops that occupied the Manila Hotel in an unsuccessful effort at destabilization in July 1986 were pardoned after performing thirty push-ups!

Furthermore, there was little change in the attitudes and morale of the bulk of NAFP units in the countryside. As Armitage noted, "The majority of the NAFP that is stationed far from Manila . . . did not share to the same degree in the revolutionary events. The excitement and euphoria, which are palpable in Manila, are much diluted in the provinces where soldiers must worry about basic needs and, indeed, survival."[45]

Factionalism, poor equipment, politicization, and low morale led newly installed Defense Minister Ileto to remark in early February 1987: "Before I got into this job, I thought it would take about a year or two to reform the military, unite everybody, and weed out the bad ones. Now I'm convinced it will take 20 years—a generation."[46] The U.S. National Security Council reportedly echoed similar frustration in a 1987 assessment of the military that concluded that the AFP still lacked "the unity, morale, equipment, and level of professionalism needed for a nationwide push against the rebels and . . . an all-out military option would not succeed at the moment."[47]

Washington's call for a counterinsurgency campaign that integrates military with political and economic initiatives has generally found little resonance in the Armed Forces of the Philippines. Firepower and repression continue to be the military's basic approach to the conflict, with the military command deploying more combat battalions against the NPA and Muslim secessionists in 1986 than in 1985, Marcos's last year in office. (With the redeployment of units formerly stationed in Metropolitan Manila for presidential security, NAFP battalions in the countryside rose from fifty-six to around sixty-seven.[48]) In some areas, including Cagayan, Negros, and Davao, the Army launched major new counterinsurgency campaigns that entailed air strikes, food blockades, resettlement programs, and torture—a grim reminder to the peasantry that there was nothing new about the New Armed Forces of the Philippines.[49]

Indeed, in some respects, the situation had worsened since the ouster of Marcos. Particularly troubling is the emergence of armed vigilante groups which seek to purge communities of NPA and Communist Party (CPP) sympathizers. Most of these groups, such as the notorious "Alsa Masa" ("Masses, Arise") organization in Davao City, appear to have been set up or actively encouraged by the military.[50] Many suspected leftists have been tortured and assassinated by such groups, leading alarmed observers to view their emergence as the prelude to the "Salvadoranization" or "Guatemalanization" of the counterinsurgency campaign—alluding to the conspicuous role of right-wing "death squads" in those tortured nations.

Clearly, the rise of vigilante groups in the Philippines poses some critical questions for U.S. policy-makers. In El Salvador, military-backed "death squads" have so discredited the Army and the government that they have aided in the spread of insurgency rather than its containment.

A similar situation could arise in the Philippines: if the present government fails to curb these groups, the legitimacy and popularity of Aquino—America's key weapon in the struggle against the insurgents— could very well erode as vigilante abuse and terror spread. "We have to be very careful about this one," a senior State Department official observed in June 1987 when asked about the Filipino vigilantes. "I mean some of this is fine as long as it is, you know, kept under control so to speak." But, given the risk of uncontrolled violence, "one has to be careful about such groups."[51]

PROSPECTS FOR U.S. INTERVENTION

At this point, the Philippines have all the ingredients for a deepening U.S. role in counterinsurgency: a strategic location housing important U.S. military bases; a relatively potent Marxist insurgency; and an inept military establishment. In the short run, however, U.S. involvement is likely to develop along the lines laid out in the 1984 National Security Study Directive, with an emphasis on strategic advice, training, military assistance, and logistical support. Such an approach would, of course, be wholly consistent with the broad outlines of current American LIC doctrine as spelled out in Chapter 3.

Strategic advice: On the advisory level, U.S. strategists are seeking to forge a coherent response to the NPA's growing military prowess and archipelago-wide reach. One hint of the emerging U.S.-NAFP strategy is found in a recent intelligence assessment suggesting that "the nation-wide spread of the CPP/NPA is vulnerable to a region-by-region [antiguerrilla] campaign since it has thinly overextended itself and is not capable of reinforcing or putting up a stand on that basis."[52] According to one report, the Pentagon has advised that military firepower be concentrated on a single island in a "decisive show of force against the insurgents." Reportedly, the island under consideration for such a drive is Negros, where the NPA has experienced a rapid rate of growth in recent years.[53]

This approach may have some appeal to strategists in Washington, but reveals the Pentagon's continuing inability to understand a fundamental characteristic of the insurgency: that it has been carried out by an organizationally decentralized force whose units are expected to be entirely self-reliant. Hence, isolating Negros will not hamper NPA operations in the rest of the archipelago. But the NPA's most likely response—stepped-up attacks in other parts of the Philippines—will prevent the NAFP from concentrating its resources on Negros for any length of time.

Civic action: To fortify the NAFP's civic-action capabilities, the Pentagon is providing bulldozers and other heavy equipment to upgrade its engineering battalions. According to Armitage, the NAFP could "make a substantial contribution to the government's efforts to revitalize the rural economy if it had the resources to procure the engineering equipment that would be used to build bridges and roads."[54] The United States is also expected to enlarge the civic-action component of joint U.S.-Philippine military exercises, including the annual "Tangent Flash" maneuver, and to step up civic-action operations around U.S. military bases in order to defuse the strong NPA presence in these areas.

Psychological operations: Another area where increased U.S. involvement is likely is in psychological and political warfare. President Reagan has reportedly authorized stepped-up clandestine CIA operations against the left in the Philippines, and has authorized a $10 million allocation to the NAFP for enhanced intelligence-gathering operations.[55] In addition, the CIA has beefed up its station in Manila, adding 12 more agents to its current roster of 115 operatives. The rise of vigilante groups is suspected by many Filipinos to be an example of CIA-inspired psychological warfare. And while there is no proof yet of direct U.S. aid for the vigilantes, "fear that such outside support is available has been stoked by signs that the vigilante organizations are coordinated on a nationwide scale."[56]

As in El Salvador, U.S. counterinsurgency efforts in the Philippines also entail stepped-up support for propaganda operations of various sorts. As a model of counterrevolutionary propaganda, Pentagon officials cite the activities of General Rodolfo Biazon when he was still in Davao as commander of the of the 3rd Marine Brigade. Through "dialogue sessions," films, and propaganda depicting the NPA as another Khmer Rouge, Biazon sought to prevent linkages between "middle forces" and the left. These propaganda efforts were aided, moreover, by the local

office of the U.S. Information Agency.[57] Now superintendent of the
Philippine Military Academy, Biazon is training a new generation of
officers in these and other counterinsurgency techniques.[58]

The activities of the American-Asian Free Labor Institute
(AAFLI)—an arm of the AFL-CIO—also constitute a part of U.S.
psychological and propaganda operations. According to AAFLI Director
Charles Grey, its programs "have evolved beyond traditional trade union
activities" to encompass developmental and organization activities in
"just those areas where the communists are most active, such as Mindanao, Negros, Iloilo, and Cebu."[59] In 1985, the AAFLI spent up to
$4 million on such programs in the Philippines, with the bulk of these
funds coming from the National Endowment for Democracy, a private
agency created by Congress that has supported right-wing causes around
the world.

Military assistance: Politics and propaganda are vital, but at the end of
the day (to paraphrase Armitage) the NPA will have to be defeated in
the field of battle. In 1986, the U.S. Congress removed Marcos-era
restrictions on sales of "lethal equipment" to the Philippine military.
Over the course of the year, $64 million—the highest level of U.S.
security assistance in the last five years—reached the Philippines.[60]

Most of the equipment provided through this channel was not heavy
weapons or sophisticated aircraft, but items that would enable the AFP
to "move, shoot, and communicate" in counterguerrilla operations. Particular stress was placed on ground and air mobility. The 1986 aid plan
included 665 military trucks, 10 refurbished UH-1 "Huey" helicopters,
and spare parts for the large complement of counterinsurgency aircraft
now in the NAFP inventory. (The Philippine Army currently possesses
about 45 Bell UH-1 helicopters, while the Air Force possesses some 60
UH-1s plus 12 AC-47 gunships, 18 OV-10 "Bronco" counterinsurgency
aircraft, and 32 T-28D ground-support planes).[61] The United States is
also supplying large quantities of small arms, ammunition, and other
basic combat gear.

In line with prevailing LIC doctrine, U.S. assistance is intended to
improve the NAFP's ability to defeat the guerrillas on their own, without conspicuous U.S. involvement. However, should it become necessary in Washington's view to stiffen Philippine forces with American
personnel, there are a variety of specialized U.S. counterinsurgency
capabilities *in the area* that could be used for this purpose. Specifically,

there are a number of special operations units at Clark Air Base and Subic Bay Naval Base.

U.S. assets at Clark currently include the MC-130E "Combat Talon" aircraft of the Air Force Special Operations Squadron. These planes are capable of clandestine, day and night infiltration, exfiltration, and reconnaissance in hostile territory (see Chapter 4). In the 1960s, Clark-based aircraft occasionally provided reconnaissance for AFP troops hunting down guerrillas. And while there have been no confirmed reports of these craft being employed in such operations in the current period, it is significant to note that two MC-130s were hit by small-arms fire while on "routine low altitude training missions" in 1985.[62]

Another U.S. counterinsurgency "asset" is the Navy SEAL team currently based at Subic Bay. The SEALs regularly exercise with Filipino units, and have reportedly provided training to NAFP counterinsurgency forces in antiguerrilla "riverine" operations. That the SEALs are less than detached in their attitude toward the current insurgency was revealed by one patrol boat pilot formerly posted at Subic Bay:

> We had a number of operations cancelled because of NPA guerrilla activity. We would carry live ammo on board depending on how far we were going and what intelligence told us. There was often a good chance that we'd take fire from the NPA's.

He added that "these PBR [river patrol] boats would be perfect for the Philippines if we have to go back there again."[63]

Clearly, Washington would much prefer that the NAFP—armed and aided as necessary by the United States—take full responsibility for the antiguerrilla struggle in the Philippines. Should the NAFP prove unequal to this task, U.S. leaders would face an agonizing and difficult choice: while direct U.S. military intervention in the Philippines would undoubtedly provoke widespread opposition in both countries, it is hard to imagine any future U.S. leader acceding to a Communist takeover in such a large and strategically located country—and one which has historically been viewed as a special preserve of the United States. If, therefore, the NPA gains strength in the years ahead and Cory Aquino is unable to wield effective control over the military, more direct forms of U.S. intervention—both political and military—must be considered highly likely. The degree and nature of U.S. involvement will largely depend, therefore, on the course of events in Manila itself.

THE STRATEGIC OUTLOOK

The distinctive characteristic of America's LIC experience in the Philippines has been its emphasis on political and ideological manipulation. Often referred to as the "third-force" strategy, this approach rests on the emergence and promotion of a populist, reformist leader; the advocacy of fair elections as a means of defusing popular pressures; the cultivation of the traditionally pro-Western middle strata; and stress on America's record as a "supporter" of democratization.

In the early 1950s and again in 1985–86, key U.S. officials were instrumental in encouraging the growth of a centrist alternative to a corrupt right-wing regime on one hand and the revolutionary left on the other. Corazon Aquino certainly is no U.S. puppet, and her ascendancy cannot be traced solely to U.S. moves; nevertheless, her rise to power would not have occurred without the U.S. pressure on Marcos to open up the political system and hold fair elections. American officials may have been surprised by the chain of events to which their acts contributed, but one thing is certain: the pragmatist faction of the U.S. foreign policy bureaucracy believed that Cory Aquino and the "democratic center" she represents is the most potent weapon that America wields in its continuing struggle against the insurgent left.

Strip the revolutionary movement of its legitimacy and initiative, then supplement this political-ideological offensive with military action: this has been the core of U.S. counterinsurgency strategy in the Philippines. Even when focused on the military realm, the main thrust of this strategy has been the manipulation of images: the old visage of an Army prone to abuses and corruption would be replaced by an image of a "new" Army committed to civic action. True, the honing of traditional military skills has not beeen neglected. But rather than enlarge the Army and provide it with massive firepower, as was the case in Vietnam, here the Pentagon has emphasized "streamlining" the AFP into an effective, modern counterguerrilla Army.

How well will this strategy perform in the years ahead? For now, it appears to be meeting with some degree of success. The combination of Cory Aquino's Joan of Arc image, the pro-American stance of the middle class, and the U.S. image as a pillar of democratic restoration has proven to be a very powerful force indeed. In 1985, the leftist National Democratic Front exuded massive political confidence and appeared to hold the political initiative; now, only a few years later, Aquino has the political and moral initiative while the left is on the defensive, struggling to counter both the weariness of war and the evident appeal of Aquino's reformist message.

There are, however, limits to the effectiveness of political and ideological manipulation. Aside from the coming of age of new generations of Filipinos who do not share the pro-U.S. attitudes of their parents, there are other factors at work that make a repeat of the 1950s counterinsurgency success unlikely.

To begin with, today's generation of insurgents have proved to be far more sophisticated practitioners of guerrilla warfare than were the Huks. They have patiently rooted themselves in peasant and working-class populations, and have relied primarily on political organizing and ideological persuasion rather than on military means to expand their influence. Now a political force in almost all areas of the Philippines, the NPA continues to enjoy an infrastructure of support that reformist promises and NAFP assaults will find difficult to destroy. The counterinsurgency effort has also suffered from the fact that the government has substituted a nebulous "land reform" decree for an effective land transfer program—a matter of vital concern to the 70 percent of the population that lives in the countryside and constitutes the largest reservoir of potential support for the NPA.

Secondly, unlike the AFP of the 1950s, today's military establishment is proving very difficult to reform. Under Marcos, the Army became the principal instrument of political control; in return for their loyalty, the dictator provided senior officers with a host of economic privileges. Today, as President Aquino and the Reagan administration have discovered, the military elite will not easily relinquish its prerogatives—and until that occurs, the image of a reformed military bowing to civilian authority will be difficult to sell.

Finally, the economic situation is very different from the 1950s, both in the United States and in the Philippines. The U.S. budget deficit will make it very difficult for the Department of Defense to obtain the funds it seeks for the NAFP. In Fiscal 1987, the administration's $100 million military aid request for the Philippines was cut in half by congressional budget cutters seeking to reduce the national deficit. Nor is the Philippine economy in any position to pick up the slack. Unlike the 1950s, when industry was growing by some 12 percent a year, today the Philippines is saddled with a $28 billion debt and is gripped by persistent stagnation. Hence, the economic underpinning for a successful counterinsurgency program simply does not exist. Indeed, the economic crisis can only exacerbate demands for a fundamental overhaul of property relations—especially on the part of the estimated 40 percent of the Philippine work force that is either unemployed or underemployed.

In sum, political and ideological manipulation may register some temporary successes in containing the insurgency, but how lasting these gains will prove to be is open to question. Provided they can keep their head above water in the face of the powerful moral-political tide of Cory Aquino's "Yellow Revolution," the left is likely to find that time is on its side. This being the case, the United States may find it more and more difficult to avoid direct involvement in the counterinsurgency struggle. And while Washington may find it expedient to eschew intervention in other LIC battlefields, it is hard to imagine that U.S. policymakers—no matter which party is in control of the White House—will countenance the ascendancy of a Marxist guerrilla army in the Philippines.

AFGHANISTAN:
SOVIET INTERVENTION,
AFGHAN RESISTANCE,
AND THE AMERICAN ROLE

SELIG S. HARRISON

AFGHANISTAN, once one of the world's most isolated, untouched societies, has been brutally transformed by the Soviet occupation into a superpower military testing ground. In other countries where the Reagan Doctrine has been applied, both superpowers have been involved by proxy. In the Afghan conflict, American-backed resistance fighters have been pitted not only against a local Marxist regime, as in Nicaragua, but also against Soviet forces. The Afghan experience thus provides a unique—and macabre—case study of what happens when American low-intensity warfare doctrine and Soviet counterinsurgency strategy meet in a Third World setting. At the same time, the Afghan case underlines the built-in danger that pursuit of the Reagan Doctrine can lead to a direct Soviet-American confrontation.

For the Soviet Union, the Afghan struggle is a "bleeding wound," as Premier Gorbachev has formally acknowledged.[1] The Soviet military presence has steadily grown since the war began in 1979, reaching a total of 120,000 men in 1987, and Soviet forces have increasingly taken over the brunt of the fighting from their Afghan allies. Afghanistan, with its social and political fragmentation and its location adjacent to Soviet territory, has offered a relatively favorable testing ground for Soviet counterinsurgency warfare. Nevertheless, while the Soviet-supported Democratic Republic of Afghanistan (DRA) is solidly entrenched in Kabul and several other urban enclaves, the Communist regime controlled at most eight thousand out of twenty-six thousand rural villages in 1986.[2] Moscow is not likely to consolidate a durable DRA infrastructure so long as Afghan resistance groups can continue to use neighboring Pakistan as a conduit for American military aid and can operate base camps there. With each passing year, the Soviet Union will be under growing pressure to upgrade its military presence and to carry the war into Pakistani territory, risking American intervention.

For the United States, the Afghan war has led to the largest covert operation by the Central Intelligence Agency since the Vietnam period. Congressional appropriations for aid to the resistance totaled some $750 million from 1980 to 1986, five times more than the amount of the more publicized aid program for the Nicaraguan contras,[3] and reportedly jumped to $630 million for FY1987 alone.[4] As the Afghan stalemate has intensified, so have pressures in the United States for a more wide-ranging American commitment to the Afghan resistance and to the defense of Pakistan. Under its 1959 mutual security agreement with Islamabad, the United States is required to "take such appropriate action, including the use of armed forces, as may be mutually agreed upon" in the event of armed Communist aggression.[5]

Western perceptions of the Afghan war have generally focused on the inconclusive character of the military struggle while ignoring the equally important reality of a political stalemate. In this simplistic imagery, there is a sharp dichotomy between an illegitimate Kabul regime, unable to establish its writ beyond the capital, and an alternative focus of legitimacy collectively provided by the resistance fighters, who are seen as controlling most of the country's land area. It is true that the Kabul regime does not have a firm grip on much of the countryside, but neither does the resistance. In reality, most of Afghanistan, now as in past decades and centuries, is governed by freewheeling local tribal and ethnic warlords.

While most of these warlords would like to get Soviet forces out of their areas and out of Afghanistan, relatively few of them are firmly committed to the resistance. Some of them are opportunists who take payoffs from both sides, smuggle narcotics, and sell weapons in the black market. Others cooperate with one or another of the resistance factions but are constrained by fear of Soviet reprisals. Still others, smaller in number, are trying to come to terms with the Communist regime but are afraid that helping Kabul would bring punishment from the resistance. For most villages, trapped between increasingly efficient Soviet-cum-Afghan forces and increasingly well-equipped resistance fighters, the issue is simply how to survive.

PRELUDE TO CONFLICT

Until its destruction in 1973, the monarchy had provided the sole focus of political legitimacy and authority in Afghanistan for more than three centuries. The Afghan state was just barely a state. It was loosely superimposed atop a decentralized polity in which separate ethnic and tribal communities paid obeisance to Kabul only so long as it accorded them substantial autonomy.

From the start, this polity has been torn by endemic tensions between the largest ethnic group, the Pashtuns, and a variety of conquered ethnic minorities. The Pashtuns have been increasingly unable to assert the position of unchallengeable dominance to which they feel entitled as the "true" Afghans. Non-Pashtuns constituted at least 35 percent of the population of Afghanistan prior to the Soviet occupation—possibly as much as 45 percent—and their relative strength has grown in the wake of the large-scale Pashtun refugee movement to Pakistan.

The number of politicized Afghans who wanted to create a centralized state has always been minuscule in relation to the total population. During the decades immediately preceding the establishment of Communist rule in 1978, this politicized elite consisted of three distinct groups: Western-oriented intellectuals, who made up the largest segment; Soviet-oriented Communist factions; and Islamic fundamentalist elements with Moslem Brotherhood links in the Persian Gulf and the Middle East. None of these groups had substantial independent organizational networks in the countryside. They were all equally dependent on alliances with the local tribal and ethnic leaders who held the real power then and who continue to hold the real power in Afghanistan today.

The concept of legitimacy has little relevance to the present struggle against the backdrop of recent Afghan political history. The destruction of the monarchy in 1973 left a political vacuum in which no consensus existed concerning the future of the Afghan polity, and no single organized group could make a more clear-cut claim of greater legitimacy than another. Neither the Communists nor the Islamic fundamentalists claimed more than a few thousand members each when the monarchy fell. But even a few thousand disciplined, highly motivated members loomed large in what was such a limited political universe.

In addition to posing ideological challenges to the Western-oriented elite, the Communist and fundamentalist movements were vehicles of social protest by disadvantaged elements of the Afghan populace. The Parcham (Flag) Communist faction represented many of those in the detribalized Kabul intelligentsia and bureaucracy who felt shut out of power by the narrow dynastic in-group that dominated both the monarchy and the republic set up in 1973 by former King Zahir Shah's jealous cousin, the late Mohammed Daud Khan. The rival Khalq (Masses) faction had more of a Pashtun tribal base. By contrast, the strongest fundamentalist cadres were organized in ethnic minority areas, notably the predominantly Tajik Pansjer Valley.

The intractability of the political stalemate in Afghanistan today can only be understood if one recognizes that the present conflict began as a civil war and continues to have some of the aspects of one. The fall of the monarchy opened the way for a polarization of Afghan political life between the Communists at one extreme and the Islamic fundamentalists at the other, both of them opposed to the ineffectual, corrupt Daud Khan republic. When the fundamentalists fled to Pakistan to escape Daud's repression, the Communists had a clear field to exploit popular dissatisfaction with the Daud regime, which lacked the legitimacy of the monarchy but was nonetheless dominated by a pro-Daud monarchist coterie.

Many Afghans initially welcomed the Communist revolution of April 1978. They hailed the end of royal family dominance and hoped that the Communists would bring rapid modernization. Communist leader Hafizullah Amin mixed his Marxism with a militant Pashtun nationalism that won applause in the tribal areas. But Amin gradually alienated many of the new regime's non-Communist sympathizers with his brutality and his overzealous reforms. Amin sought to centralize the country overnight, riding roughshod over the autonomy traditionally enjoyed by both the Pashtun tribes and by nontribal ethnic minorities. His attempts to replace established local power structures with a Communist administrative network aroused the armed resistance that helped to set the stage for the Soviet occupation. Amin also alienated businessmen, merchants, and small and medium-sized landowners with his doctrinaire land-reform and economic policies. Most important, he directly challenged the power and prerogatives of Islamic dignitaries, provoking the active intervention of Islamic fundamentalist groups throughout the Persian Gulf and the Middle East in support of the nascent anti-Communist insurgency.

Most Afghans today feel that the Communist leaders who succeeded Amin have lost their patriotic credentials by collaborating with the Soviet occupation forces. At the same time, it would be a mistake to think of the Afghan struggle in black-and-white terms as one between the Russians on one side and all Afghans on the other. The essence of the Afghan dilemma lies in the fact that a significant minority of Afghans either support or tolerate the Communist regime.

SOVIET STRATEGY:
THE POLITICAL DIMENSION

In implementing its counterinsurgency strategy both politically and militarily, Moscow can rely first and foremost on the Afghan Communist Party, known as the People's Democratic Party (PDPA). Founded in 1965, the PDPA split into separate Parcham and Khalq organizations until it was reunited under Soviet pressure in 1976. Communist sources claim that the party membership rose from its 1978 level of some 5,000 to 150,000 in 1986. A U.S. government intelligence analyst contends that 75,000 would be a more accurate number but acknowledges, in any case, that "the P.D.P.A. is unmistakably growing. Expansion of membership among peasants and soldiers has meant a smaller pool of capable, committed activists for the resistance to draw on."[6]

Based on a visit to Kabul in 1984 and other sources, my own estimate is that the party has between 25,000 and 35,000 hard-core activists, allowing for the fact that many new recruits are ideologically unreliable job seekers. But even 25,000 reliable Afghan activists is a crucial asset for the Russians in holding together their extensive Afghan administrative and military network. Moreover, the number of Communist true believers is continually enlarged by the return of at least 20,000 Afghan youths who have been sent to the Soviet Union for training. The number of Afghans on the Soviet-subsidized payroll of the Kabul regime appears to be some 350,000, including about 60,000 in the Army, another 75,000 in various paramilitary forces, and at least 25,000 in the secret police. Communist activists have been installed in key positions of control throughout the DRA hierarchy, with 64 percent of the party membership concentrated in military and paramilitary command posts.[7]

During numerous conversations in Kabul I was reminded that dedication and a patriotic self-image are not a monopoly of the resistance fighters. The Afghan Communists see themselves as nationalists and modernizers carrying forward the abortive modernization effort launched by the reformist King Amanullah from 1919 to 1929. They rationalize their collaboration with the Russians as the only way available to consolidate their revolution in the face of foreign "interference." As German journalist Andreas Kohlschutter of *Die Zeit* reported after a visit to Kabul, the commitment of the Communists to rapid modernization enables them to win a grudging tolerance from many members of "the modern-minded middle class, who feel trapped between two fires: the Russians and fanatic Muslims opposed to social reforms."[8] Confronted with a choice between the Communists and the Islamic fundamentalist leaders of the major resistance groups, such Afghans simply sit on the sidelines, acquiescing in the Communist regime despite their distaste for the Soviet occupation. In Kabul I found a widespread ambivalence toward the post-1980 Communist leaders, who are often seen as "moderates" trying to live down Amin's extremist mistakes.

In contrast to the excesses of the Amin period, post-1980 Communist leaders have pursued soft-line policies designed to undercut the insurgency. In particular, Kabul has now adopted a system of local government consciously structured to avoid a collision with grass-roots tribal and ethnic elites. On paper, at least, the tribes as such have representation in local government machinery in accordance with their numerical strength. The Communist Party promises not to run candidates for local bodies below the level of the *woleswali*, or district, roughly equivalent to several counties in the U.S., which will give the tribes de facto autonomy if the promise is kept.

Kabul makes an unabashed appeal to tribal self-interest, arguing that participation in the emerging local government setup will bring economic benefits and political rewards while a boycott will lead to punishment. As an incentive for tribal participation, Kabul pays salaries to tribal leaders for local governmental tasks and turns over central government economic development outlays directly to tribal-dominated local bodies. These financial inducements within the formal governmental framework are supplemented by personal payoffs and economic largesse to politically cooperative local power brokers. Conversely, tribal groups that refuse to join the new local bodies are subject to a variety of reprisals. The ubiquitous Khad, or secret police, systematically uses governmental authority to exploit ancient internecine tribal feuds. For example, if a tribe in one district refuses to join, pressure is applied by giving authority over the district in question to the rival group next door. In cases where a locality not only seeks to remain neutral but actively helps the resistance, Soviet or DRA troops often engage in punitive military action. The most horrendous of such cases, reminiscent of the My Lai tragedy in Vietnam, have been marked by the wholesale depopulation of clusters of villages, including the destruction of crops and livestock.

Apart from its offers of local autonomy, the DRA has also sought to moderate the image of monolithic Communist rule at the national level associated with Amin by emphasizing its character as a "national democratic revolution" in which non-Communist Afghans can share power. On December 22, 1985, *Pravda* signaled this new emphasis on power-sharing, conceding that "far from all people in Afghanistan, even among working sections of the population, accepted the Revolution."[9] Soon thereafter, twelve non-Communists were appointed to highly visible but relatively powerless government positions. A non-Communist business-man replaced a top Communist leader as president of the National Fatherland Front, the regime's major organizational link with coopera-tive non-Communists. In a move heralded as paving the way for new political parties, the governing Revolutionary Council announced that non-Communist "organizations and socio-political groups" could be formed, provided they were ready to cooperate with the Fatherland Front.[10] Communist Party secretary Najibullah Ahmadzai announced plans in 1986 for a popularly elected, bicameral parliament, to be chosen following adoption of a pending constitution. But it remains to be seen whether such ambitious plans can be implemented while the fighting continues. After launching its projected local elections with great fan-fare in mid-1985, the DRA reported a year later that it had been able to complete them in eight out of twenty-nine provinces.[11]

To counter the accusation by resistance groups that it is anti-Islamic, the DRA emphasizes that it has spent $25 million since 1980 to revital-ize Islamic worship. The lion's share of this sum has been used to rebuild 1,118 mosques and to construct 118 new ones. But the regime's pub-lished documents reveal that a significant share has also gone to provide new houses and other emoluments to the imams or presiding dignitaries of the mosques, as well as stipends to 11,570 other functionaries of mosques and religious schools.[12] Land owned by religious dignitaries and their institutions is exempt from land reforms.

In place of Amin's harsh land-redistribution measures, Kabul now permits peasants to own up to thirty-five acres, focusing its agricultural policy on price subsidies and services for farmers, such as motor and tractor pools, agricultural banks, and the distribution of fertilizer. Similarly, in an effort to win over businessmen and merchants, DRA leaders issued decrees in 1980 guaranteeing private property rights and granting tax holidays up to six years for new investments, together with customs-free imports of machinery. There is not much Marxism in the thriving Kabul bazaars, where I found American dollars freely exchanged at twice the official rate. Kabul continues to be a favorite center for laundering black money from the Persian Gulf, India, Pakistan, and Iran. Japanese goods are everywhere. Trade with Pakistan has been largely unaffected by the war, though truckers complain that they now have to make bigger payoffs to the border tribes to get safe passage. Now, as in past decades, the government winks at smuggling pipelines that run through the country from Europe and the Gulf to the border areas adjoining Pakistan, a massive source of additional profit for the canny border tribes.

SOVIET STRATEGY:
THE MILITARY DIMENSION

Soviet military strategy in Afghanistan has been governed by the fact that the DRA does not face an institutionalized political or military challenge. The disparate resistance groups have not yet attempted to establish a rival government in a liberated zone comparable to Yenan in the Chinese civil war. With the exception of the Pansjer Valley, they have not maintained localized underground government machinery in areas where they have won military victories. They have not been able to set up a unified military command structure or an effectively centralized national political alliance. The nature of the counterinsurgency challenge confronted by Moscow has thus differed fundamentally from the challenge that was presented by the National Liberation Front in Vietnam, the FLN in Algeria, and other successful guerrilla movements. Since the resistance does not seek to secure and occupy territory, it has not been necessary for the Soviet Union to emulate the costly "clear and hold" strategy pursued by the United States during the climactic phase of its Vietnam involvement. Soviet and DRA forces have had four difficult but more limited objectives: to reinforce DRA control of urban centers, transportation networks, and forward military garrisons; to punish and, if necessary, to depopulate localities that help the resistance; to destroy resistance weapons stockpiles; and to cut off resistance supply lines from Pakistan and Iran.

At the beginning of the war, Soviet forces in Afghanistan attempted to use conventional textbook tactics that had been devised to defeat NATO in Western Europe and Chinese troops on the plains of Manchuria. Soviet motorized rifle and tank units often conducted large-scale mechanized offensives that looked like parade-ground exercises. Moving in clumsy formations completely unsuited to the rough, mountainous terrain, they were confined to the few good roads in Afghanistan, where they were vulnerable to mines and to harassment by guerrillas operating out of concealed mountain redoubts. Hiding behind boulders, an Afghan resistance unit of forty men, armed with three RPG-7 antitank guns, crippled an entire motorized battalion in a celebrated 1980 victory in Paktia Province. Surprisingly, Soviet motorized offensives in 1980 and 1981 often lacked effective close air support, which reportedly demoralized DRA forces assigned to play a vanguard role in combined operations.

Soviet convoys were frequently overwhelmed in ambushes during this period. A British journalist witnessed a typical ambush of Soviet forces on the road from Kabul to Jalalabad in which a band of eighteen Afghans destroyed a fuel truck in a convoy escorted by two Soviet motorized companies. As the British observer reported, the Afghans had so ineptly positioned their ambush force that an infantry flank attack would have surrounded and destroyed them, but the mechanized forces adhered rigidly to their standard, road-bound tactics, "driving up and down the highway, firing their turret armament, with the motorized riflemen blazing away through their gunports with few hits until the convoy moved on, leaving the blazing fuel truck."[13]

In a 1982 analysis, a U.S. Army specialist on Afghanistan wrote that "Soviet tactics still tend toward an overreliance on motorized rifle and tank troops employed in 'sweep' or 'hammer and anvil' operations."[14] However, as the war has progressed, the Russians have gradually modified their tactics in the light of bitter experience, introducing new equipment and weaponry suited to Afghan conditions. Special company-sized units trained for unconventional warfare, known as *raydoviki,* were attached to each motorized division, equipped with the AGS-17 automatic grenade launcher, a weapon powerful enough to demolish the rock fortifications characteristically erected by the guerrillas. Small commando units known as *spetsnaz*, often trained in local languages and disguised as Afghans, stage surprise raids on resistance camps, assassinating key leaders. To provide better close support of infantry operations, Moscow has deployed the SU-25 Frogfoot aircraft, armed with cluster bombs, generally accompanied by high-flying MIG-21 decoys that seek to deflect heat-seeking missiles by releasing flares. Most important, Soviet strategists have attempted to achieve greater tactical maneuverability and mobile firepower by using paratroops, helicopter-borne air-assault troops, and attack helicopters.

The cutting edge of the Soviet military presence in Afghanistan has increasingly been the MI-24 Hind attack helicopter. There were some 250 of these helicopter gunships in Afghanistan in 1986, together with another 400 MI-6 and MI-8 transport helicopters used for troop-ferrying and resupply missions. Apart from their devastating impact on the resistance in their close support role, the MI-24s have made it easier for the Russians to avoid ambushes when moving their troop columns or supply convoys. As military analyst David C. Isby observes, the Russians have "adapted the old British Indian Army tactic of 'cresting the heights.' As the convoy moves along a road in the valley, Hinds will scout ahead of the convoy and then land troops to hold key positions until the convoy passes, while the other Hinds are ready to support them in case of ambush. Once the convoy has passed, the troops are picked up and re-inserted further along the convoy route."[15]

The rapid movement made possible by the use of helicopters often enables the Russians to cordon off areas before the resistance can evacuate or reinforce. But a former DRA Air Force officer who defected in 1984 told a British journalist that many ambushes still occur because the resistance units, with their intimate knowledge of the terrain, can often escape detection. When the Hinds search for them, the helicopters expose themselves to heavy machine-gun fire.[16]

An Afghan Army major described the problem of ambushes in a conversation with a *Pravda* reporter:

> Usually they operate in groups of 30 to 40 men. They prefer to stage ambushes near bridges or in narrow defiles. They destroy the bridge or block the road and then open fire from the commanding heights. If a strong army

unit is moving, they allow the reconnaissance and the combat security detachment to go by. All of a sudden, they open up with volleys of well-aimed fire and then rapidly withdraw. They mine the roads, then cover the mined areas with small arms fire. The hand of professional foreign instructors can be felt at work.[17]

To punish localities that provide help and sanctuary to the resistance, Soviet and DRA forces have utilized not only ground offensives backed by SU-25s and helicopters but also high-altitude bombing with SU-24 Fencers and TU-16 Badgers. The most dramatic instance of carpet bombing occurred during the Pansjer offensive of 1984. In many cases, the indiscriminate brutality of Soviet punitive sweeps and bombing attacks has suggested a deliberate effort to depopulate areas regarded as firmly committed to the resistance by driving their surviving inhabitants to seek refuge in Pakistan.

Confronted with Soviet control of the air, the resistance forces have emphasized night operations, sometimes with considerable success. When Soviet armored units pitched their tents at night in the first days of the 1982 Pansjer offensive, resistance units armed only with RPG-7 antitank guns and machine guns inflicted heavy losses on tanks and personnel. A Soviet officer wrote soon thereafter that "command and control of diversified forces in night combat operations continues to be a stumbling block for some officers."[18] However, Soviet forces have since cut down on the mobility of the resistance at night by air-dropping large numbers of PFM-1 "butterfly" mines and by using transport aircraft to provide battlefield illumination.

Since 1984, Soviet strategy has focused on relieving beleaguered garrisons in the critical border areas adjacent to Pakistan as part of a broader, continuing effort to destroy resistance stockpiles and to disrupt resistance supply lines from base camps in Pakistan. The most spectacular Soviet success of the war came in April 1986, when a combined Soviet-DRA force routed resistance fighters defending an elaborate complex of concealed supply depots at Zhawara in Paktia Province. This operation was unusually significant because the ground-fighting was carried out largely by DRA units with Soviet air cover.[19] Despite earlier mass desertions and mutinies, the Afghan Army numbered fifty-five thousand in 1986 and has become a useful adjunct to the Soviet military machine, augmented by another forty-five thousand men in various paramilitary forces, tribal militias, and the Air Force.[20] In the absence of a negotiated settlement, it is unlikely that the DRA forces can be more than an adjunct to a continued Soviet military presence. But the importance of their supportive role should not be underestimated in assessing the present and potential military balance in Afghanistan.

A "NATION IN ARMS"?

Summing up the military aspects of the Afghan struggle after the first five years of fighting, Pentagon intelligence specialist Elie Krakowski concluded that while the combat effectiveness of the resistance had improved, "the central factor . . . is not absolute but relative performance, and in the latter, the Soviets have widened the gap in their favor."[21] This assessment offered a sobering contrast to the romanticism of many observers, who have compared the resistance struggle with the earlier battles of Afghan insurgents against British interlopers. Such comparisons are invalidated, in part, by the civil-war aspects of the present conflict, which arise from an ideological battle that does not have a precedent in the nineteenth century. More important, however, even in strictly military terms, changes in military technology fundamentally distinguish the two situations. The resistance uses classic small-unit guerrilla tactics, striking at lines of communication, engaging in sabotage, and generally avoiding pitched battles. It was one thing to use hit-and-run tactics against British artillery, but it is quite another to do so in the face of the rapid mobility and vastly superior firepower of Soviet aircraft and armored units.

The inequality of the contest in Afghanistan is underlined by the disparity in the number of organized fighting men fielded by the two antagonists. As indicated above, Soviet forces numbering 120,000 men are supported by Afghan Army, Air Force, and paramilitary forces totaling another 100,000. Estimates of organized resistance fighters in the field at any one time vary widely, but an authoritative figure has been suggested by a leading U.S. Army expert on counterinsurgency warfare with access to government intelligence information, Colonel Rod Paschall, director of the Army's Military History Institute. Rebutting an analyst who suggested a two-to-one counterinsurgent-to-guerrilla ratio in Afghanistan, Colonel Paschall wrote in 1986 that "since only 20,000 guerrillas are in active opposition at any one time, a better figure is ten-to-one."[22] This figure apparently refers to the U.S.-funded and -equipped units that shuttle in and out of Pakistani base camps operated by the Pakistan Inter-Services Intelligence Directorate in cooperation with seven resistance exile factions. In the same vein, a high CIA operations official concerned with this program referred to thirty thousand "actives" in a 1983 conversation with me. These figures do not take into account additional thousands of men linked to the loosely organized bands inside the country operating under local tribal leaders and field commanders. At the same time, it is important to distinguish between locally based fighters, who function on an ad hoc, intermittent basis, often with primitive equipment, and the more disciplined, better-equipped units based in Pakistan. To characterize Afghanistan as a "nation in arms," as some observers do, blurs this distinction and ignores the fact that millions of Afghans are not actively helping either the Russians or the resistance. As an analysis in the *Armed Forces Journal* concluded, "If the Soviets can militarily or politically seal off the sanctuaries in Pakistan, the intensity and effectiveness of the guerrilla activity will fall to a level of tolerable annoyance."[23]

The resistance is weakened by tensions between the Pakistani-based exile factions and local field commanders inside the country. These tensions have been reinforced by the same ethnic and tribal divisions that have impeded the emergence of a coherent Afghan nationalism since the seventeenth century. To complicate matters further, the relatively recent rise of Islamic fundamentalism has introduced a new and even more debilitating element of internecine strife into Afghan society: the conflict between Islamic fundamentalist resistance factions and rival resistance elements led by traditional Islamic dignitaries and tribal chieftains.

Of the seven resistance exile leaders operating out of Pakistan, four espouse differing types of Islamic fundamentalist doctrine while three others are traditionalist Muslim divines with tribal alliances. The principal role of all seven leaders is to act as conduits for foreign assistance, channeling aid to local commanders who give them allegiance. Periodically, they mobilize their followers in the refugee camps for ad hoc, commando-type forays in and out of Afghanistan in support of local field commanders. In order to press their case for foreign help more effectively, the seven leaders have formed a tenuous coalition known as the Islamic Unity of Afghan Mujahidin (Freedom Fighters).

The fundamentalist leaders receive the lion's share of foreign aid but do not have a significant base inside the country except in the Pansjer Valley. Inspired by the pan-Islamic Moslem Brotherhood, with its roots

in Egypt, and by orthodox Wahabi groups in Saudi Arabia, the fundamentalists had a negligible organization in Afghanistan prior to the
Communist takeover in 1978 and the Soviet occupation in December
1979. They were arrayed against the monarchy; against the entire traditional Moslem clergy, identified with the Hanafi school of Islamic law,
and various Sufi sects; and against both Western-oriented and Communist modernizers alike. Above all, they had alienated the powerful tribal
hierarchy among the Pashtuns by calling for the abolition of tribalism
as incompatible with their conception of a centralized Islamic state.
Despite harsh repression, the fundamentalists, who numbered perhaps
fifteen hundred, survived as an underground movement until 1973,
when most of them fled to Pakistan. There they forged an alliance with
Pakistani fundamentalist groups and Pakistani intelligence agencies that
was to become increasingly important in the context of the Afghan
conflict.

In seeking to gauge the strength of the fundamentalists, it is neces-
sary to bear in mind that Afghan society is primarily tribal in character.
In Iran, the Ayatollah Ruhollah Khomeini's power has rested on solid
Shiite institutional foundations. Shiism requires the faithful to pay substantial taxes to the mosques, which has enabled the Islamic Republican
Party in Iran to build grass-roots political machines. By contrast, Sunni
Islam is more loosely organized, and in predominantly Sunni Afghanistan, Sunni religious leaders have little or no institutional base, though
they enjoy widespread popular respect. Their status depends on a cooperative relationship with the tribal maliks.

Although the advent of the Communist regime aroused widespread
alarm throughout the Moslem world, it was the fundamentalist elements
in the Gulf and the Middle East who reacted most purposefully and
made the Afghan issue their own. The fundamentalists saw the war as
a golden opportunity to build up organizational cadres among the Afghan refugees in Pakistan with an eye to eventually supplanting the
entire preexisting social and political hierarchy of the country. This
meant that their enemies were not only the Soviet troops and Afghan
Communist infidels, but also most of the nonfundamentalist resistance
elements.

Most U.S. and Saudi aid to the resistance has been dispensed under
the control of Pakistani officials who are beholden to the fundamentalist
Jamiat-i-Islami of Pakistan, a key ally of the Zia Ul-Haq regime. The
Jamiat, in turn, works closely with the powerful leader of the orthodox

Wahabis in Saudi Arabia, Abdul Bin Baz, who has long supported its political activities in Pakistan. The Wahabis and the Jamiat channel aid largely to the four like-minded exile groups in the refugee camps. Moslem Brotherhood elements in other parts of the Gulf and the Khomeini regime in Iran also have direct contacts with some of the fundamentalist groups.

The fundamentalists dole out some weaponry, money, and supplies to selected local commanders inside Afghanistan who are already trusted ideological allies—such as Ahmed Shah Massoud in the Pansjer Valley—or who are regarded as potential allies. But they keep much of it to develop their own Pakistani-based paramilitary cadres. These are partly for use in missions in Afghanistan and partly to provide a reserve gendarmerie for the Zia regime in the turbulent Northwest Frontier Province.

The fundamentalist paramilitary cadres have proved useful for carrying out commando missions in cooperation with locally based resistance fighters. As outsiders operating out of base camps in Pakistan, however, they are inherently disqualified from playing a follow-up political role that could translate military successes into lasting control of the countryside. Indeed, they have no desire to see an underground political infrastructure established under the control of the nonfundamentalist tribal leadership that prevails in most parts of Afghanistan.

Analyzing the tribally based field commanders inside the country, Edward Girardet, a perceptive journalistic observer of the war, has emphasized that they, too, have generally failed to consolidate their military victories with political action. "Only a handful," he reported, "have established infrastructures comparable to those of U.N.I.T.A. in Angola or the E.P.L.F. in Eritrea, by operating their own schools, literacy programs, medical dispensaries and relief and agricultural facilities."[24] Pointing to the lack of coordination between the seven Pakistan-based resistance groups and the field commanders inside the country, a non-Communist Afghan scholar writing in a resistance publication complained that the field commanders "have the power to tax and retax the population under their control, and any action by their nominal leader in Pakistan to stop them from harassing the local population would result in a shift of loyalties to another party whose leaders would always welcome them."[25] Another Afghan who supports the resistance observed that "if one group receives help from a resistance party, the rival groups in the area attach themselves to other parties, and infighting starts."[26]

Opposition from Pakistani-based fundamentalist groups and like-minded elements in Saudi Arabia was directly responsible for frustrating the promising effort to unify the resistance made during 1984 and 1985 by former King Zahir Shah. Ruling out the return of the monarchy or any personal role for himself, the ex-king attempted to create an Afghan National United Front in which the field commanders inside Afghanistan, the fundamentalists, and the traditionalist exile factions would all be represented.

The former king viewed the proposed front as a step toward some form of accommodation with the Soviet Union and the Afghan Communists that would lead to a Soviet withdrawal. This largely explains the fundamentalists' bitter antagonism toward him and his plan. For them the goal of the war is the complete destruction of all Soviet and Communist influence in Afghanistan—and its replacement with a fundamentalist brand of Islamic polity—even if this takes several generations. They are banking on a protracted struggle and are seeking long-term foreign support to set up schools and even a university in Pakistan for the training of future Afghan leaders. By contrast, many of the field commanders and others inside the country who are suffering most directly from the war are more disposed to compromise with the Afghan Communists and the Soviets so long as Soviet forces withdraw. They are prepared to consider some form of coexistence with a more broadly based Kabul regime in which tribal autonomy is honored and non-Communist elements have a significant share of power.

THE CIA AND THE AFGHAN WAR

American policy toward the Democratic Republic of Afghanistan has evolved in three distinct stages.

The United States recognized the Communist government when it was established in April 1978, and conducted normal diplomatic relations with the new regime until the assassination of Ambassador Adolph Dubs in February 1979, maintaining but not extending existing economic aid links. During Dubs's brief tenure, he met with Foreign Minister Hafizullah Amin fourteen times. This posture of active dialogue reflected his privately expressed hope that the United States could forestall the complete dependence of the regime on the Soviet bloc and encourage it to move in a national-Communist direction.[27]

The Dubs assassination, together with the Khomeini revolution in

Iran, marked the start of a second, transitional stage in the development of American policy that continued until the Soviet occupation in December 1979. The United States has not sent a new ambassador since Dubs but continued to conduct normal diplomatic relations with the DRA government until the occupation. At the same time, against a background of growing insurgent activity based in Pakistan and covertly aided by the Pakistani government,[28] the Carter administration began to identify the United States with the insurgent cause.

Former National Security Adviser Zbigniew Brzezinski states in his memoirs that "in April, 1979, I pushed a decision through the SCC [Special Coordinating Committee] to be more sympathetic to those Afghans who were determined to preserve their country's independence. Mondale was especially helpful in this, giving a forceful pep talk, mercilessly squelching the rather timid opposition of David Newsom, who was representing the State Department."[29] Brzezinski is deliberately opaque with respect to the ways in which American sympathy was to be expressed. Nevertheless, he invites speculation as to whether covert American weapons or other aid to the insurgents began during this period. Alluding to Brzezinski's disclosure, Raymond L. Garthoff comments that "while he does not note what this decision entailed, it clearly went beyond a sympathy card."[30] In early September, Brzezinski notes, he "consulted with the Saudis and the Egyptians regarding the fighting in Afghanistan," and on December 28, immediately following the Soviet occupation, "plans were made to *further enhance* our cooperation with Saudi Arabia and Egypt regarding Afghanistan."[31] (Emphasis added.) Zalmay Khalilzad, a member of the State Department Policy Planning Staff, writes that the CIA smuggled tapes of speeches by anti-Communist insurgent leaders into Afghanistan during 1979; Pakistan provided "some weapons"; and Saudi Arabia, Iran, Libya, and Egypt also gave "some aid."[32] In any event, the April policy reversal led to the active worldwide U.S. government dissemination of detailed information concerning insurgent activity and atrocities committed by Soviet-assisted DRA counterinsurgency forces. Initially, this took the form of media background briefings. On September 26, 1979, Assistant Secretary of State Harold Saunders told a congressional committee that the United States was "especially disturbed by the growing involvement of the Soviet Union in Afghan affairs" and had "important differences with the Afghan government, including our deep concern about the human rights situation in Afghanistan." While the United States had reduced its embassy staff and withdrawn the dependents of U.S. government personnel from Kabul, Saunders said, "we have continued to express to the Government of Afghanistan our desire for normal and friendly relations."[33] On October 1, 1979, the last of the American economic aid programs was phased out.

The third stage in American policy toward the DRA, beginning with the Soviet occupation in December 1979, has been marked by steadily growing American weapons assistance to Afghan resistance groups. Whatever the extent of the CIA role in 1979, it is clear that the Carter administration did begin to provide significant aid in early 1980. Significantly, however, the United States and the Communist government continued to maintain diplomatic relations. While recognizing the DRA, the State Department explains, "the U.S. does not conduct normal relations with the Kabul regime. The small U.S. embassy in Kabul, headed by a chargé d'affaires, deals with the Afghan Government on the administrative and consular level only."[34]

The Soviet occupation rapidly transformed the character and scope of the Afghan resistance struggle. What had previously been a significant but limited insurgency, based on local resistance to centralized rule and religious opposition to a Marxist-Leninist regime, soon became a broader nationalist resistance against a foreign occupation force. As the fighting intensified, the American commitment burgeoned. During the period from 1980 to 1986, the U.S. orchestrated an expanding multilateral program of some $1.2 billion in weapons aid to the resistance involving at least $750 million in congressional CIA appropriations together with additional help from China, Saudi Arabia, Egypt, and others.[35] This governmental aid effort was supplemented by a significant separate pipeline from orthodox Wahabi groups in Saudi Arabia and Muslim Brotherhood factions in the Persian Gulf and the Middle East.

From the start, the U.S. government has been broadly divided into two camps with respect to the purpose of the covert aid program: those who view aid as part of a two-track policy in which the United States simultaneously pursues a Soviet force withdrawal through a negotiated settlement, and others who discount the possibility of a withdrawal but support unlimited weapons aid for its own sake as a means of raising the costs of the occupation. The "bleeders" have clearly been stronger in the Reagan administration than they were during the Carter period. Thus, both the quantity and quality of U.S. weapons aid have escalated, amid continuing internecine controversy within the administration over American goals in Afghanistan.

Initially, the U.S. program provided only Soviet-model equipment that was either replicated in specially adapted factories in Egypt or purchased from erstwhile Soviet aid recipients. The resistance, which often captured Soviet weapons, could then say that all of its weapons were prizes of battle, and the United States could deny any involvement. In addition to AK-47 Kalashnikovs and RPG-7 antitank guns, the U.S. supplied Soviet-model heavy antiaircraft machine guns, ground-to-air missile launchers, sophisticated land mines, and portable, heat-seeking Sam-7 missiles.[36] This policy of relying exclusively on Soviet-model weaponry reflected the dominant influence of relatively moderate CIA elements led by then Deputy Director John McMahon, who emphasized the importance of "plausible deniability" of American involvement. McMahon and like-minded officials argued that it would be counterproductive to provoke Soviet escalation by introducing sophisticated American weaponry. These officials were skeptical that the factionalized resistance, with its lack of technically trained personnel, could do more than harass the Soviet forces. The CIA program during the early years of the war was designed to raise the costs of the occupation just enough to get Moscow to the bargaining table while avoiding a provocative, overt U.S. role that might prompt Soviet retaliatory pressures against Pakistan.

As the war has dragged on, "bleeders" in Congress and the administration have objected more and more angrily to what they consider excessive restraints on the Afghan aid program by the CIA and the State Department. "It's so damn obscure what the policy is," exploded Senator Malcolm Wallop of Wyoming. "McMahon himself has told me straight out that U.S. aid cannot be successful."[37]

Charging that the U.S. was giving "just enough aid for Afghans to fight and die but not enough to win," congressional supporters of the resistance in both parties launched a campaign in late 1983 for a larger and more direct American role in the war. Their first move was the introduction of a joint House-Senate resolution calling for "material assistance, as the United States considers appropriate, to help the Afghan people to fight effectively for their freedom." CIA and State Department witnesses testified in executive session that Pakistan's willingness to serve as a conduit for covert aid would be undermined by such an overt

202

confirmation of the CIA role. Former Senator Charles Mathias of Maryland warned that it could become another Gulf of Tonkin resolution, opening the way for escalating American involvement. Mathias waged a successful holding action in the Senate Foreign Relations Committee for nearly a year, but in October 1984 the resolution was adopted with marginal concessions to its critics. This breakthrough was accompanied by the first of a series of congressional initiatives to provide more and better weaponry from more varied sources, especially an antiaircraft missile that would be more effective against the dreaded MI-24 than the Sam-7, which the Soviets know how to deflect with flares. In late 1984, while continuing to resist demands for the Stinger missile and other American weaponry, the administration responded to congressional pressures by purchasing experimental quantities of the Swiss Oerlikon antiaircraft cannon, a bulky weapon that proved unsuited for Afghanistan.

It was in April 1985 that President Reagan openly aligned himself with the "bleeders" for the first time in the form of National Security Decision Directive 166, calling for efforts to drive Soviet forces from Afghanistan "by all means available."[38] This set the stage for a major increase in administration budgetary allotments for Afghanistan in October 1985. Going beyond some $250 million already appropriated for the year, the White House bypassed the appropriation process by reprogramming $200 million of fiscal 1985 funds left unspent in a secret Defense Department account, precipitating "several weeks of heated debate in the House and Senate intelligence committees" before the maneuver won grudging congressional approval.[39] At this stage, the administration was still resisting the use of American weapons but was studying the British Blowpipe missile as an answer to the Soviet helicopters. By March 1986, however, amid growing emphasis on the Reagan Doctrine as a central theme of the president's foreign policy, it was decided at an interagency meeting to provide Stingers for insurgents in Afghanistan and Angola along with upgraded aid for the Nicaraguan contras and the resistance in Cambodia.[40] CIA Deputy Director McMahon resigned in a thinly veiled protest a week later.

Implementation of the Stinger decision was delayed for nearly a year by a variety of factors. Training Afghans in the use of the missiles took much longer than expected. In contrast to the bulky Oerlikon, the thirty-four-pound Stinger is readily portable; and unlike the Blowpipe, which must be guided with radio controls, the Stinger is a "fire and forget" weapon that automatically homes in on its target. While it is relatively simple to operate, however, the Stinger requires complicated maintenance and temperature controls. Apart from training problems, other factors contributing to the delay were foot-dragging by Pakistani leaders, who feared Soviet retaliation, and congressional concern that the missiles might be diverted to anti-American terrorist groups. It was not until early 1987 that Stingers were being deployed in Afghanistan in significant numbers.

The Stinger decision reflected a broader escalation of American involvement in Afghanistan that culminated in the leap from $470 million in the 1986 CIA budget to $630 million in 1987.[41] An increased flow of information concerning both the scope and *modus operandi* of the CIA's Afghan program trickled out of congressional intelligence committees during the protracted controversy over arms sales to Iran and the diversion of funds from these sales to the Nicaraguan contras. American and Saudi funds earmarked for the Afghan conflict had been deposited in a secret Swiss bank account that was also used as a source of funds for weapons aid to Nicaragua and Angola.[42] The Saudis reportedly contributed $525 million for Afghanistan in 1985 and 1986.[43] The CIA drew on this Swiss account for purchases of Soviet-model weaponry from China, Israel, and international arms dealers. For example, an authoritative source told me in 1986 that the United States had paid Israel $35 million for a variety of Soviet-model weaponry captured in the 1982 Lebanon fighting. The CIA arranged regular airlifts of Afghanistan-bound weapons to Pakistan, where the arms were distributed by the Inter-Services Intelligence Directorate in close cooperation with the CIA station in Islamabad. The same Swiss account was the repository for the Iran arms profits that were diverted to the contras. Were funds intended for Afghanistan also diverted to Nicaragua? The Iran-contra controversy provoked widespread suggestions, not yet firmly authenticated, that such diversions had taken place and that aid funds had been misappropriated on a large scale by intermediaries handling the massive CIA Afghan operation.

In addition to the CIA weapons aid program, the burgeoning American role in Afghanistan has included a "humanitarian assistance" program administered by the Agency for International Development. The controversial AID program, which received appropriations totaling $18 million in 1986 and $15 million in 1987, operated inside Afghanistan in partnership with resistance groups. Its objectives are frankly political as well as humanitarian. "By helping the Afghans to develop networks of resistance social services," said the AID budget request to Congress for fiscal 1987, "our assistance will help the *mujahidin* to protect and take care of the people who support them."[44] In addition to providing "nonlethal" goods such as surplus U.S. military boots, sleeping bags, and a variety of equipment for schools and medical clinics in areas chosen by the resistance, AID also makes cash payments for food purchases. All of this assistance is channeled through Pakistan-based resistance groups to field commanders inside Afghanistan. Critics have charged that the multitiered AID distribution network invites corruption. Even if aid were given directly to field commanders, it is argued, AID would be unable to monitor what happens to its money and supplies, and the problem is aggravated by the network of middlemen.[45]

Advocates of a more ambitious American role in Afghanistan have focused on the goal of establishing a rival government that would be officially recognized by the United States and could receive open U.S. military aid. Leaders of the Pakistan-based coalition of seven resistance groups, the Islamic Unity of Afghan Mujahidin, asked President Reagan to recognize the alliance as a government in exile when it visited Washington in June 1986. Reagan refused, saying that the United States would not consider such a step until the alliance had won recognition from "a large section of the international community."[46] Nevertheless, advocates of an expanded American role have continued to press for either a government in exile or the establishment of a rival government in a liberated zone inside Afghanistan. The premise underlying proposals for the liberated-zone strategy is that the proposed zone could be defended with adequate antiaircraft capabilities, together with enlarged units of resistance fighters organized in regular formations instead of in guerrilla bands. But the more cautious, prevailing view was expressed by a State Department Afghan specialist who carried the intragovernment argument to the pages of *Foreign Affairs*, contending that the Soviet victory at Zhawara in April 1986,

> can provide a valuable lesson to the mujahedeen. They are not strong enough to hold or deny territory to the Soviets. Regardless of the antiaircraft weapons the mujahedeen may acquire, the Soviets will always be able to destroy static bases: they can mass air assets sufficient to overcome any such defense. Thus, no matter how well-intentioned, pressuring the mujahedeen to escalate their resistance to a higher or conventional level, to hold land, or to determine tactical details from afar seriously risks the collapse of the struggle.[47]

The continuing divisions in the Reagan administration over Afghanistan have been reinforced by growing doubts concerning the prospects of the resistance as well as increasing awareness of the scope of corruption and black-marketing in aid funds and weapons. Reports that some resistance groups grow opium destined for the American market to help finance their activities have aroused particular indignation.[48] More important, Soviet expressions of interest in a settlement have grown increasingly credible since Gorbachev's rise to power.

The administration has been cool to United Nations–sponsored negotiations on a Soviet combat force withdrawal that have been underway between Pakistan and the DRA since 1983. The U.N. formula for a settlement is anathema to the "bleeders" because it links a Soviet force withdrawal with a termination of aid to the resistance. More important, it would legitimize the DRA, while leaving open the possibility for its evolution into a more broad-based regime.[49] However, following the 1985 Soviet-American summit, the United States gave conditional support to four draft agreements that had resulted from the three-year U.N. effort. The announcement of this policy reversal on December 13, 1985, led to an intense counterattack by former Assistant Secretary of Defense Richard Perle and other influential "bleeders,"[50] and by mid-1986, the United States had openly conditioned support for the U.N. agreements on a new, transitional regime dominated by non-Communists, to be followed by elections.

In pressing for greater American involvement in the war, the "bleeders" have encountered opposition not only from supporters of a negotiated settlement but also from others anxious to avoid American combat involvement in defense of Pakistan. The danger of such involvement is underlined by the fact that the multiservice U.S. Central Command, which coordinates U.S. forces in much of the western Indian Ocean/Persian Gulf region, has included Pakistan and Afghanistan among the nineteen countries within its "area of responsibility." The Central Command's role in Pakistan is formally legitimized by the 1959 U.S.-Pakistani mutual security agreement.

American capabilities for combat intervention and intelligence surveillance in South Asia have improved dramatically since President Richard Nixon sent the aircraft carrier *Enterprise* to the Bay of Bengal in 1971. As the U.S.-Soviet military competition has escalated in the Indian Ocean and the Persian Gulf, the United States has deployed most of its additional increments of naval strength in the immediate vicinity of Pakistan. An American carrier battle group with nuclear-equipped aircraft usually is on permanent patrol in the northern Arabian Sea and the Gulf of Oman. On the Indian Ocean island of Diego Garcia alone, the Deployment Force maintains seventeen giant military container ships loaded with enough tanks, rocket launchers, and amphibious armored personnel carriers to enable 12,500 U.S. Marines to fight for thirty days without resupply.

The possibility of American military intervention on the Pakistan-Afghanistan border has grown steadily as Moscow has deployed more of its troops near the border, as Washington has stepped up its weapons aid to the resistance, and as the diplomatic stalemate has dragged on. At the very least, heightened tensions on the Afghan border would mean ever-higher requests for U.S. military aid to Pakistan. As the quantity and quality of aid increase, so would the likelihood of operational assistance, such as the dispatch of American-manned advanced radar aircraft to help warn against Soviet air strikes at resistance base camps, which could easily lead to the involvement of American personnel in quasi-combat. Worst-case scenarios envisage direct "hot pursuit" by Soviet commandos to destroy base camps in Pakistan. Should American combat forces come to the aid of Islamabad, some influential U.S. military analysts have even suggested that the United States might have to use tactical nuclear weapons.[51] In short, by seeking to apply the Reagan Doctrine to Afghanistan, the United States invites grave risks of a direct confrontation with the Soviet Union that could lead, in turn, to multiplying Soviet-American military tensions throughout the explosive Indian Ocean/Persian Gulf region.

THE COSTS AND PERILS OF INTERVENTION

RICHARD J. BARNET

"LOW-INTENSITY conflict," which Secretary of Defense Caspar Weinberger has called "the most immediate threat to free-world security for the rest of this century," has become fashionable. Inside the Pentagon, the planners and practitioners of low-intensity warfare are once again winning the bureaucratic battles, getting a bigger share of the military budget, and achieving reputations as the strategists with answers to the security problems of our age.

Though some of the weaponry developed for low-intensity warfare is new, neither the concept of "little wars," war to exert "psychosocial pressures," or war limited to a geographic area is a novel notion. In the 1950s John Foster Dulles's prescription for the maintenance of American power in the Pacific was "to let Asians fight Asians." In 1966 Secretary of Defense Robert McNamara saw "limited war" as a promising way to deter the Communists without "the necessity of arousing the public ire." The new element in "low-intensity conflict" strategy is the extention of the military's domain over what used to be the functions of the police: antidrug operations, rescuing kidnap victims, and dealing with bomb throwers and extortionists.

The rebirth of "counterinsurgency warfare" and rollback doctrine in modern dress is an effort to make the U.S. military relevant. Just as the initial preoccupation in the Kennedy administration with "counterinsurgency," "winning the hearts and minds of the people," and "civic action" followed a major military buildup, so once again in a time of escalating Pentagon budgets there is a strong need to demonstrate credible missions for the armed services in a world too dangerous for all-out war. Although the principal arguments for the escalation in military spending of the 1980s had to do with the impact such a commitment would have on Soviet "perceptions" and those of other adversary nations, the high levels of spending could not be maintained unless the public felt that it was getting some increased measure of security for its money.

What the Reagan administration says that the taxpayer is buying when Congress votes for aid to the contras or military assistance to the government in El Salvador or to the rebels in Afghanistan is protection for their sons. The starkly presented alternatives are invisible wars fought by others or heartbreaking wars fought by young Americans. Still traumatized by the Vietnam experience, the U.S. military establishment has served notice by means of an explicit statement of Secretary of Defense Weinberger that the armed forces will not go willingly into wars which the American people do not wholeheartedly embrace. But the Vietnam syndrome, as the Reagan administration calls it, is a chronic condition; polls show a consistent reluctance of the American electorate to support large-scale military interventions involving American troops—not even in the "backyard" of Central America. Blocked by public opinion in carrying out conventional warfare, military planners have staked out as new territory the threats which most concern the average American even as they promise to carry on the war against revolutionary nationalism painlessly, with new weapons and new zeal.

The Reagan worldview has helped considerably to make low-intensity warfare fashionable once more. The official "lesson" of Vietnam is not that the American military was asked to carry out tasks which could not be performed, given the nature of the government that the U.S. was aiding, the risks of widening the war, and the failure of two presidents to make the case that defeating Communism in Vietnam was worth tens of thousands of American lives. Some of the literature on low-intensity conflict reflects views expressed by the president and some of his top political advisers that the "noble war" was lost because the media and the peace movement paralyzed the will to win. The public gave up on the war in Vietnam because it forgot whom the United States was really fighting—the Soviet Union. "They" had to be stopped in Vietnam, so went Lyndon Johnson's appeal, or "they" would be in San Francisco. (Actually, President Kennedy and his top advisers who recommended the original commitment of U.S. troops to Vietnam thought they were fighting a preventive war against "a billion Chinese armed with nuclear weapons.")

Once again the official worldview has been resurrected in which a variety of indigenous nationalist movements are simply stipulated to be creations of Moscow, and once again it is possible to fight the Soviet Union safely, if ineffectively, in places like El Salvador, Grenada, and Libya. Terrorists of all sorts, even fanatical religious anti-Communist bombers and hijackers, are swept into Moscow's global army, despite the fact that the Soviet Union is ideologically opposed to terrorism as a strategy of revolution and is probably the last power to employ unstable, uncontrollable splinter movements to advance its global interests.

But a global program for engaging in low-intensity conflict requires belief in something like a revolutionary international. Mobilizing the armed forces of the world's most powerful nation to plant land mines that blow up schoolchildren, to plot assassinations, or to bomb the countryside of desperately poor countries is no "strategy" at all unless one believes that guerrillas constitute one great global army of the disaffected. But there is no evidence to support that view. The grievances that drive men and women to the variety of desperate political acts now labeled "terrorism" grow out of specific political and religious struggles over particular pieces of real estate. Military establishments are peculiarly ineffective resources for dealing with such an "army," for armed forces are designed to fight nation-states, not to police them. The military establishment is a blunt instrument to persuade governments to capitulate by breaking the will of their people. For terrorism to become a military problem, rather than the essentially political problem it is, the enemy must be turned into a state. So the terrorists are assumed to be "state-supported." While it is true that some states, such as Libya, Iran, and Syria do employ terrorists, and that many movements get some outside support, that is not the critical dimension. Rather, it is the breakdown of state power and state legitimacy that creates the soil of desperation and disorder in which terrorism flourishes.

Few strategists in the inner recesses of the Pentagon would admit to holding the simplistic view that immobilizing the Soviet Union or any other state would end terrorism; yet while most contemporary military planners pride themselves on their sophistication, the very language in which the doctrine of "low-intensity warfare" is cast indicates how shot through it is with apolitical and ahistorical thinking.

When the United States intervenes in age-old struggles within nations, like El Salvador, where old elites battle the new democratic consciousness of our age, or in complex regional struggles as in the Middle East, it is like an actor wandering onto the stage in the middle of the third act without a script. The latest efforts of the United States to modernize its strategy of intervention are based on no clearer a view of what revolutionary nationalism is and what it is becoming than was reflected in the Pentagon Papers of the Vietnam War era. The "new" strategies are unlikely, therefore, to be any more successful than the strategies of the past. More important, the costs of failure will be greater than in the past.

Since the end of World War II, it has been an axiom of American foreign policy that national security required a continuing commitment to intervene—by military means, if necessary—in internal wars and insurgencies, mostly in the Third World, in order to prevent revolutionary political change and "Marxist-Leninist" models of economic development. In the 1950s and the early 1960s, the United States used its military power or paramilitary power on an average of once every eighteen months either to prevent a government deemed undesirable from coming to power or to overthrow a revolutionary or reformist government considered inimical to America's interests. The CIA helped overthrow the government of Iran in 1953 and put the shah back on the throne. In 1954, it bombed the capital of Guatemala and installed a colonel in place of the elected president, who had dared to redistribute the land. Military or paramilitary interventions occurred in British Guiana, Lebanon, and the Dominican Republic. An invasion of Cuba was attempted. In the early 1970s, destabilization efforts were conducted against the elected Popular Unity government of Chile.

Today, under the so-called Reagan Doctrine, which ascribes virtually all revolutionary impulses in the Third World to the Soviet Union, the United States is giving military support to insurgent forces fighting leftist governments in such places as Angola and Nicaragua and is also supporting insurgents fighting Soviet troops in Afghanistan. In the past, American military interventions in civil wars and insurgencies have been motivated by the traditional concerns of imperial powers: maintaining order and stability, scoring points against a rival superpower, and, most importantly, demonstrating to revolutionary movements in other coun-

tries that they cannot succeed. In the absence of ˌ
Nations to play that role, the United States still see
policeman. Though the epithet is to be avoided beca
nineteenth-century imperialism, the policeman's task ha
ered honorable, even necessary, by every administration sin
But the American responsibility, as it is sometimes called, is ˌ   ..ngly
hard to explain to the American people. The problem is that policing
works only under two conditions: the gendarme must be seen as having
legitimate authority *and* a near monopoly in the effective use of violence
or such overwhelming superiority that he is rarely challenged. Even in
domestic society the police function breaks down when officers find
themselves engaged in a continual shoot-out.

The United States still has a greater accumulation of military power
than any other nation. But it has no monopoly, and as the low-intensity
war theorists correctly argue, much of it is intended to meet implausible
threats. So the search for usable military power goes on. But despite the
unprecedented emphasis on military power in American foreign policy
and the sacrificial cost of the military establishment, there have been few
victories in the wars which the United States has felt impelled to fight.
Indeed, the last clear-cut triumph on the battlefield was in 1950 when
Douglas MacArthur's brilliant landing at Inchon saved the American
forces in Korea and pushed the North Koreans out of South Korea.
(That victory was then reversed by pushing it too far in the hopes of
destroying North Korea, an escalation that provoked the Chinese into
entering the war. The final result was a stalemate that achieved the
original but not the enlarged U.S. war aims.) But since that time, despite
the bravery and skill of America's fighting forces, the record of military
performance has not been impressive. The reasons have less to do with
bungling, waste, and incompetence, as so often alleged by military
critics, than with conceptual failures and misconceived missions. The
reality, as the Soviets are discovering in Afghanistan, is that military
solutions do not come easily in the struggles for freedom and independence that characterize our time.

What in fact is the record of past success to support the increasing
militarization of American foreign policy? The Indochina War is of
course the greatest failure, but neither the *Mayagüez* incident where
more were lost than were rescued, the tragic helicopter mission in the
Iranian desert, nor the Bay of Pigs Invasion is a glorious chapter in
American military history. Where interventions by American military

⌐⌐s have been most successful in achieving their objectives, combat ۱as been avoided: U.S. forces played a successful police role in restoring order in Lebanon in 1958 (but not in 1983), and they were instrumental in setting up a pro-U.S. government in the Dominican Republic in 1965. Paramilitary operations have worked better than large-scale military operations. In the 1950s the United States supported a victorious antiguerrilla war in the Philippines, and, as mentioned, overthrew governments in Iran and Guatemala.

Decades of "stability" may seem like a considerable accomplishment by the reckoning of an administration. (Secretary of State Dean Rusk once said his ambition was to leave the problems of the world to his successor in no worse shape than he found them.) But the "successes" of past military and paramilitary interventions have brought neither stability, democracy, nor in the long run increased American influence. After almost thirty-five years of bloody repression, Guatemala is still a human rights nightmare. The Philippines face a bigger insurgency than ever before. The revolutionaries in Iran—fanatics, not moderates like the ones overthrown in 1953—have surpassed the pro-American shah in brutality, but they see the United States as the Great Satan, and in their thirst for revenge they have managed to inflict grievous wounds on two American presidents.

In the Reagan administration, military operations have been defended after the fact for having achieved goals quite unrelated to their original stated purposes. These purposes have almost nothing to do with the war zone itself but with the perceptions of various audiences in other places. One audience is the American people. The invasion of Grenada, first presented as a rescue mission for American medical students, was celebrated six weeks later as a triumph of American arms over the Soviet Union and Cuba. With the press kept out in the first critical hours, it was used as a piece of theater to make Americans feel better. "Our days of weakness are over," declared President Reagan. The humiliation of Vietnam had been overcome. "Our military forces are back on their feet and standing tall."

In fact, as Edward Luttwak has shown, Operation "Urgent Fury" demonstrated weakness, incompetence, and bad planning. Months later, the Catch-22 flavor of the splendid little war began to emerge. The invasion of the island about the size of Martha's Vineyard with a barely functioning government, already abandoned by Cuba, was conducted in such a way as to leave the "hostages" in the hands of the Grenadians two full days after the troops landed, and it almost got the governor-general killed. Over half the American casualties were the result of accident or "friendly fire." Communications were so bad that one officer gave up in despair and used his VISA card to make a phone call. Yet the drama elicited an outpouring of patriotic pride, and President Reagan's "approval rating" climbed. Indeed, the administration's chief claim to success in foreign policy has been to restore American pride and confidence in the wake of the Vietnam and Iran setbacks, and the Grenada affair, though not a famous victory, had much to do with changing American self-perceptions, at least for a time.

The bombing raid on Qaddafi in 1986 is another example. Ostensibly punishment for an act of terrorism, the operation was defended a year later as a strategic temper tantrum. While the United States was still unable to come up with convincing proof of Qaddafi's complicity in the particular bombing that led it to attack his living quarters—and indeed evidence pointed to other culprits, such as Syria and Iran, that would have been much more dangerous to attack—administration officials now argued that the raid was a great success because it shocked the Europeans into taking belated antiterrorist precautions. The idea of conducting military operations against third nations in order to induce behavior modification in one's allies is a new concept in warfare. As the psychological dimension of warfare assumes greater importance, victories are becoming easier to assert even as they are proving harder to achieve.

Most occasions for employing strategies of low-intensity warfare are political struggles in underdeveloped countries where governments are faced with indigenous nationalist movements. Although in the past the United States has engineered coups to bring about a change of government, the Reagan administration is the first to undertake a global program of supporting guerrilla wars against the government in power. The Reagan Doctrine proclaims a global military struggle in the name of democracy. But in none of the struggles—Nicaragua, Afghanistan, Cambodia, Angola—is there even a remote possibility that the rebel forces supplied by the United States can win without the massive engagement of U.S. forces themselves. This is so obvious that the interventions must have some purpose other than victory.

In the case of Afghanistan, the purpose is to put pressure on the Soviets and to show that the Soviets are not the only superpower capable of supporting rebels. While the supply of the *muhajidin* may well have encouraged Soviet interest in ending a war which has been a heavy political and military cost for them, the more involved militarily the United States becomes on the border of the Soviet Union, the less likely the Soviets are to pick up and leave. Military support for the rebels in Afghanistan and Nicaragua has been presented to the Congress as a war for peace. But even where, as in Nicaragua, the target government meets the original demands, even a whiff of victory causes the covert warriors to escalate their war aims. The more covert the war, the less the war aims have been thrashed out in public debate, the more contradictory the strategy will be.

By necessity, the collaboration between a global superpower and a splinter group seeking to get power, as in Afghanistan, or to take back power, as in Nicaragua, will be an uneasy partnership because the interests of the two are not the same. One of the costs of abortive interventions, like the ill-fated 1961 invasion of Cuba, is that the "freedom fighters" turn on the United States. Veterans of the Bay of Pigs fiasco have made their displeasure at being abandoned all too clear by setting off a large number of bombs in Florida over the last two decades.

Obviously, the greatest danger that extensive military interventions in the Third World pose to American security is nuclear war. There is no more plausible scenario for the outbreak of nuclear war than a superpower confrontation in or over some underdeveloped Third World country, quite possibly starting at sea. In Afghanistan and Lebanon, to take two recent examples, Soviet and American forces confront one another in a battle zone neither entirely controls. Each could be drawn into a wider war neither wanted. The 1983 Lebanon operation illustrates the dangers. A small American force is sent to a country located in a region where the Soviets have ground superiority. It comes under attack by forces supported by the Soviet Union. A nuclear-capable battleship is sent to the area as the secretary of defense warns of escalation. The American barracks are blown up with heavy loss of life. The president, faced with the choice of humiliating retreat or escalation, feels politically strong enough to take the prudent course and retreat. In that case, he was able to cover his tracks with a dramatic but much less dangerous military operation in Grenada a few days later. Would the decision to withdraw have been made had the president felt as politically vulnerable as he did four years later after the Iran-contra scandal?

Superpower confrontation in "proxy wars" is a growing threat despite the caution both have shown in the past. The Soviet Union is steadily adding to its naval capabilities for opposing U.S. military operations in various parts of the world. Gorbachev's interest in reducing confrontation with the United States is clear, but should present efforts at improving U.S.-Soviet relations fail and the Cold War heat up again, the risks that one or the other superpower may stumble will be greater than before.

But even if no such confrontation ever occurs, the strategy of intervention is damaging to U.S. national security. In the first place, the objectives are neither realizable nor clear. And the result is a loss of credibility, prestige, and influence. Are Americans really prepared to use military power to install regimes of our choice all over the world? Why, given the record, do we think we can succeed? If the strategy is to be applied only to some countries, which ones? Why? The Reagan administration was no closer to its stated objectives in Nicaragua and El Salvador at the end of its term of office than it was at the beginning.

Interventions require a reckless disregard of international law and treaty obligations. Jurisprudential fig leaves, such as the "Uniting for Peace" resolution passed by the U.S.-controlled United Nations in 1950 under which the United States went into Korea, are no longer easily available. (The mysterious organization of Caribbean islands that sanctioned the Grenada invasion—of which nothing further has been heard—did little to legitimate it in anyone's eyes but the invaders' themselves.) But why take international law seriously? One reason is the Constitution. Treaties are the supreme law of the land. Solemn commitments of past presidents with two-thirds of the Senate consenting cannot be simply sloughed off or ridiculed by subsequent administrations, as the Reagan administration has done with respect to the United Nations Charter, the Rio Treaty, and obligations undertaken to respect the jurisdiction of the World Court without damaging the Constitution itself. When governments break the law, it does nothing to encourage others to respect it. As the nation with the most to lose from international anarchy, the United States has a vested interest in promoting international law, not destroying it.

For uncertain objectives in underdeveloped countries, the United States is sacrificing a crucial objective, the commitment to development. The readiness to conduct low-intensity conflict to prevent models of development that the United States opposes for ideological reasons telegraphs a clear message: this country prefers *no* development to what we consider the wrong path to development. In the years during which the United States has been financing and advising the counterinsurgency war against the guerrillas in El Salvador, unemployment has risen from 21 percent to 33 percent, illiteracy from 43 percent to 51 percent, and households without drinking water from 56 percent to 81 percent. The strategy for conducting low-intensity war strikes at the very heart of the development process, and that is its purpose. The physical attack on the infrastructure of development, roads, dams, etc. with the inevitable "collateral" damage to houses, schools, and hospitals, is accompanied by a psychological attack on precisely those aspects of the revolutionary government's program that establish its legitimacy and popularity. Thus, agricultural, health, and literacy workers in Nicaragua are specifically targeted. The greatest obstacle to development in poor countries is disorganization, suspicion, and conflicting loyalties; enlisting local businessmen, unions, and newspapers in destabilization campaigns planned in Langley, Virginia, has the effect of further polarizing the targeted societies and paralyzing development efforts.

The revolutionary government's response to outside interference—bribery, assassination, arms shipments, conspiracy, etc.—is of course predictable. It becomes more repressive. And that is an objective of the strategy. Squeezing revolutionary regimes into austerity and frightening them into becoming repressive is intended to cause a loss of popular support and international appeal. Indeed, the more legitimate the revolutionary government appears—Chile and Nicaragua are prime examples—the more it has become a U.S. national security objective to cause the revolution to lose its positive image—in short, to self-destruct. The strategy works, sometimes well enough to cause a change of government.

But to what end? Surely the victory in Chile of one of the bloodiest dictators of the age, his vaunted economic miracle in ashes, has made whatever failures of democracy that characterized the Allende government appear insignificant by comparison. It is clear that neither the left nor the right has a ready answer to the economic problems of poor countries. When countries with revolutionary governments or popularly based reform movements find themselves at war with the United States, they of course become poorer. And so do the surrounding countries. It is not possible to tear down Nicaragua and build up El Salvador at the same time, though that is American policy. Both tiny nations are part of the same regional economy. Nation-building, whatever the model of development, requires extraordinary efforts of the population, but war leaves the people demoralized, apolitical, and in a permanent state of terror. Meanwhile, the local military "partners" of the United States carry on with their own agenda, getting and keeping power and wealth, settling scores.

But development ought to be a real goal of United States policy. Not to embrace it is to show contempt for the hopes and dreams of the vast majority of people on the planet for whom development means the right to life and the possibility of freedom. Moreover, a national security strategy with a built-in bias against development is extraordinarily self-defeating for a nation that is steadily losing its share of the world market. Promoting prosperity for masses of people rather than just a few is in the American interest. Selling necessities and amenities to countries where a majority of the world's people lives would hold more promise of creating jobs for Americans—provided those countries were actually developing—than trying to sell increasingly redundant luxury gadgets in the industrial world, where the market is saturated and the population is not growing. Ironically, the governments that the United States cele-brates as right-thinking allies, the free-enterprise autocracies, threaten American interests far more than revolutionary societies bent on build-ing up their own internal markets. The Koreas and the Taiwans with their docile labor force, having turned themselves into export machines, are damaging the American economy more than the Nicaraguans or Angolans could ever dream of doing. Moreover, these regimes are becoming increasingly unstable, and the United States risks tying its long-term interests to discredited rulers who are eventually overthrown.

In simpler times, the imperial model worked, but the United States was fated to come to preeminent power in a postimperial world. This does not mean that nations across the political spectrum do not try to dominate and exploit other nations, even to try organizing their societies for them. Demonstrably, this happens. It means rather that political and economic changes, and particularly changes in consciousness, make tra-ditional models for acquiring, projecting, and protecting power increas-ingly anachronistic. This is as true for the Soviet Union as it is for the United States.

The attempt by the United States to apply updated versions of imperial strategies in a postimperial world not only has a boomerang effect on the American economy, but it also threatens democratic insti-tutions in the United States. The American people, according to a barrage of polls, remains deeply divided about the wisdom and morality of interfering in the affairs of other nations. The Reagan administration did not find a cure for the Vietnam syndrome; not more than 40 percent

of the electorate has ever subscribed to the official worldview undergird-
ing the modernized intervention strategy or believed its major premises.
Thus, the administration, as others before it, resorted to secrecy and
deception to carry out policies that it could not defend in open political
debate.

Most foreign policy is carried on with little public participation or
interest, and the damage to the democratic process is hard to gauge. But
where a significant proportion, almost certainly a majority, of the public
cares deeply, the effort to confuse, mislead, and deceive the electorate
undermines the most fundamental democratic premises. Deliberate
deception of the voter attacks the whole notion of popular sovereignty.
Candidacy for office is an appeal for trust. The theory of our system is
that the voter's response is based on the candidate's record—his real
record, not a fiction. The reason why Ronald Reagan lost his extraordinary popularity so quickly after the revelation of the Iran arms deal was
that the actual record was shown to be totally at odds with the president's rhetoric on how to deal with terrorists. Reagan is the fourth
recent president to be severely damaged by a foreign-policy failure because the nation lacks a consensus on the national interest. The reason
is the same in each instance. There is profound disagreement about
when, where, and how to use force in the pursuit of the national interest.
(It has been forty years since these questions have been debated seriously.) So, in the absence of consensus, presidents continue to act
surreptitiously abroad to carry out policies they are unwilling to defend
openly at home.

The whole idea of low-intensity warfare is to avoid "disturbing"—a
euphemism for informing—public opinion in the United States. (In the
battle zone, the intensity can be high indeed.) The strategy depends
upon secrecy. But keeping secrets is becoming unreasonably expensive.
Never has so much money been spent on creating and guarding secrets.
Yet sensational disclosures of successful espionage operations against the
United States are becoming routine. Ironically, the most secrecy-
obsessed administration in history has been seriously wounded because
it was unable to keep the embarrassing story of the Iran arms deal from
turning up in a small Lebanese newspaper. The world is becoming better
wired and more porous, and it is now easier to steal or expose secrets than
to keep them.

Secrets differ widely in their character and importance depending
upon who is to be kept in the dark. Some secrets are designed with the

enemy in mind. Under our system, these are the only legitimate secrets. In peacetime, certain classified information usually concerns the identity of agents, the capabilities and design of weapons systems, and how and where signal-intelligence and eavesdropping operations are conducted. Many other secrets, however, have as their target the American people, and these present the greatest threat to democracy. A document may be stamped "Secret" only because the wielder of the stamp wishes to keep it from the voters. Clandestine military and paramilitary operations against countries with which the United States has ostensibly peaceful relations are almost never secrets from their targets. Nor are they meant to be. The overt "covert" war against Nicaragua is intended in fact to demonstrate the administration's determination to get rid of the Sandinistas. But the details are secret from the American people because they are ugly and because they contradict the official "spin" that the administration seeks to put on the war.

In such cases, secrecy serves a double purpose. While what is actually happening remains obscure, the administration can create official truth by presidential authority. Thus, with an earnest look, President Reagan can turn thugs and murderers into the moral equivalent of the Founding Fathers, as the story of the contras' past, the drug traffic, the mysterious financial dealings, and their plans for their country once the United States gets it back for them are stamped "Top Secret."

There is a second purpose in keeping something secret that thousands of people already know: the classification of information affords presidents the opportunity to deny responsibility. When the chief executive is called to account, secrecy permits "plausible deniability" or retreat into forgetfulness. Deniability is the exact opposite of accountability, which is the quintessential democratic value. Under representative democracy, the executive wields enormous power, but he is periodically called to account. If the president can avoid responsibility for what he does in the pursuit of national security, then the American experiment in democratic rule is over.

For a hundred and fifty years, observers of America from Alexis de Tocqueville to George Kennan have wondered aloud whether this nation can survive as a great power in the swamp of international relations and still remain a democracy. The tension between projecting power abroad and maintaining liberty at home is particularly sharp when military power is committed for purposes that the American people either do not understand or do not support. Low-intensity warfare is a strategy for fighting wars without popular support. Some military authorities believe that the strategy cannot work without censorship. A White House official explained the exclusion of the press from the Grenada rescue operation to the *Washington Post* with disarming candor: "If you get the news people into this, you lose support of public opinion." Secretary of State Shultz complained about "adversary journalism." Unlike World War II, he said, reporters these days "are always against us and so they're always seeking to report something that's going to screw things up." Some military officers are absolutely convinced that it was Walter Cronkite who single-handedly destroyed the American will to win in Vietnam by shaking his head as he showed films of napalmed children. An outraged Marine major has proposed in an article in *Military Review* that television be excluded from any combat zone, not because pictures lie but because the bits and pieces of truth they transmit with such emotional impact undermine official truth. "Television is too powerful—it has too much impact. It is clear that, if we accept this erosion of public will power, our cause, however just and necessary, is doomed." Major Cass D. Howell has put the choice between democracy and a security strategy based on fighting low-intensity wars about as well as anyone could.

In recent years the American government has split in two: in foreign affairs it acts as a secretive, fitfully accountable state run by a national security elite, while in domestic affairs it functions reasonably well as a democratic republic. After almost fifty years of Cold War, this compartmentalization of government is an accepted political reality. But the notion that the domestic and foreign branches of government can operate with radically different rules and values is corrosive. The arguments for limiting or suspending democracy in foreign affairs can be extended to domestic affairs just as easily under the right circumstances. There are all sorts of emergencies and crises that arise—the AIDS epidemic for one—to justify dictatorial behavior and the avoidance of government accountability to the citizenry. Besides, it is hard to tell where foreign affairs leave off and domestic affairs begin. Exempting foreign policy from the operation of democracy while preserving popular government in domestic affairs is becoming impossible now that the fragile membrane separating "foreign" and "domestic" issues is fast disappearing.

The democratic experience in the United States has exerted enormous positive influence around the world. The American experiment has produced unprecedented prosperity and technological development in a large nation, along with a remarkable degree of individual freedom. But if, despite our unique advantages of wealth, geography, and two hundred years of reasonably good luck, we are forced to confess that democracy does not work when national security is at issue, the American retreat from democracy would be complete. The United States is in the anomalous position of making the promotion of democracy abroad the explicit goal of its foreign policy even as democratic obligations have been recklessly evaded in the conduct of foreign policy. Reconciling national security with the requirements of democracy now poses the greatest challenge to the idea of popular government since the nation was founded.

NOTES

CHAPTER 1 THE NEW INTERVENTIONISM

1. This term is used by Secretary of Defense Caspar Weinberger in *Department of Defense Annual Report, Fiscal Year 1988* (Washington, D.C., 1987), p. 57. (Hereinafter *DOD Report FY88.*)
2. Neil C. Livingstone, "Fighting Terrorism and 'Dirty Little Wars,' " in William A. Buckingham, Jr., ed., *Defense Planning for the 1980s* (Washington, D.C.: National Defense University Press, 1984), pp. 188, 195.
3. *Taking the Stand,* the testimony of Lt. Col. Oliver L. North before the Joint House and Senate Select Committee on Iran and the Contras (New York: Pocket Books, 1987), p. 12.
4. *DOD Report FY88,* pp. 57, 62.
5. For a full transcript, see *Proceedings from the Low-Intensity Warfare Conference,* January 14 and 15, 1986.
6. Army/Air Force Center for Low Intensity Conflict (CLIC) Activation Plan, January 29, 1986, p. A-1
7. *Joint Low-Intensity Conflict Project Final Report,* Vol. I: *Analytical Review of Low-Intensity Conflict,* and Vol. II: *Low-Intensity Conflict, Issues and Recommendations,* August 1, 1986. (Hereinafter *JLIC Final Report.*)
8. John D. Waghelstein, "Post-Vietnam Counterinsurgency Doctrine," *Military Review,* May 1985, p. 46.
9. James B. Motley, "A Perspective on Low-intensity Conflict," *Military Review,* January 1985, p. 9.
10. Donald R. Morelli and Michael M. Ferguson, "Low-Intensity Conflict: An Operational Perspective," *Military Review,* November 1984, p. 15.
11. See Waghelstein's speech to the American Enterprise Institute, January 17, 1985.
12. See Reagan's speech to the nation, May 9, 1984, reprinted in the *New York Times,* May 10, 1984.
13. *JLIC Final Report,* Executive Summary, p. 3.
14. Ibid., p. 4
15. See Frank R. Barnet, et al., eds., *Special Operations in U.S. Strategy* (Washington, D.C.: National Defense University Press, 1984).
16. *JLIC Final Report,* Executive Summary, p. 4.
17. *DOD Report FY85,* p. 18.
18. Neil C. Livingstone, "Mastering the Low Frontier of Conflict," *Defense and Foreign Affairs,* January 10, 1985, p. 10.
19. Quoted in Sara Miles, "The Real War," *NACLA Report on the Americas,* April–May 1986, p. 19.
20. Miles, "The Real War," p. 19.

21. Waghelstein, "Post-Vietnam Counterinsurgency Doctrine," p. 42.
22. For discussion, see Michael T. Klare, *Beyond the "Vietnam Syndrome"* (Washington, D.C.: Institute for Policy Studies, 1981).
23. For a clear analysis of the U.S. reaction to these revolutions, see Fred Halliday, "Beyond Irangate: The Reagan Doctrine and the Third World," Transnational Institute, Amsterdam, 1987.
24. Quoted in Peter Kornbluh and Joy Hackel, "Low-Intensity Conflict: Is It Live or Is It Memorex?" *NACLA Report on the Americas,* June 1986, p. 10.
25. John Prados, *Presidents' Secret Wars* (New York: William Morrow & Co., 1986).
26. See John Lewis Gaddis, *Strategies of Containment* (New York: Oxford University Press, 1982), pp. 127–97; and Walter LaFeber, *America, Russia and the Cold War, 1945–1966* (New York: John Wiley & Sons, 1968), pp. 123–200.
27. Maxwell D. Taylor, *The Uncertain Trumpet* (New York: Harper & Row, 1960), pp. 5–6.
28. Ibid., pp. 6–7.
29. Cited in Kornbluh and Hackel, "Low-Intensity Conflict: Is It Live or Is It Memorex?" p. 9.
30. Cited in Roger Hilsman, *To Move a Nation* (Garden City, N.Y.: Doubleday, 1967), p. 415.
31. U.S. Congress, House, Committee on Appropriations, Subcommittee, *Department of Defense Appropriations 1964,* hearings, 88th Congress, 1st Session, 1963, Pt. 1, pp. 483–84.
32. Taylor memorandum to Robert S. McNamara, January 22, 1964, as reprinted in the *New York Times,* June 13, 1971.
33. Quoted in *Defense Monitor,* Vol. 4, No. 7 (1975), p. 5.
34. For an analysis of the attacks on Carter, see Jerry W. Sanders, "Empire at Bay: Containment Strategies and American Politics at the Crossroads," World Policy Institute, World Policy Paper No. 25.
35. Quoted in Joan Didion, "Washington in Miami," *New York Review of Books,* July 16, 1987, p. 22.
36. Barnett et al., *Special Operations in U.S. Strategy,* pp. 7–8.
37. See Jefferson Morley, "Ollie's Blueprint," *New Republic,* May 25, 1987, p. 16.
38. *JLIC Final Report,* Executive Summary, p. 4.
39. Barnett et al., *Special Operations in US Strategy,* p. 223.
40. Sam C. Sarkesian, "Low-Intensity Conflict: Concepts, Principles, and Policy Guidelines," *Air University Review,* Vol. 26, No. 2 (1985), pp. 7, 11.
41. Livingstone, "Fighting Terrorism," pp. 188–89.
42. *Taking the Stand,* p. 12.
43. For discussion, see: "Soviet Geopolitical Momentum: Myth or Menace?" *Defense Monitor,* Vol. 25, No. 5 (1986), pp. 1–32.
44. *DOD Report FY88,* p. 60.
45. Robert A. Doughty and L. D. Holder, "Images of the Future Battlefield," *Military Review* (January 1978), p. 67.
46. Livingstone, "Fighting Terrorism," p. 188.
47. *New York Times,* July 13, 1987.
48. *JLIC Final Report,* Executive Summary, p. 6.

CHAPTER 2 COUNTERINSURGENCY

1. To Roger Hilsman, as quoted in his *To Move a Nation* (New York: Doubleday, 1967), p. 413.
2. See, e.g., Mao Tse-tung, *Selected Works,* 4 vols. (Peking: Foreign Language Press, 1961–65); *Anthology of Mao's Writings,* ed. Ann Fremantle (New York: Mentor,

1971); Vo Nguyen Giap, *People's War, People's Army* (New York: Vintage, 1963), each published in an earlier translation by the U.S. government.
3. Spelled out in W. W. Rostow, *Stages of Economic Growth* (Cambridge: At the University Press, 1960).
4. E.g., peasant uprisings in Mexico before and during the Mexican Revolution, 1912–26; the slaughter of miners in Bolivia and Chile, 1920s; the killing of APRISTA sugar workers in Peru, 1944; the *matanza* of 32,000 peasants in El Salvador, 1932; and recent appalling massacres of Indian villagers in Guatemala, 1980–85.
5. On counterinsurgency in general, see Sir Robert K. G. Thompson, *Defeating Communist Insurgency* (New York: Praeger, 1966), and *Revolutionary War in World Strategy* (New York: Taplinger, 1970).
6. For a recent review of counterinsurgency in Malaya, see Maj. Daniel S. Challis, "Counterinsurgency Success in Malaya," *Military Review*, February 1987, pp. 56–69.
7. On May 16, 1961.
8. Brig. Gen. Edward M. Lansdale, USAF in OSD; the writer in the Office of the Secretary of State. The term "internal defense" was preferred by the State Department to either "internal security" or "counterinsurgency" and eventually became government-wide usage in the Kennedy administration.
9. See U.S. Army, *Field Service Regulations* (Washington, D.C.: GPO, 1905) and *Infantry Drill Regulations* (Washington, D.C.: GPO, 1911).
10. NSAM-124 of January 18, 1962.
11. See Douglas S. Blaufarb, *The Counterinsurgency Era* (New York: Free Press, 1977).
12. In the Annex to NSAM-124.
13. NSAM 182 of August 24, 1962.
14. Ibid., pp. 2, 11.
15. Ibid., p. 25.
16. JCS publication of April 1962, still classified. Superseded by the OIDP.
17. JCS memo of July 17, 1962. The first incumbent of this post was Maj. Gen. Victor H. Krulak, USMC, who subsequently played a key role in advising Secretary of Defense McNamara on the Vietnam War.
18. These courses are identified in *Military Counter-Insurgency Accomplishments Since January 1961*, Report from the Chairman of the Joint Chiefs of Staff to the President's National Security Advisor, July 21, 1962.
19. Col. Rod Paschal, USA, "Low-Intensity Doctrine: Who Needs It?" *Parameters*, Vol. XV, No. 3 (Autumn 1985), p. 42.
20. Ibid., p. 45.
21. E.g., Guatemala, 1954; Brazil, 1964; Uruguay and Chile, 1973; Argentina, 1976; El Salvador, 1979.
22. Drafted by the writer and personally submitted, June 1962.
23. NSAM-177 of August 7, 1962. An earlier presidential directive, NSAM-132 of February 19, 1962, urging AID to "give consideration" to support of foreign police forces, was stonewalled by the AID bureaucracy.
24. AID Public Safety Program Annual Reports, 1969–73.
25. See, e.g., U. Alexis Johnson (department undersecretary of state) "Internal Defense and the Foreign Service," *Foreign Service Journal*, July 1962; for a later view, Charles Maechling, Jr., "Our Internal Defense Policy: A Reappraisal," *Foreign Service Journal*, January 1969.
26. NSAM-182 of August 24, 1962.
27. The Senior Interdepartmental Group (SIG), established June 1966 with a far broader mandate than the Special Group (CI).
28. See n. 2.
29. See n. 2, Giap.
30. On the Vietnam War, see in particular Stanley Karnow, *History of the Vietnam War* (New York: Penguin, 1984); Douglas S. Blaufarb, *The Counterinsurgency Era* (Free

Press, 1977); Roger Hilsman, *To Move a Nation;* and Col. Harry G. Summers, *On Strategy: The Vietnam War in Context* (U.S. Army War College, April 1981).
31. For the best account of the strategic hamlet program see Hilsman, *To Move a Nation.*
32. Ibid.
33. Ibid.
34. August 24, 1963—this was the famous cable that gave the green light to the generals. See William G. Rust, *Kennedy in Vietnam* (New York: U.S. News and World Report Books, 1985).
35. Joint Resolution of Congress, 1964.
36. William A. Nighswonger, *Rural Pacification in Vietnam* (New York: Praeger, 1966).
37. See Summers, n. 30, p. 55.
38. Gen. William C. Westmoreland, *A Soldier Reports* (New York: Doubleday, 1976), p. 142.
39. See Summers, n. 30, p. 106.
40. Gen. Fred C. Weyand, in *Commander's Call,* July–August, 1976.
41. For the effects of the war on Vietnamese society, see Frances FitzGerald, *Fire in the Lake* (Boston: Little, Brown, 1972).
42. According to its director, Robert Komer, in *Bureaucracy Does Its Thing* (Rand Corp., August 1972), p. 123.
43. Blaufarb, Chap. 7, n. 30.
44. Ibid.
45. Summers, p. 70, quoting statements of North Vietnamese generals.

CHAPTER 3 THE INTERVENTIONIST IMPULSE

1. Robert H. Kupperman Associates, Inc., *Low Intensity Conflict,* prepared for U.S. Army Training and Doctrine Command, Vol. I, Main Report, July 30, 1983. (Hereinafter Kupperman, *Low Intensity Conflict.*)
2. The author first discussed this phenomenon in "The New U.S. Strategic Doctrine," *The Nation,* December 28, 1985, pp. 697, 710–16.
3. Col. James B. Motley, "A Perspective on Low-Intensity Conflict," *Military Review,* January 1985, pp. 7–8.
4. Caspar Weinberger, *Annual Report of the Secretary of Defense,* Fiscal Year 1986 (Washington, D.C., 1985), p. 41.
5. Col. John D. Waghelstein, "Post-Vietnam Counterinsurgency Doctrine," *Military Review,* May 1985, p. 46.
6. See Department of Defense, *Proceedings of the Low-Intensity Warfare Conference,* January 14–15, 1986. (Hereinafter *LIC Proceedings.*) See also *New York Times,* January 20, 1986; and *Army Times,* January 27, 1986.
7. Army/Air Force Center for Low Intensity Conflict, *Activation Plan,* January 29, 1986.
8. See Jefferson Morley, "Ollie's Blueprint," *New Republic,* May 25, 1987, pp. 16–18. For proceedings of the 1983 NDU conference, see Frank R. Barnett, B. Hugh Tovar, and Richard H. Shultz, eds., *Special Operations in US Strategy* (Washington, D.C.: National Defense University Press, 1984). On the "revitalization" of SOF, see Richard Halloran, "Military Is Quietly Rebuilding Its Special Operations Forces," *New York Times,* July 19, 1982; Noel C. Koch, "Why We Must Rebuild Our Special Operations Forces," *Defense/83,* July 1983, pp. 8–13; "America's Secret Military Forces," *Newsweek,* April 22, 1985, pp. 22–29; and "America's Secret Soldiers: The Buildup of U.S. Special Operations Forces," *Defense Monitor,* Vol. 14, No. 2 (1985), pp. 1–16.
9. U.S. Army Command and General Staff College, *Low-Intensity Conflict,* Field Circular 100-20 (Fort Leavenworth, Kans., 1986). (Hereinafter USACGSC, FC 100-20.)
10. U.S. Joint Chiefs of Staff, *Department of Defense Dictionary of Military and Associated Terms,* JCS Pub. 1, (Washington, D.C., 1984), p. 119.

11. For background on this effort, especially as applies to Central America, see Allan Nairn, "Endgame," *NACLA Report on the Americas* (May–June 1984), pp. 20–33; and Sarah Miles, "The Real War," *NACLA Report on the Americas* (April–May 1985), pp. 18–48.

12. N. C. Livingstone, "Fighting Terrorism and 'Dirty Little Wars,'" in William A. Buckingham, Jr., ed., *Defense Planning for the 1990s*, 10th National Security Affairs Conference, National Defense University, October 1983 (Washington, D.C.: National Defense University Press, 1984), pp. 185, 195.

13. See, for instance, Mr. Reagan's address at West Point on May 27, 1981 (as recorded in the *New York Times*, May 28, 1981), in which he speaks of the Vietnam syndrome as an "aberration" that was gradually receding.

14. Cited in *LIC Proceedings*, p. 99.

15. U.S. Army Training and Doctrine Command, *US Army Operational Concept for Low Intensity Conflict*, TRADOC Pamphlet No. 525-44 (Fort Monroe, Va., 1986), p. 2. (Hereinafter TRADOC Pam. 525-44.)

16. Maj. Mitchell M. Zais, "LIC: Matching Missions and Forces," *Military Review*, August 1986, p. 79.

17. Waghelstein, "Post-Vietnam Counterinsurgency," p. 42.

18. Maj. Robert J. Ward, "LIC Strategy," *Military Intelligence*, January–March 1985, p. 52.

19. Lt. Col. Peter A. Bond, "In Search of LIC," *Military Review*, August 1986, p. 80.

20. Lt. Col. John M. Oseth, "Intelligence and Low-Intensity Conflict," *Naval War College Review*, November–December 1984, p. 19.

21. Maj. Gen. Donald R. Morelli and Maj. Michael M. Ferguson, "Low-Intensity Conflict: An Operational Perspective," *Military Review*, November 1984, pp. 3–4.

22. *LIC Proceedings*, p. 10.

23. The full citation for the JLICP report is: Joint Low-Intensity Conflict Project, *Joint Low-Intensity Conflict Project, Final Report* (Fort Monroe, Va.: U.S. Army Training and Doctrine Command, August 1986). (Hereinafter *JLICP Final Report*.)

24. TRADOC Pam. 525-44, p. 13.

25. USACGSC, FC 100-20, Chap. 3, p. 1.

26. Zais, "Matching Missions," p. 93.

27. For discussion of classical U.S. counterinsurgency strategy, see William F. Barber and C. Neale Ronning, *Internal Security and Military Power* (Columbus: Ohio State University Press, 1966); Douglas S. Blaufarb, *The Counterinsurgency Era* (New York: Free Press, 1977); Harry Eckstein, ed., *Internal War: Problems and Approaches* (New York: Free Press, 1964); Frank Kitson, *Low-Intensity Operations* (Harrisburg, Pa.: Stackpole, 1971); Michael T. Klare, *War Without End: American Planning for the Next Vietnams* (New York: Knopf, 1972); John S. Pustay, *Counterinsurgency Warfare* (New York: Free Press, 1965); and Sir Robert Thompson, *Defeating Communist Insurgency* (New York: Praeger, 1966).

28. For discussion, see Jeffrey Race, *The War Comes to Long An* (Berkeley: University of California Press, 1972).

29. Ward, "LIC Strategy," p. 53.

30. *JLICP Final Report*, Vol. I, Chap. 4, p. 7.

31. For discussion, see USACGSC, FC 100-20, Chap. 3.

32. Ibid., Chap. 4, p. 1. See also Alvin H. Bernstein and Col. John D. Waghelstein, "How to Win in El Salvador," *Policy Review*, Winter 1984, p. 52.

33. For discussion, see *JLICP Final Report*, Vol. I, Chaps. 4, 11.

34. Ibid., Vol. I, Chap. 4, pp. 12–13.

35. USACGSC, FC 100-20, Chap. 3, p. 7.

36. William M. LeoGrande, "Counterinsurgency Revisited," *NACLA's Report on the Americas*, January–February 1987, p. 5.

37. TRADOC Pam. 525-44, Glossary, p. 3.

38. See USACGSC, FC 100-20, Chap. 4, pp. 7–9; Edward B. Glick, *Peaceful Conflict: The Non-Military Use of the Military* (Harrisburg, Pa.: Stackpole, 1967).
39. TRADOC Pam. 525-44, Glossary, p. 3.
40. See USACGSC, FC 100-20, Chap. 4, pp. 4–7; and *JLICP Final Report*, Vol. I, Chap. 14; Vol. II, Sec. G. See also Alfred H. Paddock, "Psychological Operations, Special Operations, and U.S. Strategy," in Barnett et al., *Special Operations in US Strategy*, pp. 229–51.
41. USACGSC, FC 100-20, Chap. 4, p. 3.
42. For discussion, see *JLICP Final Report*, Vol. I, Chap. 12; Vol. II, Sec. E.; Oseth, "Intelligence and LIC," pp. 19–36; and Ward, "LIC Strategy," pp. 56–60.
43. USACGSC, FC 100-20, Chap. 4, p. 13.
44. Ward, "LIC Strategy," p. 55. See also USACGSC, FC 100-20, Chap. 4, pp. 17–18.
45. USACGSC, FC 100-20, Chap. 4, pp. 20–21.
46. Capt. Steven E. Daskal, "The Insurgency Threat and Ways to Defeat It," *Military Review*, January 1986, p. 34.
47. See Edward N. Luttwak, "Notes on Low-Intensity Warfare," *Parameters*, December 1983, pp. 13–15; Waghelstein, "Post-Vietnam Counterinsurgency," pp. 48–49; and Zais, "Matching Missions," pp. 94–95.
48. See Tammy Arbuckle, "Same Hardware, Same Tactics, Same Conclusion in El Salvador?" *Armed Forces Journal*, December 1986, pp. 46–58. On Salvadoran air strikes, see the *New York Times*, July 18, 1985; January 13, 1986.
49. Morelli and Ferguson, "Low-Intensity Conflict," p. 14.
50. *JLICP Final Report*, Vol. II, Sec. A1, p. 1.
51. The Reagan quote and the first known use of the term "Reagan Doctrine" appeared in a column by Charles Krauthammer in the *Washington Post*, July 19, 1985. For discussion, see Sidney Blumenthal, "The Doctrine Is In," *Washington Post*, July 14, 1986; Michael Ledeen, "Fighting Back," *Commentary*, August 1985, pp. 28–31; and Patrick E. Tyler and David B. Ottaway, "Reagan's Secret Little Wars," *Washington Post National Weekly Edition*, March 31, 1986.
52. Address by George Shultz before the Commonwealth Club of California, San Francisco, Cal., February 22, 1985 (U.S. Department of State Current Policy No. 659), p. 5. (Hereinafter Shultz, San Francisco address.)
53. Ibid., p. 1.
54. See the *Los Angeles Times*, August 31, 1986; the *New York Times*, November 4 and 23, December 11, 1985, February 19, May 25, 1986; and the *Washington Post*, November 3, 1985, January 10 and 13, 1986.
55. Shultz, San Francisco address, p. 3.
56. George P. Shultz, "New Realities and New Ways of Thinking," *Foreign Affairs*, Spring 1985, pp. 706–7. For an elaboration of this theme, see Jeane J. Kirkpatrick, *The Reagan Doctrine and U.S. Foreign Policy* (Washington, D.C.: Heritage Foundation, 1985).
57. *New York Times*, April 9, 1986.
58. See note 54 and the *Los Angeles Times*, September 1, 1986; the *New York Times*, December 11, 1985, February 21, 1986; and the *Washington Post*, March 9 and 31, 1986.
59. See *The Tower Commission Report*, The Full Text of the President's Special Review Board, John Tower, Chairman (New York: Bantam Books and Times Books, 1987).
60. See *New York Times*, December 2 and 4, 1986; January 20, 1987.
61. USACGSC, FC 100-20, Chap. 9, p. 6.
62. U.S. Army Training and Doctrine Command, *US Army Operational Concept for Special Operations Forces*, TRADOC Pamphlet No. 525–34 (Fort Monroe, Va., 1984), pp. 8–9.
63. Ibid., p. 9.
64. Ibid., p. 11.

65. USACGSC, FC 100-20, Chap. 9, p. 1.
66. Caspar Weinberger, Remarks prepared for delivery before the American Newspaper Publishers Association Meeting, Chicago, Ill., May 5, 1981 (U.S. Department of Defense News Release).
67. *JLICP Final Report*, Vol. I, Chap. 6, p. 1.
68. Ibid., Vol. I, Chap. 6, p. 7.
69. Ibid., Vol. I, Chap. 6, p. 9.
70. Ibid., Vol. I, Chap. 6, pp. 9–13. See also USACGSC, FC 100-20, Chap. 9, pp. 4–6; Bond, "In Search of LIC," pp. 84–85; and Zais, "Matching Missions," pp. 91–93.
71. *JLICP Final Report*, Vol. I, Chap. 6, pp. 8–9. See also USACGSC, FC 100-20, Chap. 9, pp. 3–4.
72. U.S. Army Training and Doctrine Command, *US Army Operational Concept for Terrorism Counteraction*, TRADOC Pamphlet No. 525-37 (Fort Monroe, Va., 1984), p. 2. (Hereinafter TRADOC Pam. 525-37.)
73. Ibid.
74. George Shultz, address before the Park Avenue Synagogue, New York, N.Y., October 25, 1984 (U.S. Department of State Current Policy No. 629), pp. 1–2.
75. Ibid., pp. 4–5.
76. Robert C. McFarlane, "Deterring Terrorism," *Journal of Defense and Diplomacy*, June 1985, p. 7.
77. Ibid., p. 8. See also David C. Morrison, "The 'Shadow War,' " *National Journal*, May 10, 1986, pp. 1100–1105; the *Los Angeles Times*, April 15, 1984; and the *Washington Post*, April 18, 1984.
78. TRADOC Pam. 525-37, pp. 14–25.
79. See the *New York Times*, April 15 and 16, 1986. See also Morrison, "The 'Shadow War.' "
80. Quoted in the *New York Times*, April 16 and 24, 1986.
81. See Seymour Hersh, "Target Qaddafi," *New York Times Magazine*, February 22, 1987, pp. 17–26, 48, 71–84.
82. Quoted in David C. Morrison, "The Pentagon's Drug Wars," *National Journal*, September 6, 1986, p. 2105.
83. R. Dean Tice, "Fighting the Drug Flow," *Defense/86*, May–June 1986, pp. 14–15.
84. Ibid., p. 15. See also Morrison, "The Pentagon's Drug Wars," pp. 2105–7.
85. "Enlarged Role for the Military in Drug Interdiction Campaign," *Army*, August 1986, p. 73.
86. See Morrison, "The Pentagon's Drug Wars," p. 2107; and the *New York Times*, July 16, 17, and 18, September 24, 1986.
87. Tice, "Fighting the Drug Flow," pp. 15–17.
88. See Morrison, "The Pentagon's Drug Wars," pp. 2105–7.
89. Col. John D. Waghelstein, "A Latin-American Insurgency Status Report," *Military Review*, February 1987, pp. 46–47.
90. *JLICP Final Report*, Vol. I, Chap. 7, p. 1.
91. TRADOC Pam. 525-44, p. 11.
92. For discussion, see *JLICP Final Report*, Vol. I, Chap. 7; Bond, "In Search of LIC," pp. 83–84; and Zais, "Matching Missions," pp. 90–91.
93. Sam C. Sarkesian, "Low-Intensity Conflict: Concepts, Principles, and Policy Guidelines," *Air University Review*, January–February 1985, p. 2.
94. *JLICP Final Report*, Vol. I, Chap. 4, p. 8.
95. *LIC Proceedings*, p. 47. See also Luttwak, "Notes on Low-Intensity Warfare," p. 16.
96. Motley, "A Perspective on LIC," p. 9.
97. Capt. Ralph Peters, "Kinds of War," *Military Review*, October 1986, pp. 20–23.
98. See the *New York Times*, June 5, 1985.
99. Livingstone, "Fighting Terrorism," p. 195.
100. Sarkesian, "Low-Intensity Conflict," pp. 5, 7, 11.

CHAPTER 4 THE WARRIORS AND THEIR WEAPONS

1. "A World at War—1987," *Defense Monitor*, forthcoming.
2. Quoted in written statement by Senator William S. Cohen at Senate Armed Services Committee Hearing on S. 2453, August 5, 1986, p. 2. (Hereinafter SASC.)
3. For a description of these units, see *New York Times*, June 21, 1985.
4. *Newsweek*, April 22, 1985, p. 24.
5. Caspar Weinberger, *Secretary of Defense, Annual Report to Congress Fiscal Year 1985* (1984), p. 276.
6. Ibid.
7. DOD Fact Sheet, "SOF Expansion," provided by Office of Noel Koch, principal deputy assistant secretary of defense, December 1984, p. 1.
8. A good summary of the 1981–1985 SOF buildup is provided by Noel Koch in House Appropriations Committee [hereinafter HAC], *Department of Defense Appropriations for 1986, Hearings,* Part 6, pp. 602–8. The two most comprehensive reports on SOF are "A Report to the Committee on Appropriations, US House of Representatives, on the Special Operations Forces of the Department of Defense," Surveys and Investigations Staff, February 1986, reprinted in HAC, *Department of Defense Appropriations for 1987, Hearings, Part 6,* pp. 543–635, and "America's Secret Soldiers: The Buildup of US Special Operations Forces," *Defense Monitor*, Vol. 14, No. 2 (1985), pp. 1–16.
9. Sec. Def., *Annual Report FY1987*, p. 53; HAC, *DOD App. 1987*, Pt. 8, p. 631; Sec. Def., *Annual Report FY1988*, p. 296.
10. See *Armed Forces Journal International*, April 1986, p. 20. (Hereinafter *AFJI*.)
11. HAC, *DOD App. 1986*, Pt. 6, p. 604; *Joint Chiefs of Staff Posture Statement FY1986*, p. 68.
12. HAC, *DOD App. 1986*, Pt. 6, pp. 605, 617.
13. See notes 45–50.
14. Of the numerous press accounts noting SOF participation, see particularly the *Washington Post*, November 9, 1984; *Newsday*, August 13, 1984; *Philadelphia Inquirer*, December 3, 1984; *New York Times*, October 23 and December 4, 1984, and January 3, 1985; *Los Angeles Times*, November 15, 1983; *Defense Week*, December 3, 1984; *Navy Times*, December 17, 1984; and Asst. Sec. Def. Michael Burch, ABC *Nightline* transcript, October 24, 1984. Other important sources include William Lind, "Report to the Congressional Military Reform Caucus," April 5, 1984; General Vessey, "Analysis of the Lind Report," June 6, 1984; and CINCLANT Operations Urgent Fury Report.
15. See Chap. 6.
16. Koch statement to HAC, April 10, 1984, p. 4; HAC, *DOD App. FY1985*, Pt. 8, p. 788.
17. Dr. Spiro Manolas, senior training adviser, DSAA, "IMET: A Study of Program Management," *DISAM Journal*, Vol. 7, No. 2 (Winter 1984–85), p. 76.
18. Koch to HAC, April 10, 1984, p. 4.
19. Statement by Gen. William Moore to HASC, September 13, 1984, p. 13; MTT Status Report, June 1984, pp. 24–38; *Army*, October 1983, p. 248.
20. HAC, *DOD App. FY1985*, Pt. 8, pp. 799–801.
21. These initiatives are discussed by Koch in his statements to HAC, April 10, 1984, p. 11, and to HASC, September 6, 1984, p. 4.
22. See Rep. Dan Daniel, "The Case for a Sixth Service," *AFJI*, August 1985, pp. 70–75.
23. *AFJI*, November 1986, p. 20.
24. *Army Posture Statement FY1987*, p. 19. For general organizational details, see HAC, *DOD App. FY1987*, Pt. 6, pp. 563–88; U.S. Army, "A History of Special Forces."
25. Joint Special Operations Support Element Briefing, MacDill AFB, August 24, 1982; *Defense and Foreign Affairs*, September 1984, p. 26; William Arkin, "IPS Fact Sheet

on Special Operations," February 22, 1984; author's interviews with active and retired U.S. military personnel.

26. HAC, *DOD App. FY1987*, Pt. 1, p. 139; interview with Maj. Gen. Leroy Suddath, Jr., Commander 1st Special Operations Command, in *Jane's Defence Weekly*, July 26, 1986, p. 125.

27. SAC, *DOD App. FY1984*, p. 208.

28. *New York Times*, August 21, 1986.

29. *The Elite and Their Support*, extracts from Vol. 1, 1984, p. 20.

30. DOD news release, April 9, 1984; Gen. Moore to HASC, September 13, 1984, p. 5.

31. For background on Delta, see Col. Charlie Beckwith, USA (ret.), and Donald Knox, *Delta Force* (New York: Dell, 1983).

32. *JCS Posture Statement FY1986*, p. 68, refers to a "battalion-size unit"; *Wall Street Journal*, June 10, 1986, citing "government estimates," says 300; *Washington Post*, November 21, 1985, says 300; *St. Louis Post-Dispatch*, June 17, 1985, says 200; "NBC Nightly News" transcript, January 2, 1985, p. 10, says 160; *Washington Post*, May 18, 1980, in wake of Iran failure, says 200–300.

33. Most of the following deployments were revealed in an "NBC Nightly News" investigation of Delta, aired January 2, 1985 (see transcript, pp. 10–11). Other lists of deployments appeared in the *Washington Post*, December 5, 1985; *Washington Times*, June 17, 1985; and *St. Louis Post-Dispatch*, June 17, 1985. See also HAC, *DOD App. 1985*, Pt. 8, p. 805 (Dozier, 1982, and Olympics, 1984); *Newsweek*, April 22, 1985, p. 22 (Sudan, 1983); *Washington Times*, January 3, 1985, and *New York Post*, December 18, 1984 (Kuwaiti airliner in Iran, 1984); *Washington Post*, November 21, 1985 (Beirut, 1985); *National Journal*, May 10, 1986, p. 1103, *Washington Post*, December 3, 1985, and *New York Times*, October 11, 1985 (*Achille Lauro*, 1985); and *Newsweek*, September 15, 1986, p. 26 (Pakistan, 1986).

34. *Washington Post*, November 21, 1985.

35. A good article on TF-160 appeared in *Newsweek*, April 22, 1985, p. 24.

36. Gen. Moore to HASC, September 13, 1984, p. 7.

37. *Army Posture Statement FY1987*, p. 19; HAC, *DOD App. FY1987*, Pt. 1, p. 165.

38. Joint Chiefs of Staff, *Department of Defense Dictionary of Military and Associated Terms*, JCS Pub. 1, (Washington, D.C., 1984, p. 230.

39. *Wall Street Journal*, June 16, 1986, citing "government estimates." HAC, *DOD App. FY1987*, Pt. 6, p. 566, says 97 percent of CA is in the Army Reserves.

40. *Wall Street Journal*, June 16, 1986; HAC, *DOD App. FY1987*, Pt. 6, p. 566, says 89 percent of PSYOP is in the Army Reserves.

41. HAC, *DOD App. FY1987*, Pt. 6, p. 564; *Army Posture Statement FY1987*, p. 19.

42. 1st Special Operations Command Briefing at the JFK Center for Military Assistance, undated (1981?), p. 12; Army Field Manual 33-5.

43. Army Field Manual 33-5.

44. See Chap. 5.

45. *The Elite and Their Support*, extracts from Vol. 1, 1984, p. 42; 1st Special Operations Command Briefing at JFK Center for Military Assistance, undated (1981?), p. 17.

46. 1st Special Operations Command Information Packet, Ft. Bragg, N.C., January 1, 1984, p. 1.

47. HAC, *DOD App. FY1986*, Pt. 6, p. 644.

48. HAC, *DOD App. FY1987*, Pt. 6, pp. 571, 664; *Jane's Defence Weekly*, January 26, 1985, p. 158.

49. *Army RDT&E Supporting Data FY1987*, Vol. 2, pp. 74–75.

50. HAC, *DOD App. FY1987*, Pt. 6, pp. 653–55, 668–69, 671.

51. DOD Fact Sheet, "SOF Expansion," December 1984, p. 1; HAC, *DOD App. FY1986*, Pt. 6, p. 604; *JCS Posture Statement FY1986*, p. 68.

232

52. HASC, *DOD Authorization FY1984*, Pt. 6, p. 54; *Combat Arms*, November 1984, p. 86.
53. *All Hands*, April 1985, p. 7.
54. HASC, *DOD Auth. FY1984*, Pt. 6, p. 57; HAC, *Mil. Con. App.*, *FY1982*, Pt. 1, p. 939; SAC, *Mil. Con. App. FY1986*, p. 139.
55. HASC, *DOD Auth. FY1984*, Pt. 6, p. 57; HAC, *DOD App. 1986*, Pt. 6, p. 604.
56. HAC, *Mil. Con. FY1982*, Pt. 1, p. 939; "NBC Nightly News" transcript, January 2, 1985, p. 10; *New York Times*, June 8, 1985.
57. HASC, *DOD Auth. FY1984*, Pt. 6, p. 65; *Defense and Foreign Affairs*, September 1984, p. 26; *Glasgow Herald*, November 18, 1981.
58. HAC, *DOD App. FY1986*, Pt. 6, p. 604; *Defense and Foreign Affairs*, September 1984, p. 26.
59. The new unit will be called SEAL Team 8. See *DOD App. FY1986*, Pt. 6, p. 647; Statement by Capt. T. E. Grabowsky to HASC, July 30, 1985, p. 4.
60. HAC, *DOD. App FY1987*, Pt. 6, p. 553.
61. HASC, *DOD Auth. FY1984*, Pt. 6, pp. 62–63; *The Elite and Their Support*, extracts from Vol. 1, 1984, p. 30.
62. HASC, *DOD Auth. FY1984*, Pt. 6, pp. 62, 72.
63. Author's interview with Capt. Ted Lyon (ISA/Special Plans), February 22, 1985.
64. HAC, *Mil. Con. App. FY1982*, Pt. 1, p. 939; SAC, *DOD App. FY1981*, Pt. 4, p. 381.
65. Capt. Lyon, February 27, 1985; HAC, *DOD App. FY1987*, Pt. 6, p. 680.
66. *JCS Posture Statement FY1987*, p. 63; Capt. Lyon, February 27, 1985; *Proceedings*, May 1984, pp. 174–75; Sen. Sasser in *Nation*, July 14, 1984, p. 10; *Washington Post*, January 4, 1985; "NBC Nightly News," January 2, 1985; *Jane's Defence Weekly*, January 12, 1985, p. 96; author's interview with Ms. Judy Van (CHINFO), February 14, 1985; HASC, *DOD Auth. FY1984*, Pt. 6, p. 72.
67. *JCS Posture Statement FY1986*, p. 68; Capt. Lyon, February 27, 1985.
68. *Military Technology*, Vol. VI, No. 5 (1982), p. 32.
69. HAC, *DOD App. FY1986*, Pt. 6, p. 604; Capt. Lyon, February 22, 1985; HASC, *DOD Auth. FY1984*, Pt. 6, p. 59.
70. HAC, *DOD App. FY1986*, Pt. 6, p. 604; HAC, *DOD App. FY1986*, Pt. 4, p. 467; HAC, *DOD App. FY1987*, Pt. 6, p. 554; Statement of Capt. Grabowsky to HASC, July 30, 1985, p. 5; *Jane's Defence Weekly*, December 15, 1984, p. 1057.
71. DOD Fact Sheet, "SOF Expansion," December 1984, p. 1; *Wall Street Journal*, June 10, 1986; Koch to HAC, April 10, 1984, p. 11; *Air Force*, January 1984, p. 78.
72. HAC, *DOD App. FY1987*, Pt. 6, p. 590.
73. Ibid, pp. 590, 600; HAC, *DOD App. FY1986*, Pt. 6, p. 605.
74. HAC, *DOD App. FY1987*, Pt. 6, pp. 590, 597, 599, 600; HAC, *DOD App. FY1986*, Pt. 6, p. 605; SASC, *DOD Auth. FY1985*, Pt. 8, p. 3918; Gen. Smith to HASC, April 7, 1983; 1st SOW FY84 Economic Impact Statement; *Defense and Foreign Affairs*, September 1984, pp. 26–27.
75. HAC, *DOD App. FY1987*, Pt. 1, p. 639, and Pt. 6, pp. 594–95, 655, 699; HAC, *DOD App. FY1986*, Pt. 6, p. 598.
76. Good details in HAC, *DOD App. FY1987*, Pt. 6, pp. 590–91 and HAC, *DOD App. FY1986*, Pt. 6, p. 636. See also DOD, *Program Acquisition Costs FY86*, p. 44. Missions described in HAC, *DOD App. FY1987*, Pt. 6, pp. 590–91; SASC, *DOD Auth. FY1985*, Pt. 8, p. 3918; Sec. Def., *Annual Report FY86*, p. 182; DOD, *Program Acquisition Costs FY86*, p. 44.
77. HAC, *DOD App. FY1986*, Pt. 6, pp. 617, 623, 636–37; HAC, *DOD App. FY1987*, Pt. 6, p. 685.
78. HAC, *DOD App. FY1987*, Pt. 6, p. 687; *USAF Posture Statement FY1986*, pp. 47–48; *Aviation Week and Space Technology*, January 14, 1985, p. 85.
79. DOD, Selected Acquisition Report as of June 30, 1986, cites total services buy of 608

for $19.8 billion, or $32.6 million per copy. AF total of 80 cited in HAC, DOD App. 1987, Pt. 6, p. 687.

80. The Marine initiative was first publicly revealed in a HASC press release dated August 5, 1985. See also *AFJI,* October 1985, pp. 24–25.

81. *Navy Times,* August 19, 1985, p. 3; *Jane's Defence Weekly,* December 7, 1985, p. 1235; HAC, *DOD App. FY1987,* Pt. 6, p. 678.

82. 1st Special Operations Command Briefing at JFK Center for Military Assistance, undated (1981?), p. 15.

83. NSWG1 Staff Manual, September 11, 1981, pp. 2–20.

84. See Field Manuals 31-21, 31-21A, 5-26.

85. 1st Special Operations Command Briefing at JFK Center for Military Assistance, undated (1981?), p. 15.

86. Thomas Cochran et al., *Nuclear Weapons Databook, Volume I: US Nuclear Forces and Capabilities* (Cambridge, Mass.: Ballinger, 1984), pp. 60, 311.

87. Ibid; "NBC Nightly News" transcript, January 3, 1985.

88. "America's Secret Warriors," *Newsweek,* October 10, 1983, pp. 38–39; *New York Times,* June 11, 1984, July 7, 1986.

89. *New York Times,* July 7, 1986.

90. *New York Times,* June 11, 1984; *Newsweek,* October 10, 1983, p. 38.

91. *Newsweek,* October 10, 1983, p. 38.

92. *New York Times,* July 7, 1986.

93. *Newsweek,* October 10, 1983, pp. 38–41.

94. *Newsweek,* October 10, 1983, pp. 41, 46.

95. *Nation,* July 14, 1984, p. 10.

96. *New York Times,* November 29, 1984.

97. *Washington Post,* September 5, 1984.

98. *New York Times,* August 21, 1986.

99. See *Washington Post,* August 17, 1986, "The Trouble with Covert Action," by Rep. Lee Hamilton, chairman of the House Permanent Select Committee on Intelligence.

100. Jim Wooten, "Special Operations Forces: Issues for Congress," Congressional Research Service Report No. 84-227F (December 14, 1984), pp. vi, 14–17.

101. *Washington Post,* August 17, 1986.

102. *Los Angeles Times,* November 18, 1984.

103. Army officials cited in Michael Gordon, "The Charge of the Light Infantry," *National Journal,* May 19, 1984, p. 968.

104. HAC, *DOD App. FY1987,* Pt. 1, pp. 141, 143.

105. SASC, *DOD Auth. FY1985,* Pt. 2, p. 1248.

106. Michael Gordon, "The Charge of the Light Infantry," p. 968. See also SASC, "Army's Light Division" (hereinafter "ALD"), June 20, 1985, p. 37.

107. "Light Infantry Division," *Air Defense Artillery,* Fall 1985, p. 38.

108. SASC, "ALD," p. 23; DOD news release, March 11, 1986.

109. SASC, "ALD," p. 23; HAC, *DOD App. FY1987,* Pt. 1, p. 142.

110. Maj. Scott MacMichael, "Proverbs of the Light Infantry," *Military Review,* September 1985, pp. 22–28.

111. HAC, *DOD App. FY1987,* Pt. 1, p. 143.

112. Sec. Def., *Annual Report FY1987,* p. 155; *Army Times,* August 19, 1985, pp. 7, 30, and September 30, 1985, p. 3; DOD news release, March 11, 1986; *Army Times,* April 17, 1986, p. 10; General Accounting Office, "Information on Stationing Army's 6th Infantry Division," August 1986, p. 4; *Army Times,* September 30, 1985, p. 3; *Washington Times,* August 23, 1985; *AFJI,* November 1985, p. 24.

113. *Army Posture Statement FY1987,* p. 18.

114. Sec. Def., *Annual Report FY1987,* pp. 155–56.

115. *Army Times,* September 9, 1985, p. 6.

116. *Army Times,* September 8, 1986, p. 12.

117. *Army Posture Statement FY1987*, p. 17; *Army Times*, August 19, 1985, p. 38.
118. *Army Times*, April 14, 1986, p. 18; *Army Times*, April 7, 1986, p. 10; DOD news release, March 11, 1986.
119. Good sources for LID weapons and equipment include: SASC, "ALD," pp. 46–47; *Military Technology*, May 1985, p. 89; *Military Logistics Forum*, May 1985, p. 30; *Military Intelligence*, April–June 1985, p. 11; *National Defense*, November 1984, pp. 57–58; *Army Times*, September 15, 1986, pp. 27, 30; *Army*, October 1986, p. 410.
120. LTV Aerospace Defense, HMMWV Technical Information Sheet (August 1984), and Hummer M998 Series Brochure (July 1986).
121. Donald Gilleland, "To Drive It Is to Love It," *Defense Systems Review*, No. 5, 1985, p. 40.
122. *Defense Week*, March 31, 1986, p. 3.
123. *Army Times*, April 7, 1986, p. 10.
124. *Aviation Week and Space Technology*, April 28, 1986, pp. 43, 68–83; U.S. Army, *Army Weapons Systems 1984*, p. 77; *Defense Systems Review*, July–August 1984, p. 14.
125. *Army Times*, September 15, 1986, pp. 27, 30; *Army*, October 1986, p. 410.
126. Maj. J. F. Holden-Rhodes, "Light Infantry: New Applications of an Old Concept," *Military Intelligence*, April–June 1985, p. 11; SASC, "ALD," p. 24; *Army*, October 1986, p. 411.
127. *Defense News*, February 10, 1986, p. 4.
128. SASC, "ALD," pp. 41, 54; *Army*, October 1986, pp. 422, 424.
129. Wickham *White Paper 1984*.
130. SASC, "ALD," p. 29.
131. Holden-Rhodes, "Light Infantry," p. 11.
132. Sec. Def., *Annual Report FY1987*, p. 238.
133. Sec. Def., *Annual Report FY1986*, p. 41.
134. Gen. George Crist (Commander in Chief Central Command), statement to SASC, March 11, 1986, p. 26.
135. Sec. Def., *Annual Report FY1987*, p. 240.
136. Crist to SASC, p. 53.
137. Sec. Def., *Annual Report FY1987*, p. 242.
138. Sec. Def., *Annual Report FY1986*, p. 200.
139. *AFJI*, April 1985, p. 16.
140. *Navy Times*, March 24, 1986, p. 8.
141. Sec. Def., *Annual Report FY1987*, p. 238.
142. Information on all of the following is from DOD, *Selected Acquisition Report* (June 30, 1986), and Sec. Def., *Annual Report FY1987*, pp. 240–41.
143. DOD, *Selected Acquisition Report*, June 30, 1986.
144. Watkins statement to HAC, February 26, 1986, p. 40.
145. Sec. Def., *Annual Report FY1986*, p. 200. See also Watkins to HAC, p. 39.
146. Sec. Def., *Annual Report FY1987*, p. 242.
147. Ibid.
148. Ibid.
149. Sec. Def., *Annual Report FY1986*, p. 157.
150. *AFJI*, July 1986, p. 76.
151. Secretary of the Navy John Lehman's Report to HAC FY1987, February 26, 1986, p. 38.
152. Center for Defense Information Fact Sheet, "Detailed Costs of One New CVN Aircraft Carrier Battlegroup Over 30 Years," June 1982; HAC, *DOD App. FY1983*, Pt. 2, p. 124.
153. DOD, *Selected Acquisition Report*, June 30, 1986.
154. *Navy Times*, March 31, 1986, pp. 25, 28.

155. Sec. Def., *Annual Report FY1987,* p. 182.
156. Ibid., p. 183.
157. DOD, *Selected Acquisition Report,* June 30, 1986.
158. Sec. Def., *Annual Report FY1987,* p. 183.

CHAPTER 5 EL SALVADOR

1. Reagan ambassador to Costa Rica Lewis A. Tambs and Lt. Com. Frank Aker, "Shattering the Vietnam Syndrome: A Scenario for Success in El Salvador" (unpublished ms., 1983), p. 11.
2. Col. John D. Waghelstein, "El Salvador: Observations and Experiences in Counterinsurgency," Study Project, U.S. Army War College, January 1, 1985. (Hereinafter Waghelstein study).
3. See Galvin's presentation at the American Defense Preparedness Association Conference, "Low-Intensity Conflict for Industry," March 4, 1987.
4. See Michael McClintock, *The American Connection, Volume 1: State Terror and Popular Resistance in El Salvador* (London: Zed, 1985), for exhaustive documentation of the U.S. role in constructing the modern "national security state" in El Salvador since 1960.
5. For the history of this network, see Allan Nairn, "Behind the Death Squads," *Progressive,* May 1984, p. 21.
6. Quoted in Raymond Bonner, *Weakness and Deceit: U.S. Policy and El Salvador* (New York: Times Books, 1982) p. 208.
7. Nairn, "Behind the Death Squads," p. 24.
8. Ibid., p. 23
9. Thomas Enders, before the Senate Foreign Relations Committee, February 2, 1983. Cited in *"In Contempt of Congress: The Reagan Record of Deceit and Illegality on Central America,"* Institute for Policy Studies, 1985, p. 35. See Fiallos' testimony before the Foreign Operations Subcommittee of the House Appropriations Committee, April 29, 1981, ibid., p. 35.
10. U.S. diplomat quoted in "Why Death Squads Still Spread Terror," *U.S. News and World Report,* February 27, 1984, p. 30.
11. For figures on political killings by death squads and Army forces between 1979 and 1983, see "As Bad As Ever: A Report on Human Rights in El Salvador," Americas Watch/American Civil Liberties Union, January 31, 1984, pp. 8–9; Joaquin Villalobos, "The Current State of the War in El Salvador and Outlook for the Future," *Estudios Centroamericanos,* May 1986.
12. Salvadoran Defense Minister Vides Casanova said that a reduction in death squad killings was "worth billions of dollars of aid for the country." James LeMoyne, "A Salvador Police Chief Vows an End to Abuses," *New York Times,* July 1, 1984.
13. *Amnesty International Report, 1986,* (London: Amnesty International Publications, 1986), p. 152.
14. See Richard Millet, "Praetorians or Patriots? The Central American Military," in Robert S. Leiken, ed., *Central America: Anatomy of Conflict* (New York: Pergamon, 1984), p. 75.
15. Waghelstein study, p. 34.
16. Ibid., p. 49.
17. Author's interview with Col. Aron Royer, Defense Security Assistance Agency (DSAA), June 27, 1986.
18. "U.S. Aid to El Salvador: An Evaluation of the Past, A Proposal for the Future," a report of the Arms Control and Foreign Policy Caucus, from Rep. Jim Leach (R-Iowa), Rep. George Miller (D-Calif.), and Sen. Mark Hatfield (R-Ore.), February 1985, p. 96.

19. Department of Defense reports, "U.S. Training Teams in El Salvador as of 31 August, 1982," and "U.S. Training Teams in El Salvador as of 25 October, 1982."
20. Interview with John Waghelstein, July 29, 1986.
21. See the *New York Times*, March 28, 1983.
22. "A Turn for the Worse," *Newsweek*, December 12, 1983, p. 54.
23. Chris Hedges, "Salvador Rebel Leaders Admit Army Has Thrown Them Off Balance," *Christian Science Monitor*, August 28, 1984.
24. 1987 figure provided by Major Mike Blatti, staff assistant, Defense Security Assistance Agency (DSAA), in author's interview, June 17, 1987.
25. Robert McCartney, "U.S. Reconnaissance Helps El Salvador Increase Bombing," *Washington Post*, April 12, 1984.
26. "Managing the Facts: How the Administration Deals with Reports of Human Rights Abuses in El Salvador," Americas Watch, December 1985, p. 27. "Basically, we feel if you don't carry a gun you are a noncombatant," said U.S. embassy spokesperson Don Hamilton. "But the guerilla relationship with the 'masas' complicates matters, so it is a sad fact of life in El Salvador that civilians do get killed in bombings." Marc Cooper, "Duarte Bombs in El Salvador," *L.A. Weekly*, July 26–August 1, 1985.
27. Author's backround interview with former high-level U.S. military adviser in El Salvador.
28. Waghelstein's study, p. 35.
29. See Waghelstein's speech, "Low-Intensity Conflict in the Post-Vietnam Period," January 17, 1985, at the American Enterprise Institute, Washington, D.C.
30. Royer interview.
31. State Department cable, April 3, 1985.
32. Robert McCartney, "Salvadoran Rebel Area Gets U.S. Aid," *Washington Post*, December 18, 1983. The *Christian Science Monitor*, commenting on the plan's failures, concluded, "The guerrillas seem as much involved in applying American aid as do local officials." Chris Hedges, "Rebels Pull Strings of U.S. Aid Program in El Salvador Province," *Christian Science Monitor*, December 9, 1983.
33. Author's interview with State Department official, June 30, 1986.
34. Army Chief of Staff General Blandón quoted in "El Salvador: How Much Change Is Possible?" Kenneth Sharpe, *World Policy Journal*, Fall 1986.
35. El Salvadoran Armed Forces, "Campana de Contrainsurgencia 'Unidos para Reconstruction,'" March 1986, secret, p. 22.
36. Ibid. p. 16.
37. Ibid.
38. *New York Times*, July 3, 1985.
39. Waghelstein study, App. 8b.
40. Tim Golden, "War for Minds Opens New Front in Salvador," *Miami Herald*, July 14, 1985.
41. Edward Cody, "U.S. Backs Salvadorans In Psywar Campaign," *Washington Post*, August 5, 1985; Golden, "War for Minds,"
42. Alfonso Chardy, "U.S. Fighting Secret Battles Worldwide," *Miami Herald*, December 16, 1986.
43. Ibid.
44. Golden, "War for Minds."
45. Marjorie Miller, "Salvador Aims Psychological Fire at Rebels," *Los Angeles Times*, September 9, 1985.
46. Ibid.
47. Ambrose Evans-Pritchard, "Salvador Village Defenders," *Washington Times*, July 26, 1985.
48. Latin America Regional Reports, "Ochoa Mutiny: Bring Me the Head of Guillermo Garcia," January 19, 1983, cited in McClintock, *The American Connection*, p. 341.

49. Mary Jo McConahay, "El Salvador: Hopes Ebb for Early End to War," *Latinamerica Press*, August 29, 1985.
50. Robert S. Greenberger, "Military's Return to Humanitarian-Aid Business Raises Concerns About Using Food as a Weapon," *Wall Street Journal* June 16, 1987.
51. Dan Williams, "Salvador Villages Resist Army's Call for Militias," *Los Angeles Times*, January 9, 1985.
52. Capt. Robert S. Perry, "Civic Action and Regional Security," *Journal of International Security Assistance*, Spring 1983, p. 36.
53. The Lawyers' Committee for International Human Rights and Americas Watch, *El Salvador's Other Victims: The War on the Displaced* (New York, 1984), pp. 84–89; and Eva Gold, "The New Face of War in El Salvador" (American Friends Service Committee, National Action Research on the Military Industrial Complex, February 1986), pp. 4–5.
54. Author's interview with Dick Nelson, June 30, 1986.
55. Greenberger, "Military's Return to Humanitarian-Aid Business."
56. Ibid.
57. Author's interview, AID, Latin and Caribbean Division, September 25, 1986.
58. Defense Department Task Force Report on Humanitarian Assistance, approved by the Secretary of Defense on June 19, 1984.
59. Waghelstein study, p. C-9.
60. U.S. State Department, Special Report No. 148, August 1986. 1986 figures refer to allocations.
61. Tom Barry and Deb Preusch, *The Central America Fact Book* (New York: Grove Press, 1986), p. 28.
62. Leach, Miller, and Hatfield, "U.S. Aid to El Salvador," p. 41.
63. "U.S. Aid and the Economy of El Salvador," testimony by Jorge Sol Castellanos before the Subcommittee on Foreign Operations of the House Appropriations Committee, April 21, 1987.
64. Ivan Santiago, "Salvadorans Resist Paying Price of 'War Economy,' " *Latinamerica Press*, May 22, 1986.
65. Cable from William Hallman, Political Officer at the U.S. Embassy in El Salvador, January 1981, cited in Bonner, *Weakness and Deceit*, p. 189.
66. Ibid., p. 200.
67. Ibid. p. 199.
68. Tom Barry and Deb Preusch, "El Salvador: The Other War" (The Resource Center, Albuquerque, New Mexico, 1986), p. 37.
69. For an overview of the exclusionary, coercive, and fraudulent nature of the elections, see Edward S. Herman and Frank Brodhead, *Demonstration Elections: U.S.-Staged Elections in the Dominican Republic, Vietnam, and El Salvador* (Boston: South End, 1984).
70. A March 1981 Gallup poll showed only 2 percent of Americans favored sending U.S. troops to El Salvador, while less than 20 percent backed military or economic aid.
71. In May 1982, for instance, the Senate Foreign Relations Committee slashed the administration's FY1983 aid request by $100 million.
72. For discussion on D'Aubuisson's role with the death squads, see Craig Pyes, "Salvadoran Rightists: The Deadly Patriots," *Albuquerque Journal*, December 18–22, 1983, and Pyes' "Who Killed Archbishop Romero," *Nation*, October 13, 1984.
73. For a good discussion of the role of elections in the Salvador conflict, see Terry Karl's unpublished paper, "Imposing Consent: Electoralism vs. Democratization in El Salvador."
74. See Philip Taubman, "C.I.A. Said To Aid Salvador Parties," *New York Times*, May 12, 1984, and Robert J. McCartney, "U.S. Seen Assisting Duarte In Sunday's Salvadoran Vote," *Washington Post*, May 3, 1984.
75. Few in Congress remembered that Duarte presided over the military junta that killed

twenty-five thousand noncombatants during his tenure between March 1980 and March 1982.

76. Marc Cooper, "Whitewashing Duarte: U.S. Reporting on El Salvador," *NACLA Report on the Americas*, January–March 1986, p. 7.

77. National Security Planning Group, "U.S. Policy in Central America and Cuba Through FY'84, Summary Paper," April 1982.

78. Cited by John B. Oakes, "In El Salvador, A Dance of Death," *New York Times*, December 12, 1984.

79. "Salvadorans Resist Paying Price of 'War Economy,'" Ivan Santiago, *Latinamerica Press*, May 22, 1986, p. 3.

80. Of special significance, the powerful UNTS alliance included the Democratic Popular Unity (UPD), a powerful labor machine created in part by AIFLD that played a central role in mobilizing support to elect Duarte. The UPD became increasingly critical of Duarte's failure to produce promised reforms for workers, and split with AIFLD in 1985 after AIFLD officials' attempts to bribe UPD workers to support Duarte were exposed.

81. In early 1985, some U.S. embassy officials expressed backing for a rightist victory in the 1985 Assembly elections to, in the words of one U.S. embassy official, "give balance to El Salvador's democracy." See the *New York Times*, May 12, 1985, and Jonathan Kwitney, "Anti-Duarte Tilt," *Nation*, April 20, 1985.

82. Weeks before the earthquake, the *New York Times* reported that "the army is more narrowly defining the rules of the game. Civilian rule in El Salvador appears to remain an experiment in which the army may play a growing, rather than diminishing, role." James LeMoyne, "In Salvador, an Uneasy Peace Between Duarte and the Army," *New York Times*, September 21, 1986.

83. A poll conducted by the Salvadoran government in October 1986 found that 49 percent of Salvadorans were not sure if any political party in the country was capable of resolving the country's economic crisis. Marjorie Williams, "Salvador Rightists Attack Duarte Over Taxes for War," *Los Angeles Times*, January 12, 1987.

84. "Duarte's Unkept Promises," *Newsweek*, March 2, 1987.

85. See Tammy Arbuckle, "Same Hardware, Same Tactics, Same Conclusion in El Salvador?" *Armed Forces Journal*, December 1985, p. 50.

86. Gabriel Kolko, *Anatomy of a War: Vietnam, the United States, and the Modern Historical Experience* (New York: Pantheon, 1985), p. 5.

CHAPTER 6 NICARAGUA

1. See William R. Bode, "The Reagan Doctrine," in *Strategic Review*, Winter 1986, p. 26.

2. See Reagan's nationally televised speech on Central America, May 9, 1984, reprinted in the *New York Times*, May 10, 1984.

3. *New York Times*, May 3, 1987.

4. See MacMichael's testimony before the World Court, September 8, 1985, p. 8 of transcript.

5. Department of State briefing paper, "Central America," June 26, 1982.

6. See the *Miami Herald*, June 5, 1983.

7. The NSC document, "United States Policy in Central America and Cuba Through FY84, Summary Paper," is reprinted in the *New York Times*, April 7, 1983.

8. CIA, Directorate of Intelligence, "Nicaragua: Costs of the Insurgency," secret, July 26, 1983.

9. CIA Intelligence Information Report, "Fifteenth of September Movement," July 28, 1981.

10. See Woody Kepner Associates' letter to Edgar Chamorro, January 24, 1983.

11. See DIA, Weekly Intelligence Summary, July 16, 1982, p. 21.
12. These statistics are cited in David Siegel, M.D., "Nicaraguan Health: An Update," *LASA Forum*, Winter 1986, p. 30.
13. See Americas Watch, "Human Rights in Nicaragua: Reagan, Rhetoric and Reality," July 1985, p. 16.
14. For the original lesson plan, see United States Army Special Warfare School, Psychological Operations Department, Fort Bragg, North Carolina, Lesson Plan 643, "Armed Psyop," April 1968.
15. The manual has been translated and published. For quotations, see Tayacán, *Psychological Operations in Guerrilla Warfare* (New York: Vintage, 1985).
16. Clarridge's testimony is cited in the *Miami Herald,* October 20, 1984.
17. Exerpts of the CIA summary paper of attacks in Nicaragua are cited in the *Wall Street Journal,* March 6, 1985.
18. *Washington Post,* April 11, 1984.
19. This estimate was made by Nicaragua's ambassador to the OAS, Juan Gozal. See his statement to the OAS, April 24, 1984.
20. United Nations Economic Commission for Latin America, "Nicaragua: Economic Repercussions of Recent Political Events," E/CEPAL/G. 1091, September 1979, p. 24.
21. World Bank, "Nicaragua: The Challenge of Reconstruction," Report No. 3524-NI, October 9, 1981, p. 57.
22. White House press release, May 10, 1983.
23. *Washington Post,* May 8, 1985.
24. For an assessment of the embargo's impact, see the Overseas Development Council, Policy Focus, "The U.S. Embargo Against Nicaragua—One Year Later," No. 3, 1986.
25. Memorandum from Jane Hallow, assistant to the U.S. director, "Bank Policy in Nicaragua," August 24, 1983.
26. See the *Washington Post,* March 8, 1985.
27. See the Inter-American Development Bank, Secretary to Board of Executive Directors, "Nicaragua: Request for a Loan for a Global Agricultural Credit Program" (PR-1490), December 17, 1985, p. 2.
28. *New York Times,* March 30, 1985.
29. Quoted in Sara Miles, "The Real War," NACLA, April–May 1986.
30. Quoted in the *New York Times,* March 30, 1985.
31. See Robert Kupperman Associates, *Low-Intensity Conflict,* July 30, 1983.
32. See the *Washington Post,* August 6, 1983.
33. For Gorman's views on LIC, see his statement before the Senate Armed Services Committee, February 27, 1985.
34. *New York Times,* September 20, 1983.
35. See the General Accounting Office, Appendix to Comptroller General Decision B-213137, "Funding of Joint Combined Military Exercise in Honduras," p. 1.
36. See March 8, 1984, DOD letter to the GAO cited in a GAO letter to Congressman Bill Alexander, June 22, 1984. See also Nestor Sanchez's testimony before the House Subcommittee on Military Construction, March 7, 1984.
37. See the General Accounting Office, "Funding of Joint Combined Military Exercise in Honduras," p. 14.
38. Appendix I, "GAO Responses to Questions in November 14, 1983 Letter," p. 3. This appendix is undated but appears to be an attachment to the GAO's March 6, 1984, report to Congressman Alexander.
39. Ibid. p. 4. See also Sanchez's testimony before the House Subcommittee on Military Construction, March 7, 1984.
40. Colonel Comee is quoted in the "Report to Senate Democratic Leader Robert C. Byrd on a Democratic Party Staff Trip to Nicaragua, Honduras, El Salvador, Costa Rica, Guatemala, July 5–16, 1986," August 5, 1986, p. 67.

41. Statement of General Paul F. Gorman, February 27, 1985.
42. See the *New York Times*, April 23, 1984.
43. *New York Times*, June 5, 1985.
44. This document was obtained and reprinted in full in the *New York Times*, April 7, 1983.
45. Edward Gonzalez et al., "U.S. Policy in Central America" (Santa Monica, Calif.: Rand Corporation, October 1983), pp. 4,5.
46. Weinberger is quoted from his Fort McNair Conference speech. January 14, 1986.
47. See NSDD-77, "Management of Public Diplomacy Relative to National Security," January 14, 1983, p. 1.
48. According to Whittlesey, the Outreach Group endeavored to "get the American people to understand that what we are facing down there is communism in our own backyard." For a description of the group's operations see the *Washington Post*, June 17 and September 24, 1983.
49. NSC Summary Paper, "Strategy in Central America," July 6, 1983, p. 8.
50. See MacMichael's statements in the *New York Times*, June 11, 1984.
51. This evaluation, which states that there is "little likelihood of an attack on [Nicaragua's neighbors], given fear of U.S. reprisal," is cited in the *Wall Street Journal*, April 4, 1985.
52. For a thorough comparison of Reagan's claims and the facts, see Americas Watch, "Human Rights in Nicaragua."
53. As one embassy official told reporters, "We've pointed out the distortions time and time again and been totally ignored or told to shut up." See the *Boston Globe*, April 20, 1982.
54. Americas Watch, "Human Rights in Nicaragua," p. 40.
55. This quote is taken from the State Department agenda briefing paper prepared for the "Chiefs of Mission Conference, Panama, September 4, 1985," p. 4.
56. See the *Miami Herald*, November 21, 1986.
57. For an overview of the administration's harassment campaign, see Margaret Leahy, "The Harassment of Nicaraguanists and 'Fellow Travellers,' " in Thomas W. Walker, ed., *Reagan vs. the Sandinistas: The Undeclared War on Nicaragua* (Boulder, Col.: Westview Press, 1987).
58. Peter Kornbluh, "The Selling of the FDN," *The Nation*, January 21, 1987, p. 41.
59. Project No. 1001-602066, U.S. Department of State Contracts Branch, "Description/Specifications/Work Statement."
60. See "ABC World News Tonight," February 12, 1987.
61. *New York Times*, May 4, 1987.

CHAPTER 7 PHILIPPINES

1. Joint Low-Intensity Conflict Project, *Joint Low-Intensity Conflict Project Final Report, Volume II: Low-Intensity Conflict Issues and Recommendations* (Fort Monroe, Va.: U.S. Army Training and Doctrine Command, August 1986), Part C2, pp. 2–3.
2. Ibid.
3. Paul Wolfowitz, assistant secretary of state for East Asian and Pacific affairs, "Developments in the Philippines," statement at hearings of U.S. Senate Foreign Relations Committee, Washington, D.C., October 30, 1985, p. 13.
4. Memorandum to Lawrence Houston, CIA general counsel, from Allen Dulles, April 21, 1964, Dulles Collection, Mudd Library, Princeton University. See also letter of Allen Dulles to Harry Truman, January 7, 1964, from the same collection.
5. Edward Lansdale, introductory remarks at "Counter-Guerrilla Seminar," Fort Bragg, N.C., 1961.
6. Ibid.

7. Lansdale, *In the Midst of Wars* (New York: Harper & Row, 1972), p. 51.

8. David Sturtevant, "Filipino Peasant Rebellions Examined: Lessons from the Past," in *CALC Report,* Vol. XII, No. 3 (May–June 1986), p. 6.

9. Francisco Nemenzo, "Rectification Process in the Philippine Communist Movement," in Joo-Jock Lim and S. Vani, eds., *Armed Communist Movements in Southeast Asia* (Aldershot, England: Gower, 1984), p. 73.

10. For figures and types of U.S. military and economic aid, see Walden Bello and Severina Rivera, eds., *The Logistics of Repression: The Role of U.S. Military Aid in Consolidating the Martial Law Regime in the Philippines* (Washington, D.C.: Friends of the Filipino People, 1977).

11. U.S. Department of Defense, *Answers to Questions on Defense Issues Posed in the August 20, 1984, Letter of the House of Representatives Subcommittee on Asian and Pacific Affairs* (Washington, D.C., 1984), pp. 12–13.

12. James Kelly, deputy assistant secretary of defense for international security affairs, "Fiscal Year 1985 Security Assistance for the Philippines," statement to the House Subcommittee on Asian and Pacific Affairs, February 7, 1984, pp. 9–10.

13. Richard Armitage, assistant secretary of defense for international security affairs, confirmed the figure in response to a question from Rep. Stephen Solarz at hearings of the House Asian and Pacific Affairs Subcommittee on November 12, 1985.

14. Inter-Agency Task Force, *NSSD* [National Security Study Directive]: *U.S. Policy Toward the Philippines,* secret, Washington, D.C., November 2, 1984. (Hereinafter *NSSD.*)

15. Michael Armacost, speech at Foreign Service Institute, Rosslyn, Virginia, April 23, 1986.

16. Wolfowitz, statement at hearings of House of Representatives Subcommittee on Asian and Pacific Affairs, November 12, 1985.

17. *Washington Post,* October. 22, 1984.

18. For an account of Crowe's assessment, see Nayan Chanda, "A Gloomy View of Reform and Rebellion from the U.S.," *Far Eastern Economic Review,* August 30, 1984, pp. 28–30.

19. The *NSSD* was leaked by sources at the State Department to the author, who leaked it to the *Washington Post, Far Eastern Economic Review,* and other news media.

20. *NSSD.*

21. Ibid.

22. Ibid.

23. Ibid.

24. Ibid.

25. Ibid.

26. Armitage, testimony at hearings of House Foreign Affairs Committee, October 4, 1984.

27. *NSSD.*

28. Kelly, "Fiscal Year 1985," p. 4.

29. Command and General Staff College, Armed Forces of the Philippines, *The AFP Foreign Training Program for Officers: An Assessment* (Manila: AFP, 1983), pp. 25–26.

30. Armitage, reply to question at hearings of U.S. Senate Foreign Relations Committee, December 18, 1985.

31. Quoted in "Further Details on Military Shakeup," *Ang Pahayagang Malaya,* December 5, 1985.

32. Armitage, statement at hearings of House Asia–Pacific Affairs Subcommittee, November 15, 1985, pp. 1–2.

33. Nayan Chanda, "Dear Mr. President . . . ," *Far Eastern Economic Review,* October 31, 1985, p. 17.

34. Confidential cable from U.S. embassy, Manila, to Secretary of State, November 6, 1985.
35. Armitage, statement at hearings of Senate Foreign Relations Committee, December 18, 1985, p. 1.
36. Gwen Robinson, "Fraud Puts Marcos Offside with Army," *National Times*, January 31, 1986, p. 25.
37. John Monjo, "U.S. Assistance to the Philippines," statement at hearings of House Subcommittee on Asian and Pacific Affairs, May 15, 1986, pp. 8–9.
38. Michael Armacost, speech at Foreign Service Institute, Rosslyn, Virginia, April 23, 1986.
39. Ibid.
40. Armitage, statement at hearings of House Subcommittee on Asia and Pacific Affairs, March 17, 1987, p. 10.
41. Armitage, statement at hearings of Senate Foreign Relations Committee, June 3, 1986, p. 10.
42. "U.S. Wants Aquino to Toughen Stand on Insurgents," *New York Times*, September 1, 1986.
43. Armitage, statement to House Subcommittee on Asian and Pacific Affairs, March 17, 1987, p. 9.
44. *San Francisco Chronicle*, March 23, 1987.
45. Armitage, statement to Senate Foreign Relations Committee, June 3, 1986, pp. 7–8.
46. "The Hamstrung Philippine Army," *San Francisco Chronicle*, February 14, 1987, p. 9.
47. "U.S. Interference Bared," *Manila Chronicle*, February 10, 1987. This was an account of an exposé by Robin Broad, a fellow of the Council on Foreign Relations connected with the Carnegie Endownment for International Peace.
48. *Liberation* (International), September–October 1986, p. 4.
49. See among other reports *Philippine Human Rights Update*, Vol. 1, No. 11, (July 15–August 14, 1986).
50. Several good recent accounts of the rise of vigilante groups exist. See among others "Vigilantes for Aquino," *Newsweek*, March 30, 1987; and Seth Mydans, "Right-Wing Vigilantes Spread in Philippines," *New York Times*, April 4, 1987.
51. Quoted in *New York Times*, June 17, 1987.
52. Armed Forces of the Philippines, "Intelligence Estimate of the National Situation," undated, p. 7.
53. *Manila Chronicle*, February 10, 1987.
54. Annex to Armitage's statement to House Subcommittee on Asian and Pacific Affairs, May 15, 1986, p. 3.
55. *San Francisco Examiner*, March 22, 1987; see also *Newsweek*, March 23, 1987.
56. *Philadelphia Inquirer*, March 31, 1987.
57. This is based on interviews and research conducted by Erik Guyot in Davao in early 1985. For a summary of Guyot's findings, see Erik Guyot, "Hearts and Minds (Again)," *Progressive*, January 1986, pp. 28–31.
58. Thepchai Young, "Giving Philippine Military Cadets a New Direction," *The Nation* (Bangkok), reproduced in *JPRS Southeast Asia Report*, August 18, 1986, pp. 42–43.
59. Charles Grey, AAFLI executive director, statement at hearings of House Foreign Affairs Committee, May 15, 1986, p. 4.
60. Armitage, statement to the House Subcommittee on Asian and Pacific Affairs, March 17, 1985, pp. 1A, 2A.
61. Drawn from various sources, including *DMS Reports*, 1985.
62. Brian Massey, "Hurlburt Planes Hit by Gunfire," *Log* (Fort Walton Beach, Fla.), August 15, 1985, pp. 1A, 2A.
63. David Helvarg, "River Rats," *Image* (Sunday Magazine of the *San Francisco Examiner*), August 24, 1986, p. 24.

CHAPTER 8 AFGHANISTAN

1. Mikhail Gorbachev, *Political Report of the C.P.S.U. Central Committee to the 27th Party Congress*, (Moscow: Novosti Press Agency Publishing House, 1986), p. 86.
2. Najibullah Ahmadzai, then director of the Khad (secret police and intelligence service), gave this figure to Nikhil Chakravarty, editor of the New Delhi weekly *Mainstream*, in an interview in Kabul on October 15, 1985.
3. This figure is based on conversations with U.S. congressional and official sources and is less than that given in many published accounts.
4. Walter Pincus, "Panels to Probe Afghan Arms Fund," *Washington Post*, January 13, 1987.
5. The text of identical bilateral agreements concluded in 1959 between the U.S. and Iran, Turkey, and Pakistan may be found in *Documents on American Foreign Relations, 1959* (New York: Harper & Bros., 1960), pp. 397–99.
6. Craig M. Karp, "The War in Afghanistan," *Foreign Affairs*, Summer 1986, p. 1038.
7. Bakhtar News Agency, Kabul, May 14, 1986, cited in *Daily Report: South Asia*, Foreign Broadcast Information Service, May 15, 1986, p. Cl.
8. "Wir Warten Auf Unser Schicksal [We Are Waiting for Our Fate]," *Die Zeit*, December 28, 1984, p. 3.
9. *Pravda*, December 22, 1985, cited in *Daily Report: USSR International Affairs*, December 24, 1985, p. D1.
10. Declaration of the Revolutionary Council, Bakhtar News Agency, November 14, 1985, published by the Permanent Representative of the Democratic Republic of Afghanistan to the United Nations, November 29, 1985.
11. Bakhtar News Agency, Kabul, May 10, 1986, published by the Permanent Representative of the Democratic Republic of Afghanistan to the United Nations, June 1, 1986.
12. Bakhtar News Agency, Kabul, March 8, 1986, published by the Permanent Representative of the Democratic Republic of Afghanistan to the United Nations, April 1, 1986.
13. Cited in David C. Isby, "Soviet Tactics in the War in Afghanistan," *Jane's Defence Review*, Vol. 4, No. 7 (1983), p. 689.
14. Joseph Collins, "Soviet Military Performance in Afghanistan: A Preliminary Assessment," *Comparative Strategy*, Vol. 4, No. 2 (1983), p. 158.
15. David C. Isby, "Afghanistan: The Unending Struggle," *Jane's 1982–83 Military Review* (London, 1982), p. 40.
16. "Special Report: Afghanistan War," *Aviation Week and Space Technology*, October 29, 1984, p. 43.
17. *Pravda*, June 5, 1980, translated in United States Air Force, *Soviet Press: Selected Translations*, September 1981, p. 273.
18. Maj. Gen. F. Kuzmin, in *Krasnaya Zvezda*, cited in David C. Isby, "Soviet Tactics in the War in Afghanistan," p. 689.
19. Arthur Bonner, "The Slow-Motion War in Afghanistan," *New York Times*, July 6, 1986, The Week in Review, p. 2, citing sources in Peshawar. This estimate is reinforced by my own conversations with a U.S. Army intelligence specialist in Washington.
20. The latter figure is based on conversations with military attachés in well-informed European and Third World embassies in Kabul during my 1984 visit as well as subsequent conversations with U.S. and Indian intelligence specialists.
21. "Defining Success in Afghanistan," *Washington Quarterly*, Spring 1985, p. 42.
22. Rod Paschall, "Marxist Counterinsurgencies," *Parameters*, Summer 1986, Vol. XVI, No. 2, p. 10.
23. James B. Curren and Philip A. Karber, "Afghanistan's Ordeal," *Armed Forces Journal*, March 1985, p. 105.

24. Edward L. Girardet, *Afghanistan: The Soviet War*, (New York: St. Martin's Press, 1985), p. 183.
25. D. M. Khalil, "Coordination Leads to Success," *Journal of the Writer's Union for a Free Afghanistan* (Peshawar, Pakistan), Vol. 1, No. 1 (1985), p. 25.
26. A. Rasul Amin, "Unity Is the Remedy," *Journal of the Writers Union for a Free Afghanistan*, Vol. 1, No. 1 (1985), p. 13.
27. Selig S. Harrison, "Dateline Afghanistan: Exit Through Finland?" *Foreign Policy*, Winter 1980–81, pp. 170–72.
28. As one example of firsthand accounts of the Pakistani role, see Peter Niesewand, "Guerrillas Train in Pakistan to Oust Afghan Government," *Washington Post*, February 2, 1979.
29. Zbigniew Brzezinski, *Power and Principle* (New York: Farrar, Straus & Giroux, 1983), p. 427.
30. Raymond L. Garthoff, *Détente and Confrontation* (Washington, D.C.: Brookings Institution, 1985), p. 942.
31. Zbigniew Brzezinski, *Power and Principle*, pp. 427, 429.
32. Zalmay Khalilzad, "The United States and the War in Afghanistan," pp. 7, 9. Unpublished.
33. *Department of State Bulletin*, December 1979, p. 53.
34. U.S. State Department, Bureau of Public Affairs, *Background Notes: Afghanistan*, April 1983.
35. The existence of the CIA program was revealed in high-level press leaks in early 1980 (for example, see William Beecher, "What He Didn't Say," *Boston Globe*, January 5, 1980, and David Binder, "U.S. Supplying Afghan Insurgents with Arms in a Covert Operation," *New York Times*, February 15, 1980). Shortly before his death, the late Anwar Sadat confirmed Egypt's role in the program in an interview with NBC on September 22, 1981. As examples of eyewitness press accounts of U.S. weaponry in Afghanistan, see Richard Ben Kramer's articles in the *Philadelphia Inquirer* in 1980 (especially December 26, 1980); Aernout Van Lynden in the *Washington Post*, December 19, 1982; Joseph Allbright in the *Atlanta Journal*, June 15, 1983; *Newsweek*, "The Afghan Connection," October 10, 1983, p. 45; and *Time*, June 11, 1984, pp. 38–40. For reports dealing specifically with Saudi aid, see Jeff Gerth, "'81 Saudi Deal: Aid to Contras for U.S. Arms," *New York Times*, February 4, 1987, and Bob Woodward, "Saudis Gave $500 Million in Afghan Aid," the *Washington Post*, June 20, 1986.
36. Ibid.
37. David B. Ottaway, *Washington Post*, January 16, 1986.
38. Leslie H. Gelb, *New York Times*, June 19, 1986.
39. Joanne Omang, *Washington Post*, October 10, 1985. See also David Rogers, the *Wall Street Journal*, October 9, 1985.
40. David B. Ottaway, *Washington Post*, March 5, 1986.
41. Walter Pincus, "Iran Arms Cash Is Tied to C.I.A.-Run Account Aiding Afghan Rebels," *Washington Post*, December 3, 1986.
42. Ibid. See also Bob Woodward, "Saudis Gave $500 Million in Afghan Aid."
43. Ibid.
44. AID, Annual Budget Submission, FY88, *Afghanistan*, June 1986, pp. 38, 39.
45. James Rupert, "U.S. Aid to Rebels Stirs Fear of Hurting Cause," *Washington Post*, October 14, 1986.
46. Bernard Gwertzman, "Reagan Bars Ties to Afghan Rebels," *New York Times*, June 17, 1986. See also David B. Ottaway, "Administration's Signals Mixed on Afghans," *Washington Post*, June 18, 1986.
47. Craig Karp, "The War in Afghanistan," p. 1042.
48. For example, Arthur Bonner, *New York Times*, June 18, 1986.
49. For analysis of the U.N. negotiations at various stages, see Selig S. Harrison, "A

Breakthrough in Afghanistan?" *Foreign Policy*, Summer 1983; "The Afghanistan Stalemate: 'Self-Determination and a Soviet Force Withdrawal,'" *Parameters*, Winter 1984–85, pp. 38–39; "South Asia: Avoiding Disaster," *Foreign Policy*, Spring 1986, pp. 134–40; and "Toward Peace in Afghanistan," *New York Times*, March 17, 1986; "A Route out of the Afghanistan Maze," *New York Times*, May 20, 1987.

50. See "A Negotiated Settlement of the Afghan War?" an address by Elie D. Krakowski, special assistant to Perle, Heritage Foundation, January 16, 1986.

51. Anthony H. Cordesman, "U.S. Force Planning and Small Nuclear Forces in the Middle East and South Asia," in Rodney W. Jones, ed., *Small Nuclear Forces and U.S. Security Policy* (Lexington, Mass.: Lexington Books, 1984), pp. 214, 220.

BIBLIOGRAPHY

Books and Articles

Barber, Willard F., and C. Neale Ronning, *Internal Security and Military Power* (Columbus: Ohio State University Press, 1966).

Barnet, Frank, ed., *Special Operations in U.S. Strategy* (Washington, D.C.: National Defense University Press, 1984).

Blaufarb, Douglas, *The Counterinsurgency Era: U.S. Doctrine and Performance* (New York: Free Press, 1977).

Bode, William R., "The Reagan Doctrine," *Strategic Review*, Winter 1986, pp. 21–29.

Bond, Peter A., "In Search of LIC," *Military Review*, August 1986, pp. 79–88.

Cable, Larry E., *Conflict of Myths: The Development of American Counterinsurgency Doctrine and the Vietnam War* (New York: New York University Press, 1986).

Chaliand, Gerard, ed., *Guerrilla Warfare: From the Long March to Afghanistan* (Berkeley: University of California Press, 1982).

Collins, John M., *Green Berets, SEALs, and Spetsnaz: U.S. and Soviet Special Military Operations* (Washington, D.C.: Pergamon-Brassey's, 1986).

Hart, Douglas, "Low-Intensity Conflict in Afghanistan: The Soviet View," *Survival*, March–April 1982, pp. 61–68.

Hunt, Richard, and Richard Shultz, eds., *Lessons from an Unconventional War* (Washington, D.C.: Pergamon, 1982).

Iklé, Fred C., "Taking Sides in Small Wars," *Defense/86*, March–April 1986, pp. 7–13.

Kitson, Frank, *Low-Intensity Operations: Subversion, Insurgency, Peace-Keeping* (London: Faber, 1971).

Klare, Michael T., *War Without End: American Planning for the Next Vietnams* (New York: Knopf, 1972).

———, *Beyond the "Vietnam Syndrome"* (Washington, D.C.: Institute for Policy Studies, 1981).

Kornbluh, Peter, *Nicaragua: The Price of Intervention* (Washington, D.C.: Institute for Policy Studies, 1987).

———, "Test Case for the Reagan Doctrine: The Contra War," *Third World Quarterly*, October 1987.

Livingstone, Neil C., "Mastering the Low Frontier of Conflict," *Defense and Foreign Affairs*, December 1984, pp. 9–11.

———, "Fighting Terrorism and 'Dirty Little Wars,'" *Air University Review*, March–April 1984, pp. 4–16.

Luttwak, Edward N., "Low-Intensity Warfare," *Parameters*, December 1983, pp. 11–18.

Maechling, Charles, Jr., "Insurgency and Counterinsurgency: The Role of Strategic Theory," *Parameters*, October 1984, pp. 32–41.

Morelli, Donald R., and Michael M. Ferguson, "Low-Intensity Conflict: An Operational Perspective," *Military Review,* November 1984, pp. 2–16.

Motley, James B., "A Perspective on Low-Intensity Conflict," *Military Review,* January 1985, pp. 2–11.

Osgood, Robert, *Limited War Revisited* (Boulder, Col.: Westview, 1979).

Prados, John, *President's Secret Wars: CIA and Pentagon Covert Operations since World War II* (New York: Morrow, 1986).

Sarkesian, Sam C., and William L. Scully, eds., *U.S. Policy and Low-Intensity Conflict* (New Brunswick, N.J.: Transaction, 1987).

Summers, Harry, *On Strategy: A Critical Analysis of the Vietnam War* (San Francisco: Presidio, 1983).

Thompson, Robert, *Defeating Communist Insurgency* (New York: Praeger, 1966).

Taylor, William J., Jr., and Steven A. Maarenen, eds., *The Future of Conflict in the 1980s* (Lexington, Mass.: Lexington Books, 1982).

Tarr, David W., "Political Constraints on U.S. Intervention in Low-Intensity Conflict in the 1980s," *Parameters,* September 1980, pp. 51–56.

Waghelstein, John, "A Latin-American Insurgency Status Report," *Military Review,* February 1987, pp. 42–47.

———, "Post-Vietnam Counterinsurgency Doctrine," *Military Review,* March 1985, pp. 42–49.

Government Reports and Documents

Air University Library, *Low-Intensity Conflict,* Special Bibliography No. 274, Maxwell Air Force Base, Ala. January 1985.

Airpower Symposium on the Role of Airpower in Low-Intensity Conflict, March 11–13, 1985, *Proceedings,* Maxwell Air Force Base, Ala.: Air War College.

American Defense Preparedness Association, "Low-Intensity Conflict: A Conference for Business," March 4–5, 1987, *Proceedings,* Orlando, Fla., Naval Training Center.

Army War College Library, *Special Warfare: A Selected Bibliography,* Carlisle Barracks, Pa., October 1983.

Copson, Raymond W., and Richard P. Cronin, "Reagan Doctrine: Assisting Anti-Marxist Guerrillas," Congressional Research Service, November 24, 1986.

Dean, David, *Low-Intensity Conflict and Modern Technology* (Maxwell Air Force Base, Ala.: Air University Press, 1986).

Gorman, Paul F., "National Strategy and Low-Intensity Conflict," Statement before the Senate Armed Services Committee, January 28, 1987.

Johnson, W. P., and E. N. Russell, *Strategic Studies Project: U.S. Army Strategy for Low-Intensity Conflict in Central America,* Industrial College of the Armed Forces, Washington, D.C., March 1985.

Kupperman, Robert H., Associates, *Low-Intensity Conflict,* Report prepared for the U.S. Army Training and Doctrine Command, July 30, 1983.

National Defense University, *Proceedings of the Low-Intensity Warfare Conference,* Fort McNair, Washington, D.C., January 14–15, 1986.

Rand Corporation, *Terrorism and Beyond: An International Conference on Terrorism and Low-Level Conflict,* Santa Monica, Cal., December 1982.

Schlacter, D.C., "Policy, Strategy, Forces: The Sequential Basis of Military Capability for Low-Intensity Conflict," Air War College, Maxwell Air Force Base, Ala., March 1985.

Shultz, George, "Low-Intensity Warfare: The Challenge of Ambiguity," Department of State, Current Policy Report #738, January 15, 1986.

U.S. Army, *Low-Intensity Conflict—Field Manual,* U.S. Army FM 100-20, January 1981.

U.S. Army, "U.S. Army Operational Concept for Special Operations Forces," TRADOC PAM 525-34, July 26, 1984.

U.S. Army, "U.S. Army Operational Concept for Low-Intensity Conflict," TRADOC PAM 525-44, February 10, 1986.

U.S. Army, "U.S. Army Operational Concept for Terrorism Counteraction," TRADOC PAM 525-37, March 19, 1984.

U.S. Army/Air Force, Center for Low-Intensity Conflict (CLIC), *Activation Plan,* January 29, 1986.

U.S. Army Joint Low-Intensity Conflict Project, *Final Report:* vol. I, *Analytical Review of Low-Intensity Conflict,* and vol. II, *Low-Intensity Conflict Issues and Recommendations,* TRADOC, Fort Monroe, Va., August 1, 1986.

Critical Analysis

Barry, Deborah, et al., "Nicaragua: Un País Sitiado," *Criés Cuaderno,* Nicaragua, 1986.

Barry, Tom, "Low-Intensity Conflict: The New Battlefield in Central America," *Resource Center,* 1986.

Center for Defense Information, "America's Secret Soldiers: The Buildup of U.S. Special Operations Forces," *Defense Monitor,* March 1985.

Halliday, Fred, "Beyond Irangate: The Reagan Doctrine and the Third World," Transnational Institute, *Transnational Issues* 1, 1987.

Klare, Michael T., "Low-Intensity Conflict: The New U.S. Strategic Doctrine," *Nation,* December 28, 1985.

Miles, Sara, "The Real War: Low-Intensity Conflict in Central America," *NACLA,* April–May 1986.

———, "The LIC Update: An Annotated Bibliography on Low-Intensity Conflict/ Counterinsurgency," *Resource Center,* Summer–Fall 1987.

———, "The Philippines and LIC: Third-World Chameleon Infests Mindanao," *Resource Center,* Summer–Fall 1987.

Miller, Marc S., "Ambiguous War: The United States and Low-Intensity Conflict," *Technology Review,* August–September 1987, pp. 60–67.

Morley, Jefferson, "Ollie's Blueprint," *New Republic,* May 25, 1987, pp. 16–18.

Nairn, Allan, "Endgame: A Special Report on U.S. Military Strategy in Central America," *NACLA,* May–June 1984.

Reed, Gail, "Low-Intensity Conflict: A War for All Seasons," *Black Scholar,* February 1, 1986.

CONTRIBUTORS

MICHAEL T. KLARE is director and associate professor for the Five College Program in Peace and World Security Studies, a joint venture of Amherst, Hampshire, Mount Holyoke, and Smith colleges and the University of Massachusetts at Amherst. He is the defense correspondent for the *Nation,* and the author of numerous articles on U.S. military policy. His books include *War Without End, Beyond the 'Vietnam Syndrome,'* and most recently, *American Arms Supermarket.*

PETER KORNBLUH is an information analyst at the National Security Archive in Washington, D.C., specializing in U.S. policy toward Latin America. He wrote chapter 6 of this book during his tenure as a fellow at the Institute for Policy Studies. He is the author of *Nicaragua: The Price of Intervention* and a forthcoming book on U.S.-Chilean relations.

RICHARD J. BARNET is cofounder and senior fellow of the Institute for Policy Studies in Washington, D.C. During the Kennedy administration he served as an official of the State Department and the Arms Control and Disarmament Agency. He is the author of numerous books, including *Roots of War, Intervention and Revolution,* and most recently, *The Alliance: America, Europe, Japan, Makers of the Post-War World.*

WALDEN BELLO is senior analyst in Pacific and Philippine affairs at the Institute for Food and Development Policy. He is coauthor of *Development Debacle: The World Bank in the Philippines* and *American Lake: The Nuclear Peril in the Pacific.*

STEPHEN D. GOOSE is legislative assistant for foreign and military affairs for Congressman Robert J. Mrazek. He wrote chapter 4 of this book while serving as Senior Research Analyst for the Center for Defense Information in Washington, D.C. His articles have been published in the *New York Times, Chicago Tribune, Bulletin of Atomic Scientists,* and other journals and newspapers.

JOY HACKEL is a reporter for States News Service in Washington, D.C. She coauthored chapter 5 of this book as a research associate at the Institute for

Policy Studies and staff member of Policy Alternatives for the Caribbean and Central America. She is coeditor of the IPS publication *In Contempt of Congress: Reagan's Record of Deceit and Illegality in Central America.* Her articles have appeared in the *Washington Post, Los Angeles Times, Newsday, National Catholic Reporter,* and other papers.

SELIG S. HARRISON, a senior associate of the Carnegie Endowment for International Peace, has specialized in South Asian affairs and American policy problems in South Asia for thirty-five years as a foreign correspondent and author. He served as Associated Press correspondent in New Delhi from 1951 to 1954, covering India, Pakistan, Afghanistan, Sri Lanka, and Nepal, and returned as South Asia Bureau Chief of the *Washington Post,* from 1962 to 1965. His visits to Afghanistan have spanned the periods of the monarchy, the Daud Khan republic, and the Communist regimes established since 1978. Among his four books are *India: The Most Dangerous Decades* and *In Afghanistan's Shadow.*

CHARLES MAECHLING, JR., served as director for internal defense in politico-military affairs in the State Department and as staff director of the National Security Council's cabinet-level special group for counterinsurgency during the Kennedy and Johnson administrations. He served on the staff of the Joint Chiefs of Staff and was a naval attaché in Latin America. His articles on U.S. foreign policy have appeared in numerous journals, including *Foreign Policy, Foreign Affairs, Parameters, Orbis,* and the *Foreign Service Journal,* as well as numerous newspapers, including the *Miami Herald* and *Los Angeles Times.* He is currently a fellow of Wolfson College, Cambridge University.

DANIEL SIEGEL is currently director of public education at the Christic Institute, a public-interest law and policy center in Washington, D.C. He coauthored chapter 5 of this book during his tenure as a research associate at the Institute for Policy Studies. He is coeditor of *The Cuba Reader* and *In Contempt of Congress: The Reagan Record of Deceit and Illegality in Central America,* an IPS publication.